Israel
and the
British
Empire

Israel and the British Empire

A HISTORY IN BIBLICAL PERSPECTIVE

DAVID GIBSON

Copyright ©2020 David Gibson

The right of David Gibson to be identified as the author of this work has been asserted by him in accordance the Copyright, Designs and Patents Act 1988.

ISBN: 979-8-6306-5159-4

All rights reserved. This book may not be copied or reprinted for commercial gain or profit.

Unless otherwise marked, Scripture quotations are taken from The Holy Bible, New International Version (Anglicised edition). Copyright ©1979, 1984, 2011 by Biblica (formerly International Bible Society). Used by permission of Hodder & Stoughton Publishers, an Hachette UK Company. All rights reserved.

Scripture quotations marked 'NKJV' are taken from the New King James Version. Copyright ©1982 by Thomas Nelson. Used by permission. All rights reserved.

Scripture quotations marked 'NLT' are taken from Holy Bible: New Living Translation. Copyright ©2004 by Tyndale House Publishers. Used by permission. All rights reserved.

Cover Design by Justyn Hall, J8 Creative.

Interior by Wordzworth Ltd.

Contents

Acknowledgements		vii
Prologue: Everlasting Covenant		ix
Chapter 1	The Balfour Declaration	1
Chapter 2	British Mandate: Contradiction & Betrayal	35
Chapter 3	Pogroms, Prejudice & Appeasement	61
Chapter 4	Arab Uprisings 1936 – 1939	87
Chapter 5	The Broken Promise	107
Chapter 6	Ha'apala	121
Chapter 7	The Final Solution and Britain's Sin of Omission	139
Chapter 8	The Rise of Jewish Insurgency	161
Chapter 9	Haganah Exodus 1947	187
Chapter 10	Dying Embers of British Rule	203
Chapter 11	The Rise of Israel	223
Chapter 12	The Decline of Britain	259

Appendix 1 – British Palestine Mandate:
             Text of the Mandate (24 July 1922)   287

Appendix 2 – Legal Considerations Regarding
             the 'West Bank'   301

Appendix 3 – British Government Documents
             of the Mandatory Period   307

Bibliography   309

Acknowledgements

There are many people to whom thanks are due for supporting this project, chiefly family and friends who remained enduringly patient during my periods of obsession and who allowed me to bounce newly formed ideas around. Special mentions, however, are required for...

... Geoff Spence, a friend of Israel, for an incredible act of generosity that enabled me to travel to Israel for the first time, an experience that inspired the writing of this book.

... Paul Parkhouse, Development Director for International Christian Embassy Jerusalem UK, for his generosity in devoting an extraordinary amount of time to proof reading the first draft, checking facts and challenging my objectivity. Paul also introduced me to others who have helped this project come to fruition, including ...

... Roy Thurley, Director of Balfour 100 Ltd and Chairman of Hatikvah Film Trust, who freely shared his own work which opened fresh avenues of research. I am particularly indebted to Roy for sharing two DVD's produced by Hatikvah Film Trust, *"The Forsaken Promise"* and *"Partners in this Great Enterprise"*, both of which recount the story of Britain's involvement in Palestine. My account of the battle for Beersheba and details of the Christian Zionist influences in Lloyd George's war Cabinet were founded upon information recorded in *"Partners in this Great Enterprise"*, and quotations from Irgun fighter Yosef Nachmias, who took part in the attack on Deir Yassin, were transcribed directly from *"The Forsaken Promise."*

… Peter Sammons, from Christian Publications International, for providing advice about publishing options and for re-directing my thoughts about the title of the book.

Prologue: Everlasting Covenant

> *I will make you into a great nation, and I will bless you; I will make your name great, and you will be a blessing. I will bless those who bless you, and whoever curses you I will curse; and all peoples on earth will be blessed through you."*
>
> —GENESIS 12:2-3

According to ancient biblical traditions, the 'Great King' YHVH, the God of creation and Lord of heaven and earth, entered into a covenant-treaty with a wandering nomad called Abraham, a descendent of Shem who, through his son Isaac and grandson Jacob, would become the father of the Hebrew nation of Israel. By this covenant, the Lord promised to Abraham and his successors a portion of land: *"On that day the LORD made a covenant with Abram and said, 'To your descendants I give this land, from the Wadi of Egypt to the great river, the Euphrates'"* (Genesis 15:18).

Called by God to leave his place of birth, the Sumerian city-state of Ur which was situated in the south of what is now Iraq, Abraham travelled along the Fertile Crescent that linked ancient Mesopotamia to Egypt until he arrived in this land, then known as the land of Canaan, with his wife and servants. On arrival, God spoke to Abraham and made a promise, *"I will make you into a great nation, and I will bless you ... So Abram went, as the* LORD *had told him ... and they set out for the land of Canaan, and they arrived there. Abram travelled through the land as far as the site of the great tree of Moreh at Shechem. At that time the Canaanites were in the land. The* LORD *appeared to Abram and said, 'To your offspring I will give this land'"* (Genesis 12:2, 4-7).

While Abraham was still childless, the Lord confirmed that not only would he possess Canaan but he would be father to a family from which a great nation would be derived, *"All the land that you see I will give to you and your offspring for ever. I will make your offspring like the dust of the earth, so that if anyone could count the dust, then your offspring could be counted. Go, walk through the length and breadth of the land, for I am giving it to you"* (Genesis 13:15-17).

The promise was reaffirmed again when the Lord made an everlasting decree that the title deeds to this small parcel of real estate would be given on a permanent basis to the nation that would come forth from Abraham, *"The whole land of Canaan, where you now reside as a foreigner, I will give as an everlasting possession to you and your descendants after you; and I will be their God"* (Genesis 17:8).

These promises were repeated to Abraham's son Isaac and grandson Jacob, who was also called Israel (Genesis 26:23-24; 28:10-15). Thus, the land of Canaan, and the people of Israel who were the descendants of Abraham, became the inheritance of YHVH through an everlasting covenant. This covenant is reiterated in the Psalms, *"He remembers his covenant for ever, the promise he made, for a thousand generations, the covenant he made with Abraham, the oath he swore to Isaac. He confirmed it to Jacob as a decree, to Israel as an everlasting covenant: 'To you*

PROLOGUE: EVERLASTING COVENANT

I will give the land of Canaan as the portion you will inherit'" (Psalm 105:8-11).

The covenant with Abraham came with a promise to the nation that he would father, Israel, and a warning to the other nations that would deal with Israel, *"I will make you into a great nation, and I will bless you; I will make your name great, and you will be a blessing. I will bless those who bless you, and whoever curses you I will curse; and all peoples on earth will be blessed through you"* (Genesis 12:2-3).

The prophets also confirmed that the nations would be held to account for how they treated Israel. The prophet Joel, speaking of the last days in which we are now living, declared, *"In those days and at that time, when I restore the fortunes of Judah and Jerusalem, I will gather all nations and bring them down to the Valley of Jehoshaphat. There I will put them on trial for what they did to my inheritance, my people Israel, because they scattered my people among the nations and divided up my land"* (Joel 3:1-2). In a passage from Isaiah, which speaks of Israel's future glory in the coming Messianic age, the Lord makes another promise to his chosen people: *"Foreigners will rebuild your walls, and their kings will serve you. Though in anger I struck you, in favour I will show you compassion. Your gates will always stand open, they will never be shut, day or night, so that people may bring you the wealth of the nations – their kings led in triumphal procession. For the nation or kingdom that will not serve you will perish; it will be utterly ruined"* (Isaiah 60:10-12). There are many other biblical texts that relate the sin of the nations to their abuse of Israel and the Jews.[1]

History is littered with the graveyards of nations and kingdoms that have mistreated the land and the people of Israel. By so doing they have brought upon themselves the curse contained in the promise to Abraham, and the ruin that the prophets foretold. Many once great empires lie in ruin to this day because of their attitude towards God's people. Though Israel and the Jewish people have suffered terribly at the hands of such empires, they have outlasted them all and once more stand proud and strong as a nation in a portion of the land promised to Abraham.

Even the most cursory glance at the history of this relatively small tract of land reveals a litany of once great powers that have taken possession of the land and abused the descendants of Abraham whilst at their height only to decline and be supplanted by the next great power: Assyria, Babylon, Persia, Greece, Rome, the Muslim Caliphates, the European Catholic Crusaders, the Egyptian Mamluks, the Ottoman Turks.

When General Allenby captured Jerusalem from the Ottomans on 9 December 1917 during the Great War, entering the Old City on foot two days later, the British Empire became the final link in the chain of great powers to assume trusteeship of the land prior to the restoration of a Jewish State in her ancient homeland. Would Britain fare any better than those who preceded her?

This book examines the conduct of Britain's Mandatory rule over Palestine in light of the eternal covenant between the Lord and His people. There is no doubt that Britain performed many good deeds that helped the Jews and facilitated the rise of modern day Israel, primarily through the Balfour Declaration which stated that His Majesty's government viewed "with favour the establishment in Palestine of a national home for the Jewish people." Yet, by the end of the Mandate, Britain was enacting immoral immigration policies that broke faith with the promises made in the Balfour Declaration and which had devastating consequence for the Jews. Britain was eventually forced into an ignominious withdrawal from Palestine after buckling under the weight of a determined Jewish insurrection and drawing upon herself international condemnation. But before we examine the conduct of Britain's Mandatory rule, and discover why it ended so acrimoniously, a brief summary of Israel's history will help to set the scene.

PROLOGUE: EVERLASTING COVENANT

A Whistle Stop History of Israel

The modern State of Israel is located roughly on the site of the ancient kingdoms of Israel and Judah. Throughout most of the 2nd millennium BC, the land of Canaan, the land which had been promised to Abraham and which would later become known as Israel, was dominated by the Pharaohs of Egypt. The first record of the name Israel occurs in the Merneptah stele, erected to celebrate the military achievements of Egyptian Pharaoh Merneptah (son of Ramses II) circa 1209 BC, which includes a line, "Israel is laid waste and his seed is not." This reference probably relates to Israel's formative period, a time when Israel was an ethnic group rather than an organized political state.

Merneptah's reference practically coincides with the beginning of Israel's national history, for it is the Exodus from Egypt, which took place during the reign of his father, that marks Israel's birth as a nation. Many generations earlier, the descendants of Abraham, who were living in Canaan as a nomadic pastoral clan, went down to Egypt in a time of famine and settled in the Wadi Tumilat. There, they multiplied and were drafted into forced labour gangs until Moses, who came in the name of the God of their ancestors, reawakened their faith and brought them out of Egypt.

Shortly after their escape from Egypt, at the foot of Mount Sinai, the early Israelite tribes entered into a covenant relationship with the God of Abraham, Isaac and Jacob. The covenant between God and Israel, made concrete by the Tabernacle and its ritual, bound the tribes together in a cultic bond. They possessed a strong centralizing force through their monotheistic faith which, combined with a stern code of ethics, set them apart from all their neighbours. But because of their disobedience against the terms of the covenant, the people whom Moses brought out of Egypt wandered in the wilderness for a generation until all but Joshua and Caleb had perished. By the time that Moses' life was ebbing away, a completely new generation, which had not been born in slavery, had arisen during the wilderness wanderings. This generation was not shackled to a mindset of slavery like their forefathers and had been forged in the blast furnace heat of the wilderness into a formidable host who were ready, under the leadership of Joshua, to invade Canaan as conquerors and settlers.

During their wandering, Moses had organised the people into a confederacy of twelve tribes. After entering Canaan, the biblical records describe a state of constant warfare between the tribes of the Israelites and other people groups in the region, including the Philistines, believed to be a sea-people of Aegean origin, whose capital city was Gaza. But for the constant attacks launched by her neighbours, Israel would perhaps never have attained any political solidarity. As it was, salvation from their enemies lay only in union, and, after abortive attempts had been made at one-man rule, Saul became king over all of Israel (circa 1020 BC). Saul defeated the Ammonites and the Philistines but was killed in battle against the latter on Mount Gilboa circa 1000 BC and was succeeded by David from the tribe of Judah, under whose leadership Israel finally emerged as the dominant people group. David transformed Israel from an ethnic tribal confederacy into a political and national entity. This national cohesion was solidified by the establishment of a dynasty of kings in the line of David by a covenant in which the Lord promised that a successor to David would reign forever.

At the heart of the territory ruled by David stood the city of Jerusalem, one of the oldest cities in the world. It is referenced during the early Canaanite period as "Urusalima" in the ancient cuneiform, meaning "City of Peace." The mountain on which the city is founded, Mount Moriah, was the place where the Lord instructed Abraham to sacrifice his only son, Isaac. According to the biblical tradition, David conquered the city from the Jebusites and established it as the capital of Israel. David was succeeded

PROLOGUE: EVERLASTING COVENANT

by his son, Solomon, who commissioned the building of the First Temple in Jerusalem.

Solomon's reign represents the high watermark of Israelite political history. He expanded Israel's borders, amassing considerable wealth which he spent on elaborate building projects, including the Temple, the Royal Palace, and numerous fortified cities. The best known of these are Megiddo, Hazor and Gezer. But royal activities on such a grand scale cost more than was produced by foreign trade and the tribute of vassal states, and so the Israelites themselves were forced to submit to conscription in royal labour gangs and to paying oppressive taxes. This heavy-handed approach to governance was the catalyst for a revolt by the northern tribes of Israel which, after the great king's death circa 930 BC, disrupted the united monarchy. The kingdom divided into the southern kingdom of Judah, who continued to be ruled from Jerusalem by kings in the line of David, and the northern kingdom of Israel.

A stunning archaeological discovery from the period of the northern Kingdom, the Moabite Stone dated circa 840 BC, relates a story of how Chemosh, the god of Moab (located in modern Jordan), had been angry with his people and so abandoned them to subjugation by Omri, King of Israel. But at length Chemosh returned and assisted Mesha, the Moabite King, to throw off the yoke of Israel and restore the lands of Moab (compare with 2 Kings 3:4-8).

The northern kingdom survived for approximately 200 years before it was destroyed by the Assyrian king Tiglath-Pileser III around 750 BC. A succession of Biblical prophets including Joel, Amos, Hosea and Isaiah had warned the people of this impending disaster, asserting that it would be the inevitable consequence of their idolatry, denial of justice and oppression of the poor.

The Assyrians carried most of the northern Israelites into exile, thus creating the "lost tribes of Israel." A revolt by the survivors of the Assyrian conquest (724 - 722 BC) was crushed after the siege and capture of Samaria by the Assyrian king Sargon II. Finally, in the first months of 722 BC, the northern kingdom of Israel became politically extinct.

Sargon's successor, Sennacherib, tried and failed to conquer Judah. The Taylor Prism, discovered among the ruins of the ancient Assyrian capital of Nineveh, contains the Annals of Sennacherib. On the prism Sennacherib boasts that he levelled 46 walled cities in Judah and that he shut up "Hezekiah the Judahite" within his own royal city, Jerusalem, "like a bird in a cage." Interestingly, although he boasts of extracting a substantial tribute from Hezekiah, he admits that he did not actually enter Jerusalem despite expressing his anxiety to do so, and from this point onwards there was an abrupt discontinuance of Assyria's western invasions (compare with Isaiah 37:33-38). Archaeological discoveries such as the Merneptah stele, the Moabite Stone and the Taylor Prism provide spectacular demonstrations of the authenticity of Hebrew scripture, of the connections from early antiquity between the Jewish people, Jerusalem and the land of Israel, and of the dishonesty of those who deny these connections. Archaeologists continue to unearth a stream of ancient treasures that make the case for Israel's origins impenetrable.

Modern scholars believe that refugees from the destruction of the northern kingdom migrated to Judah during the rule of King Hezekiah (715 - 686 BC), greatly expanding Jerusalem and inspiring to the construction of the Siloam Tunnel to provide water during times of siege.

As the Assyrian Empire slid into a rapid decline that the Prophets attributed to its extreme acts of cruelty, the Chaldean kings of Babylonia gained strength and began to press into the void. Nabopolassar of Babylon and Cyaxares of Media defeated and divided the Assyrian Empire between them, and the former's son, Nebuchadnezzar II, gained control of Syria and Judah in swift campaigns. Babylonian and biblical sources suggest that the Judean king, Jehoiachin, ignoring the warnings of the prophet Jeremiah, made an alliance with Egypt, Babylon's principal rival, which provoked Nebuchadnezzar into launching a punitive invasion in 586 BC. He destroyed Solomon's Temple and carried the Jewish elite into exile in Babylon. Jehoiachin was eventually released by the Babylonians and according to the Bible and the Talmud, the Judean royal family continued to lead the exiled Jews in Babylon.

Babylonian hegemony was short-lived. In 539 BC, Cyrus II of the Persian Achaemenian dynasty followed up his triumph over Media by conquering Lydia and Babylonia, thus making himself ruler of the greatest Empire thitherto known. One of Cyrus' first acts was to issue a proclamation (circa 538 BC) that granted subjugated nations, which included the people of Judah, religious freedom. A large number of Jewish exiles in Babylonia, led by Zerubbabel, were allowed to return to Jerusalem, and work on constructing the Second Temple was begun. A second group of 5,000 exiles, led by Ezra and Nehemiah, returned to Judah from 456 BC to rebuild the walls of Jerusalem and reinstate religious practices, overcoming determined opposition and obstruction from non-Jews living in the land.

The Persian Empire in turn fell to the brilliant Greek general, Alexander the Great, as he pressed into the Middle East, driven by a vision to spread Greek culture throughout the world. This trend, called Hellenisation (after 'Hellas', the original name for Greece), had a major impact in the land of Israel. Alexander conquered Judea and Jerusalem in 332 BC and, after Alexander's demise, the Land came under the rule of the Hellenistic Ptolemaic and Seleucid dynasties. The last of these rulers, the tactless and neurotic Seleucid king Antiochus IV Epiphanes, desecrated the Temple in Jerusalem on the 25th day of the Hebrew month Kislev (November – December) in 168 BC, by setting up the "abomination of desolation," namely an altar of Zeus, and sacrificing swine upon the altar. Such provocation and odious profanity triggered a Jewish rebellion under the leadership of Yehuda HaMakabi (Judah the Hammer), the son of a priest, who proved himself a leader of high quality. He successfully resisted the forces sent by the Seleucid authorities and, after three years of intermittent warfare, he succeeded in purifying the Temple circa 165 BC – an event still celebrated annually in the Jewish festival of Chanukah.

The Jewish revolt against the intolerable policies of Antiochus IV expedited a return to independence for the nation, which was solidified by the establishment of the Hasmonean dynasty, who extended their rule into the neighbouring regions of Samaria, Galilee, Iturea, Perea and Idumea. However, their freedom was to be short lived because a terrifying new power was rising over the horizon that would crush their hope of independence with an iron fist: the power of Rome.

As the Roman Republic expanded into the eastern Mediterranean, seizing control over the old Hellenistic empires, the Roman general Pompey conquered the regions governed by the Hasmoneans in 63 BC. Roman rule over the region was solidified when Herod, a half Jew of Idumean descent, was appointed as a puppet king in 37 BC. Herod has been called "the evil genius of the Judean nation."[2] Though an able administrator who oversaw colossal building projects and who singlehandedly forged a new aristocracy, he was hated by the Jews because he was complicit in executing Roman policies of taxation and state terror against the populace. His greatest achievement was to massively expand the Temple Mount in Jerusalem, upon which he reconstructed a magnificent Temple.

After Herod's death in 4 BC, the Roman Emperor Augustus divided Herod's kingdom amongst his sons. Herod Antipas was made tetrarch of Galilee and Perea, while Herod Archelaus became governor of Judea and Samaria, but he was deposed by the Emperor after failing in his responsibilities and replaced by a succession of Roman Procurators, the most infamous of whom

PROLOGUE: EVERLASTING COVENANT

was Pontius Pilate (26 - 36 AD) who gained notoriety for sentencing Jesus to be crucified.

From a Jewish perspective, however, the title of most despised Procurator was claimed by Gessius Florus. In 66 AD, his administrative incompetence and anti-Jewish posture led to what became known as the 'First Jewish Revolt' as the Jews of Judea rebelled against Roman rule and declared a new state of Israel. It was a brave but ultimately futile act of resistance for it triggered a disastrous war as Vespasian, the future Roman emperor, with his son Titus, arrived from Rome with a force of 60,000 men to crush the rebellion. The events of the war, which became increasingly bitter, were described by the Jewish historian Josephus, including his accounts of the siege of Jerusalem (69 - 70 AD) and the desperate last stand at Masada under Eleazar Ben Yair (72 - 73 AD). Josephus estimated that over a million people died in the siege of Jerusalem. Herod's Temple was destroyed in an act of Roman retribution against the uprising and most of Jerusalem and Judea laid waste. The Arch of Titus, constructed in 82 AD on the Via Sacre in Rome, depicts the sacking of Jerusalem and the taking of Jewish treasure, including the Menorah, from the Temple.

In 131 AD, the Roman Emperor Hadrian renamed Jerusalem "Aelia Capitolina" and constructed a Temple to Jupiter on the site of the former Jewish Temple. Jews were banned from living in Jerusalem itself, and the Roman province, until then known as Iudaea, was joined with Syria and spitefully renamed "Syria Palaestina", a derivation from Philistia, the name given by Greek writers to the land of the Philistines. The English name for the region, "Palestine", and the Arabic form, "Filastin", are derived from this. The name changes were a calculated attempt to erase the Jewish connection to the land of Israel and the city of Jerusalem. After Roman times the region was considered part of Syria and the name "Palestine", though commonly invoked in reference to biblical events, had no official status until after World War I, when it was adopted by the Allies as a legal instrument for distinguishing the region mandated to Great Britain from the remainder of Syria mandated to the French.

Despite the devastation wrought by the Romans during the first Jewish-Roman war, which had left the population and countryside in ruins, Hadrian's actions were sufficient to spark a second major Jewish revolt against the Romans under the leadership of Simon Bar Kokhba (132 - 35 AD). Initially, the rebellion achieved surprising success, and an independent Jewish state was established, once again named Israel, which survived for three years. Many Jews at the time believed that they were entering the long hoped for Messianic age. Their excitement was short-lived; after a brief span of glory, the revolt was crushed by Roman legions led by the Emperor Hadrian himself. Vast numbers of Jews were killed – 580,000 according to the Roman historian Cassius Dio.

After suppressing the Bar Kokhba revolt, the Romans exiled all remaining Jews from Judea, though Jews were permitted to live in Galilee and a hereditary Rabbinical Patriarch was appointed (from the House of Hillel in Galilee) to represent the Jews in dealings with the Romans. The most famous of these was Rabbi Jehudah HaNasi who is credited with compiling the final version of the Mishnah (Jewish religious texts which interpret the Hebrew Bible). From this point on most of the Jewish people were dispersed among the nations of the world.

Early in the 4th Century, the Roman emperor Constantine converted to Christianity and decreed that it be made the official religion of the Roman Empire. The name Jerusalem was restored to Aelia Capitolina and it was designated as a Christian city. The emperor oversaw the building of a magnificent church on the site of the Holy Sepulchre, traditionally believed from the time of Constantine to be the site of Jesus' tomb and crucifixion. Constantine's mother, Helena, made a pilgrimage to Jerusalem and oversaw the construction of the Church of the Nativity in

Bethlehem and the Church of the Ascension in Jerusalem. Jews were still banned from residing in Jerusalem, but were permitted to visit, and it was during this period that the surviving Western Wall of the old Temple Mount became sacred to Judaism. In 362 AD, the last pagan Roman emperor, Julian the Apostate, announced plans to rebuild the Jewish Temple but he perished while fighting the Persians in 363 AD and the project was abandoned.

In 390 AD, the Roman Empire fractured along an East-West divide. The province of Palaestina became part of a newly formed Eastern Empire, dominated by the Eastern Orthodox Church. This marked the beginning of an era known as the Byzantine period (390 - 634 AD). The Byzantine church displayed little sympathy for the Jewish people because of entrenched beliefs that the Jews, by rejecting Jesus as Messiah, had themselves been rejected by God as a nation. Roman Christianity treated the Jewish people with contempt and disdain.

In the 5th Century, the collapse of the Western half of the Roman Empire generated large scale migration of Christians into Palaestina and the development of a Christian majority. Judaism was tolerated to a degree, but there were prohibitions on Jews building new places of worship, holding public office and owning slaves.

In 611 AD, Persia invaded the Byzantine Empire, capturing Jerusalem in 614 AD with help from the Jewish community. As a reward, the Persians granted autonomy to the Jews to govern Jerusalem. The Byzantine emperor, Heraclius, responded by promising to restore Jewish rights in return for their assistance in defeating the Persians. After re-conquering Palaestina he reneged on this agreement, issuing an edict banning Judaism altogether from the Byzantine Empire. In 630 AD, Heraclius marched in triumph into Jerusalem and a general massacre of Jews ensued which devastated the Jewish communities of Jerusalem and the Galilee.

According to Muslim tradition, in 620 AD, the Prophet Muhammad was taken on a spiritual journey from Mecca to the "farthest mosque", whose location is considered by many to be the Temple Mount in Jerusalem. In 634 - 36 AD, the Arabs conquered Palaestina, renaming it Jund Filastin and ending the Byzantine prohibition on Jews living in Jerusalem. This marked the beginning of the Caliphates period (634 - 1099 AD), during which Islam replaced Christianity as the dominant religion in the region.

In 691 AD, Umayyad Caliph Abd al-Malik (685 - 705 AD) constructed the Dome of the Rock shrine on the Temple Mount. The Foundation Stone at its centre is the holiest site in Judaism. Jews traditionally face towards it when praying, in the belief that it was the location of the Holy of Holies in the Temple. It is also known as the Pierced Stone because it has a small hole on the south-eastern corner that enters a cavern beneath the rock, known as the Well of Souls. A second building, the Al-Aqsa Mosque, was also erected on the Temple Mount in 705 AD.

The Caliphates period was brought to an abrupt close by the Catholic Crusaders. In 1099 AD, the first Crusade captured Jerusalem and, on Christmas Day of the following year, established a Latin kingdom known as the Kingdom of Jerusalem. During the Crusader conquest, both Jews and Muslims were indiscriminately massacred or sold into slavery. The orthodox Ashkenazi Jews still recite a prayer in memory of the death and destruction caused by the Crusades. However, in 1187 AD, Sultan Saladin defeated the Crusaders at the Battle of Hattin, taking Jerusalem and most of the former Kingdom of Jerusalem, though a weakened Crusader Kingdom, centred round Acre, survived for another century.

From 1260-91 AD the area became the frontier between Mongol invaders and the Mamluks of Egypt. The prolonged conflict between these powers devastated the land and severely reduced its population. Sultan Qutuz of Egypt eventually defeated the Mongols at the Battle of Ain Jalut in Galilee, and Al-Ashraf

Khalil eliminated the last Crusader Kingdom at Acre in 1291 AD, thereby ending the era of the Crusades in the Holy Land. The Mamluks ruled the region until 1517 AD. In Hebron, Jews were banned from worshiping at the Cave of the Patriarchs (the second holiest site in Judaism); the ban would remain until Hebron was captured by the State of Israel during the Six Day war of 1967. The collapse of the Crusader kingdom corresponded with an increase in levels of persecution against Jews in European states dominated by Catholic Christianity and their expulsion from many. These expulsions began in England (1290 AD), followed by France (1306 AD).

British medieval history is stained by anti-Semitism. The first recorded claim of the so called 'blood libel' came out of Norwich, England, in 1141 AD, as recorded in the Catholic Encyclopedia.[3] The dead body of a boy, later referred to as William of Norwich, was found on Good Friday. According to the testimony of a monk Thomas of Monmouth, who recorded the event, Jews were accused of committing the murder for ritual purposes though no proof was ever found to substantiate the accusation, some even going so far as to claim that the blood of Christian children was collected to produce the unleavened bread used for Passover. Lingering belief that the murder of William was the work of Jews provoked a crowd into attacking a Jewish delegation coming to the coronation of Richard the Lionhearted in 1189 AD.

The following year, while Richard the Lionhearted was fighting the Crusades, most of the Jews of Norwich were slaughtered and riots broke out against the Jewish community in York. Hundreds fled for sanctuary to the Royal Castle of Clifford Tower, to which the enraged mob laid siege. As food supplies dwindled, most of the Jews committed suicide out of desperation. When the Castle was eventually captured, those left alive were slaughtered. This was the worst massacre of Jews on British soil.

During the reign of Edward 1, also known as Edward Longshanks (1272 - 1307 AD), the identification of Jews became compulsory. Every Jew was required to wear a yellow badge, a sign of social stigma. This humiliating identification by a yellow badge started not in Germany under Hitler as is often assumed, but in England under a Christian king.[4] Belief in blood libels became widespread, with rumours that each year at Passover the Jews would kill Christian children and drain their blood for use in satanic rituals. When Edward 1 became the first Monarch to expel all Jews from a European state in 1290 AD, Britain was void of a Jewish presence for 350 years until Oliver Cromwell became Lord Protector in the aftermath of the English civil war and encouraged Jews to return.

In Spain, persecution of the highly integrated and successful Jewish community included massacres, forced conversions to Catholicism and the Inquisition. During the Black Death, which reached its devastating peak circa 1346-53 AD, many Jews were murdered after being accused of poisoning wells. Many millions died across Europe from this contagion, but very few Jews succumbed because of the preventative benefits of strict dietary and sanitary laws. The survival of the Jews led many to believe that they were somehow responsible and, out of anger and fear, some Jewish communities were completely destroyed and many Jews were tortured and burned to death.

Jews were expelled from Spain in 1492 AD and from Portugal in 1497 AD. These were the wealthiest and most integrated Jewish communities in Europe. Most of the expelled Spanish Jews moved to North Africa, Poland, to the Ottoman Empire and to the region of Bilad al-Sham, which corresponds roughly to the modern regions of Syria and Lebanon. In Italy, Jews living in the Papal States were required to live in ghettos.

The Ottoman–Mamluk War (1516 - 17 AD) led to the fall of the Mamluk Sultanate and the incorporation of the Levant, Egypt and the Arabian Peninsula as provinces of the Ottoman Empire. The war transformed the Ottoman Empire from a realm at the margins of the Islamic world, mainly located in Anatolia and the Balkans, to a vast Empire that encompassed the traditional lands of Islam, including the cities of Mecca, Cairo, Damascus and Aleppo.

Under Ottoman rule, Palestine was divided into four administrative districts attached to the province of Damascus and ruled from Istanbul. At the beginning of the Ottoman era, it is estimated that only 1,000 Jewish families lived in Palestine, mainly centred in Jerusalem, Nablus, Hebron, Gaza, Safed and the villages of Galilee. The community comprised Jews whose ancestors had never departed from the Land throughout the centuries of upheaval, conflict and persecution, and more recent immigrants from North Africa and Europe.

Their situation improved dramatically during the reign of the tenth and greatest Sultan of the Ottoman Empire, Suleiman the Magnificent (1520 - 66 AD), who brought orderly government to the region which stimulated renewed Jewish immigration. Under his able rule, the Ottoman fleet dominated the seas from the Mediterranean to the Red Sea and through the Persian Gulf. Most of the Jewish newcomers settled in Safed where, by the mid-16th Century, the Jewish population had risen to about 10,000. Sadly, however, Suleiman's successors proved to be bereft of his leadership abilities.

Over time, with the decline in the quality of Ottoman rule, Palestine was brought into a state of widespread neglect. By the end of the 18th Century, much of the land was owned by absentee landlords and leased to impoverished tenant farmers crippled by capricious taxation. The great forests of Galilee and the Carmel mountain range were stripped bare; swamp and desert encroached on agricultural land. The sedentary population began to yield to nomadic bands of Bedouin tribesmen. The land that had once flowed with milk and honey was a desolate and barren wasteland.

During the course of the 19th Century, the fluctuating fortunes of the Jews were revived once more by the intervention of Western powers as they jockeyed for position in the region, forcing medieval backwardness to yielded to progress. This Western power struggle was triggered by Napoleon's doomed attempt to sever Britain's link to India by landing forces in Egypt and Palestine. Napoleon's battle fleet was crushed by the British Royal Navy under the command of Horatio Nelson at the Battle of the Nile in 1798, but his invasion had thrust the entire region from Egypt to the Dardanelles into a position of vital strategic importance for Europe's imperialist strongmen.

Western involvement in Palestine opened the way for British, French and American scholars to launch academic expeditions to study biblical geography and archaeology. Britain, France, Russia, Austria and the United States opened consulates in Jerusalem. Steamships opened regular trade routes between Palestine and Europe; postal and telegraphic connections were installed; the first road was built connecting Jerusalem and Jaffa. Palestine's rebirth as the crossroads for intercontinental commerce was accelerated by the opening of the Suez Canal.

As a consequence of these developments, the condition of Palestine's Jewish community improved, and their numbers increased substantially. By the mid 19th Century, the overcrowded conditions within the walled city of Jerusalem motivated the Jews to build neighbourhoods outside the Old City walls. By 1880 AD, Jerusalem had an overall Jewish majority; land for farming was being purchased by Jews throughout Palestine; new rural settlements were created; and the Hebrew language, long restricted to liturgy and literature, was revived. The foundation stones were being laid for the modern Zionist movement.

Palestine would remain part of the Ottoman Empire until its demise was sealed by defeat to the Allies during World War I. For the best part of two millennia, the Promised Land had been

PROLOGUE: EVERLASTING COVENANT

governed by a succession of dominant empires, each of which declined and was subsequently overtaken by a new great power. The remnant of Jews who remained in the land suffered persecution and subjugation as a colonised and oppressed minority, while the vast majority were flung into dispersion among other nations where generally they fared no better. Some prospered, but most were persecuted, unwanted and impoverished. Now it would be the turn of the British Empire to occupy the Promised Land. Would she fare any better than her predecessors? Would she finally bring to the Jewish people the blessings of peace, prosperity and a place to call home, and thereby secure for herself the promised blessings of the everlasting covenant that the Lord made with Abraham? Or would she betray the Jews, and thereby bring upon herself the curse contained in the covenant and make certain of her decline like all the other once great kingdoms that had ruled in the Promised Land?

The Stage is Set

Jerusalem, the eternal city, has always held a mystical significance for Jews which is mournfully expressed in the lamenting of the exiles in Babylon, *"By the rivers of Babylon we sat and wept when we remembered Zion. There on the poplars we hung our harps ... How can we sing the songs of the Lord while in a foreign land? If I forget you, Jerusalem, may my right hand forget its skill. May my tongue cling to the roof of my mouth if I do not remember you, if I do not consider Jerusalem my highest joy"* (Psalm 137:1-6 NIV). Throughout the years of dispersion amongst the nations, Jews continued to look towards Jerusalem as their spiritual home, facing towards the Temple Mount during daily prayers and ending each Passover Seder with the hopeful declaration, 'next year in Jerusalem.' Although some deny it, the consciousness of Jewish identity has always been tied inextricably to Jerusalem and all that it symbolizes. Far more than a mere geographic site, Jerusalem is the "heartbeat" of God's ancient people, no matter where in the world they reside. Jewish history and destiny are irrevocably and forever interwoven with those of Jerusalem.

For nearly two millennia, the Jews scattered amongst the nations were praying that God would bring about their return to Zion at a time of his choosing. But the idea was little more than a pious aspiration until late in the 19th Century when, in mainland Europe, such nationalist ideals began gaining momentum.

In parallel with this rising tide of Zionism amongst European Jews, British Evangelical churches were at the forefront of a movement that took seriously prophetic scriptures that told of the restoration of Israel and were praying ardently for their fulfilment. The influences of this movement were deeply rooted in British political circles at the very moment that Allied forces under the command of General Allenby were sweeping through Palestine during World War I.

And so the destinies of Britain and Israel became intertwined in the providence of God during the birth pangs of modern Zionism. Theodor Herzl, the father of modern Zionism, confidently proclaimed to the fourth Zionist Congress held in London in the year 1900, "England, free and mighty England, whose vision embraces the seven seas, will understand us and our aspirations. It is here that the Zionist movement will soar to further and greater heights."[5] The British Christian Zionist movement was kindling the fire of modern Jewish Zionism just as Britain was on the cusp of taking control of Palestine.

Below is a list of important prophetic texts which reference the restoration of Israel as a nation in the last days. Each could be viewed in light of the return of the exiles from captivity in Babylon but appear on plain reading to be referring to a wider regathering from many nations and assert that the people will

PROLOGUE: EVERLASTING COVENANT

never again be separated from Judea and Jerusalem. These are the verses that inspired the rise of Christian-Zionism and to which the Evangelical churches in Britain were looking, though they were of lesser significance to Jewish Zionist aspirations. They speak of events which were fulfilled during the period in which Britain governed in Palestine and beyond and are essential for understanding the times in which we live. Times in which many claim that the 'West Bank', including the Old City of Jerusalem and the Judean hills, rightfully belong to an Arab Palestinian state; but see what the Lord says (all references are taken from the NLT):

> *He will raise a flag among the nations for Israel to rally around. He will gather the scattered people of Judah from the ends of the earth"*
>
> −ISAIAH 11:12.

> *'Do not be afraid, for I am with you. I will gather you and your children from east and west and from north and south. I will bring my sons and daughters back to Israel from the distant corners of the earth. All who claim me as their God will come, for I have made them for my glory. It was I who created them"*
>
> −ISAIAH 43:5-7

> *Who has ever seen or heard of anything as strange as this? Has a nation ever been born in a single day? Has a country ever come forth in a mere moment? But by the time Jerusalem's birth pains begin, the baby will be born; the nation will come forth"*
>
> −ISAIAH 66:8

> 'But the time is coming,' says the Lord, 'when people who are taking an oath will no longer say, 'As surely as the Lord lives, who rescued the people of Israel from the land of Egypt.' Instead, they will say, 'As surely as the Lord lives, who brought the people of Israel back to their own land from the land of the north and from all the countries to which he had exiled them.' For I will bring them back to this land that I gave their ancestors"
>
> —JEREMIAH 16:14-15

> 'But I will gather together the remnant of my flock from wherever I have driven them. I will bring them back into their own fold, and they will be fruitful and increase in number. Then I will appoint responsible shepherds to care for them, and they will never be afraid again. Not a single one of them will be lost or missing,' says the Lord. 'For the time is coming,' says the Lord, 'when I will place a righteous Branch on King David's throne. He will be a King who rules with wisdom. He will do what is just and right throughout the land. And this is his name: 'The Lord Is Our Righteousness.' In that day Judah will be saved, and Israel will live in safety. 'In that day,' says the Lord, 'when people are taking an oath, they will no longer say, 'As surely as the Lord lives, who rescued the people of Israel from the land of Egypt.' Instead, they will say, 'As surely as the Lord lives, who brought the people of Israel back to their own land from the land of the north and from all the countries to which he had exiled them.' Then they will live in their own land"
>
> —JEREMIAH 23:3-8

> *I will end your captivity and restore your fortunes. I will gather you out of the nations where I sent you and bring you home again to your own land"*
>
> −JEREMIAH 29:14

> *For the time is coming when I will restore the fortunes of my people of Israel and Judah. I will bring them home to this land that I gave to their ancestors, and they will possess it and live here again. I, the Lord, have spoken!"*
>
> −JEREMIAH 30:3

> *I will surely bring my people back again from all the countries where I will scatter them in my fury. I will bring them back to this very city and let them live in peace and safety"*
>
> −JEREMIAH 32:37

> *Therefore, give the exiles this message from the Sovereign Lord: Although I have scattered you in the countries of the world, I will be a sanctuary to you during your time in exile. I, the Sovereign Lord, will gather you back from the nations where you were scattered, and I will give you the land of Israel once again"*
>
> −EZEKIEL 11:16-17

> *When I bring you home from exile, you will be as pleasing to me as an offering of perfumed incense. And I will display my holiness in you as all the nations watch. Then when*

> *I have brought you home to the land I promised your ancestors, you will know that I am the Lord"*
>
> −EZEKIEL 20:41-42

> *This is what the Sovereign Lord says: The people of Israel will again live in their own land, the land I gave my servant Jacob. For I will gather them from the distant lands where I have scattered them. I will reveal to the nations of the world my holiness among my people. They will live safely in Israel and build their homes and plant their vineyards. And when I punish the neighbouring nations that treated them with contempt, they will know that I am the Lord their God"*
>
> −EZEKIEL 28:25-26

> *I will be like a shepherd looking for his scattered flock. I will find my sheep and rescue them from all the places to which they were scattered on that dark and cloudy day. I will bring them back home to their own land of Israel from among the peoples and nations. I will feed them on the mountains of Israel and by the rivers in all the places where people live. Yes, I will give them good pasture land on the high hills of Israel. There they will lie down in pleasant places and feed in lush mountain pastures"*
>
> −EZEKIEL 34:12-14

> *And give them this message from the Sovereign Lord: I will gather the people of Israel from among the nations. I will bring them home to their own land from the places where they have been scattered. I will unify them into one*

PROLOGUE: EVERLASTING COVENANT

nation in the land. One king will rule them all; no longer will they be divided into two nations"

—EZEKIEL 37:21-22

> So now the Sovereign Lord says: I will end the captivity of my people; I will have mercy on Israel, for I am jealous for my holy reputation! They will accept responsibility for their past shame and treachery against me after they come home to live in peace and safety in their own land. And then no one will bother them or make them afraid. When I bring them home from the lands of their enemies, my holiness will be displayed to the nations. Then my people will know that I am the Lord their God - responsible for sending them away to exile and responsible for bringing them home. I will leave none of my people behind. And I will never again turn my back on them, for I will pour out my Spirit upon them, says the Sovereign Lord"

—EZEKIEL 39:25-29

> 'The time will come,' says the Lord, 'when the grain and grapes will grow faster than they can be harvested. Then the terraced vineyards on the hills of Israel will drip with sweet wine! I will bring my exiled people of Israel back from distant lands, and they will rebuild their ruined cities and live in them again. They will plant vineyards and gardens; they will eat their crops and drink their wine. I will firmly plant them there in the land I have given them,' says the Lord your God. 'Then they will never be uprooted again'"

—AMOS 9:13-15

> *This is what the Lord of Heaven's Armies says: Once again old men and women will walk Jerusalem's streets with their canes and will sit together in the city squares. And the streets of the city will be filled with boys and girls at play. This is what the Lord of Heaven's Armies says: All this may seem impossible to you now, a small remnant of God's people. But is it impossible for me? says the Lord of Heaven's Armies. This is what the Lord of Heaven's Armies says: You can be sure that I will rescue my people from the east and from the west. I will bring them home again to live safely in Jerusalem. They will be my people, and I will be faithful and just toward them as their God"*
>
> —ZECHARIAH 8:4-8

It is important to note, in view of the claims of ownership to the land that lie at the heart of the Arab-Israeli conflict today, that throughout the period of Israel's dispersion the Jews continued to look towards Jerusalem as their capital which no other nation did, that a remnant of Jews always remained in the land as a persecuted indigenous minority while it was under occupation, and that none of the Empires who ruled over the land attempted to establish any other state. Since the time of King David there has never been any Palestinian state apart from Israel. And no other people group in the world today has an older claim to the land than the Jewish people. As Israel's 1948 Declaration of Independence declares, "The land of Israel was the birth place of the Jewish people. Here, their spiritual, religious and political identity was shaped. Here, they first attained statehood, created cultural values of national and universal significance and gave the world the eternal Book of Books."

Endnotes

1. See Psalms 79:1-13; 83:1-18; Isaiah 29:1-8; 34:1-3; Jeremiah 25:13-17; Zechariah 1:14-15; 12:2-3; Matthew 25:31-46.
2. Graetz, Heinrich (Hist., V. II, p. 77).
3. Douglas Raymund Webster, "St. William of Norwich," *Catholic Encyclopedia*, Vol. 15 (New York: The Encyclopedia Press, 1913).
4. The origins of a distinguishing mark for Jews go back to Caliph Omar II who, in 717 AD, ordered both Jews and Christians to wear a distinguishing mark. In 807 AD, the Persian Abbassid Caliph Harun al-Rashid ordered Jews to wear a yellow belt and Christians a blue one.
5. Walter Laqueur, *The History of Zionism 3rd Ed.* (London: Taurisparke Paperbacks, 2003), p. 112.

CHAPTER 1

THE BALFOUR DECLARATION

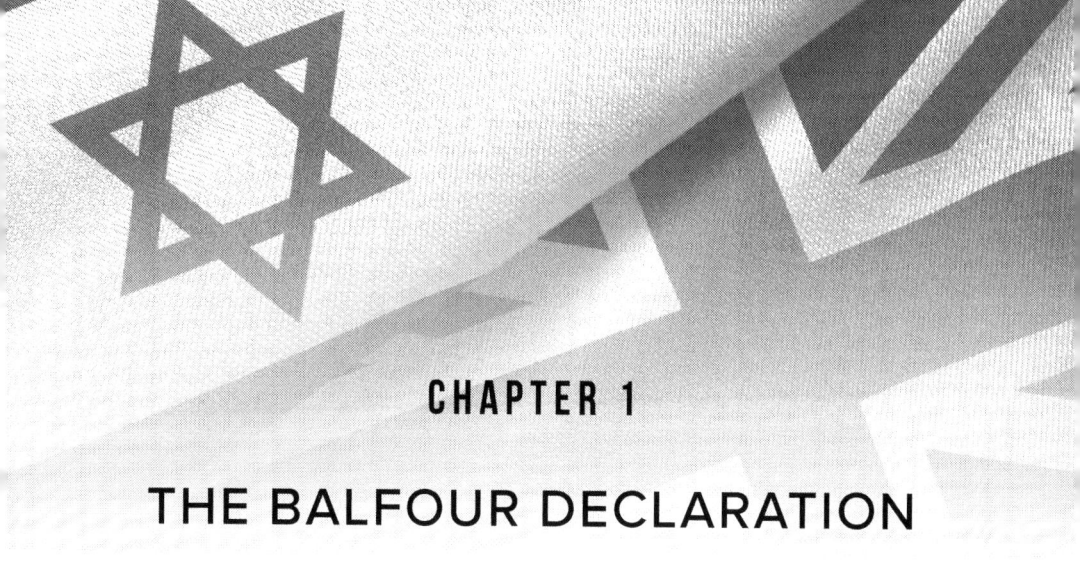

> *The Zionist leaders gave us a definite promise that, if the Allies committed themselves to giving facilities for the establishment of a national home for the Jews in Palestine, they would do their best to rally Jewish sentiment and support throughout the world to the Allied cause. They kept their word."*
>
> −DAVID LLOYD GEORGE

On 2 November 1917, the United Kingdom's Foreign Secretary Arthur James Balfour wrote a letter to Walter Rothschild, the unofficial leader of the British Jewish community, for transmission to the Zionist Federation of Great Britain and Ireland. The letter, which became known as the Balfour Declaration, is one of the most important documents in modern history. It stated:

> Foreign Office
> November 2nd, 1917

> Dear Lord Rothschild,
>
> I have much pleasure in conveying to you, on behalf of His Majesty's Government, the following declaration of sympathy with Jewish Zionist aspirations which has been submitted to, and approved by, the Cabinet.
>
> His Majesty's government view with favour the establishment in Palestine of a national home for the Jewish people, and will use their best endeavours to facilitate the achievement of this object, it being clearly understood that nothing shall be done which may prejudice the civil and religious rights of existing non-Jewish communities in Palestine, or the rights and political status enjoyed by Jews in any other country.
>
> I should be grateful if you would bring this declaration to the knowledge of the Zionist Federation.
>
> Yours,
> Arthur James Balfour

On the basis of Balfour's promise to facilitate the establishment of a Jewish homeland in Palestine, Jews around the world rallied behind the Allied cause, helping to secure victory in the Great War. Some 15 months after the end of hostilities, at an international conference held in San Remo, Italy, to determine the boundaries for territories captured by the Allies in the Middle East, it was resolved to incorporate the "Balfour Declaration" into a British Mandate for Palestine. By this resolution, Britain was made legally responsible "for putting into effect the declaration made on the 8 [sic] November 1917 by the British government and adopted by the other Allied Powers, in favour of the establishment in Palestine of a national home for the Jewish people."

Jews throughout the world celebrated the passing of this resolution with jubilant mass rallies. Arab leaders, however, considered it a violation of an earlier promise made by Britain that in the event of an Allied victory in World War I, the Arab independence movement would be granted control of the Middle Eastern territories in exchange for revolting against the Ottoman Empire. The San Remo resolution was, therefore, a significant step in the build-up to the Arab–Israeli conflict, often referred to as the world's "most intractable conflict." It would also prove to be the crucial turning point in the destinies of both Israel and Britain.

Pro-Zionists believed that the ratification of the Balfour Declaration, and its incorporation into the British Mandate for Palestine, was a providential miracle that would herald the fulfilment of Hebrew prophecies concerning the restoration of Israel in her ancient homeland. The foundation stone for the modern state of Israel had been laid and the Zionist movement had secured a guarantee of support from one of the world's great powers.

At the beginning of the Mandatory period, Britain administered the most extensive Empire the world had ever seen. The Union Jack flew over a quarter of the land surface of the planet, and she was responsible for the lives and hopes of 460 million people. She was a supremely confident nation, imbued with a sense of superiority, governed by haughty politicians and bellicose military administrators whose formative years were spent on the playing fields of Eton and Oxford, and who strode imperiously along the marbled floors and among the columns of power in Whitehall suffering not from insecurities. Governance for them was an imperial game of thrones. Such was the extent of their sphere of control, it could be said that "the Sun never sets on the British Empire." The powerful Royal Navy dominated the oceans, protecting trade routes that made London the financial capital of the world.

Twenty-Eight years later, on 14 May 1948, the leaders of the Jewish community in Palestine, led by David Ben Gurion, gathered together in Tel Aviv to declare the rebirth of the State of Israel. The

British, in contrast, were forced into an ignominious withdrawal from Palestine, accused of betraying the Jews by an act of political appeasement that had sealed the fate of hundreds of thousands of Jews in the Holocaust by severing their only escape route from the horror unfolding in Europe. In an act of ruthlessly calculated political expediency on the eve of World War II, Britain callously broke faith with the promises made in the Balfour Declaration in order to mitigate the risk of the Arabs uniting with Nazi Germany, knowing that the price of this appeasement would be paid by the blood of the Jews.

By the time Britain withdrew from Palestine, this once mighty nation was presiding over a crumbling Empire, economically ruined by the cost of victory in World War II, drained of confidence, dishonoured and humiliated. Britain's conduct of the Mandate for Palestine would prove to be a disastrous moral failure underscored by cold hearted and cynical anti-Semitic sentiments. It was a lamentable fiasco that triggered a collapse of her global reputation and for which she is still paying the price today. Truly it can be said of Britain, how are the mighty fallen in the midst of the battle! The betrayal of the Jews, by forsaking the promises of the Balfour Declaration, is an act largely glossed over by (British) revisionists and hardly spoken of in mainstream media. Yet it is arguably the darkest stain on British history.

So how did the Balfour Declaration come about? Why did Britain renege on the commitments contained therein? What were the dreadful consequences of this betrayal? This chapter examines the first of these questions. The remaining chapters of this book will answer the other two.

The Rise of Zionism

The term "Zionism" (derived from the Hebrew word 'tsiyon,' hill – referring to Jerusalem) was first coined by Nathan Birnbaum in 1890 to describe the nationalist movement for the return of the Jewish people to their homeland and the resumption of Jewish sovereignty in the land of Israel. For nearly two millennia, most Jews had lived in dispersion beyond the land of Israel, praying that God would bring about their return at a time of his choosing. But the idea was little more than a pious aspiration until late in the 19th Century when, in mainland Europe, such nationalist ideals began gaining momentum in Jewish circles as a reaction to the rising political forces of anti-Semitism.

At the outset of the 19th Century, bitter controversies had broken out amongst European Jews between those who saw Judaism as their religion and others for whom it was an expression of nationhood; the relationship between Judaism and Zionism remains a contentious issue in some quarters of the global Jewish community to this day. Most of the Jewish political elites and wealthy business classes, based in Western Europe, were opposed to nationalist aspirations and advocated for assimilation into mainstream society believing that this was the best solution to anti-Semitism. In the West, Jews were increasingly granted citizenship and equality before the law and so were inclined to reject the Zionist assertion of a distinct Jewish national identity, as they believed it encouraged the view that Jews were always strangers and aliens in their adopted home. There was little appetite among these Jews for emigration to the unknown discomforts of an uncultivated land amid a sea of Muslims. Besides which, if a Jewish home were established elsewhere, they reasoned that there would be an increased likelihood of rejection by a society deeply imbued with anti-Semitic sentiments. On this basis, intellectual Jews came to associate Zionism with anti-Semitism. Claude

Montefiore, the British born founder of progressive Judaism and an influential anti-Zionist religious teacher, commented bitterly, "all anti-Semites are enthusiastic Zionists."[1]

However, half the world's Jews lived in the Tsarist Russian Empire where, unlike in Western Europe, they were regarded as a separate and distinct entity. The Jews of Russia and Poland were downtrodden, suppressed, targets for contempt and ridicule, and subjected to legal restrictions. Eastern Europe, therefore, became a natural breeding ground for nationalist ideas. When a series of violent anti-Jewish pogroms broke out in the Russian Empire in the years 1881-84, the millions of Jews who fled the country carried the seeds of this nationalism wherever they went. It was these Russian Jews who established the Hibat Tzion (Love of Zion) pioneer associations. Their ideology of national revival generated a wave of migration to Palestine, known today as the First Aliyah, which was accompanied by a revival of the Hebrew language as a modern spoken language, a process unique in the history of linguistics which has furnished no other example of a sacred language being remodelled as a national language with millions of "first language" speakers. The intellectual driving force behind this revival in the use of Hebrew was the Jewish activist, Eliezer Ben-Yehuda.

In 1896, Theodor Herzl, a Jewish journalist living in Austria-Hungary, published a highly influential work entitled *Der Judenstaat* (*The Jewish State*), in which he asserted that the only solution to the growth of anti-Semitism in Europe, the so called "Jewish Problem", was the establishment of a national home for the Jews.

Herzl was born on 2 May 1860, and grew up in an assimilated Jewish household. As a young man, he worked as a columnist for a liberal newspaper. Anti-Semitism was a reality that he faced and struggled to overcome, but he was convinced that assimilation and liberalism were the natural solutions. This illusion, however, was shattered in late 1894 by the sensational story of a Jewish French Army Captain, Alfred Dreyfus, who was convicted by a military court of treasonously sending military secrets to Germany. Evidence soon emerged that in fact Dreyfus was innocent and had been made a scapegoat for the crimes of another. Dreyfus had been convicted because he was a Jew to protect the sullied honour of the French Army.

Reeling from shock at the rampant anti-Semitism provoked by the Dreyfus affair, Herzl set about writing *'The Jewish State'* in a frenzy of inspiration and revelation, having concluded, in a complete reversal of his former convictions, that anti-Semitism was an immutable factor in society which assimilation could never resolve. He was now persuaded that the only way that Jews would gain acceptance in the world was if they ceased being a national anomaly. Persecution would be their lot in life as long as Jews were a nation without a state, and so their plight could only be transformed by the establishment of a Jewish state with the consent of the great world powers.

Herzl's ideas marked the emergence of political Zionism, and today, he is widely recognized as the visionary behind modern Zionism and the re-institution of the Jewish homeland in the state of Israel. He proposed a programme for collecting funds from Jews around the world via a company, owned by shareholders, which would work toward the practical realisation of the Zionist goal. This organization, when it was eventually founded, was called the Zionist Organization, and at its first congress in 1897 it called for "the establishment of a home for the Jewish people in Palestine secured under public law." Measures proposed to attain that goal included the promotion of Jewish settlement in Palestine, the organisation of Jews in the Diaspora, the strengthening of Jewish feeling and consciousness, and preparatory steps to attain governmental grants. Herzl predicted at this congress that a Jewish state would be established within 50 years.

Herzl's vision of the future Jewish home was for a model state characterised by an enlightened, tolerant and progressive society.

It would be a "light unto the nations" that would arise on a cooperative basis, advancing science and technology for the benefit of the entire world and striving to realize, as Herzl termed it, the unique ethos of "an infinite ideal." Towards the end of his life, in his work titled "Our Hope", Herzl wrote, "I once called Zionism an infinite ideal ... as it will not cease to be an ideal even after we attain our land, the land of Israel. For Zionism ... encompasses not only our hope of a legally secured homeland for our people ... but also the aspiration to reach moral and spiritual perfection."[2] Herzl's vision had a great impact on the Jews of his time and became a symbol of the Zionist vision in Palestine.

Inspired by Herzl's vision, a new wave of Jewish migrants settled in Palestine, known as the Second Aliyah, during the years 1904-14. In 1908, the Palestine Office was founded to aid Jewish immigration and to purchase land for settlement. Like the First Aliyah, these migrants were mainly young Russians who were escaping persecution. In 1909, the first entirely Hebrew-speaking city, Tel Aviv, was established. Newspapers began to be published in Hebrew and Hebrew-speaking schools were founded.

While Herzl's ideas were gathering momentum, Chaim Weizmann, a Belarusian biochemist who had fled the land of his birth to escape persecution during the Russian pogroms, became active in the Zionist movement while studying in Geneva. He subsequently moved to England in 1904, taking up a post at the University of Manchester, and was elected to the General Zionist Council. Weizmann's employer in Manchester, Charles Dreyfus, was president of the Manchester Zionist Society and a leading figure in the East Manchester Conservative Association during the time that Arthur Balfour was Member of Parliament for the constituency and Prime Minister. At Dreyfus' suggestion Balfour and Weizmann first met at a constituency meeting on 27 January 1905. Weizmann would later become president of the World Zionist Organisation and the leading spokesperson for Zionism in Britain.

During their first fateful meeting, Balfour enquired about Weizmann's views regarding a scheme proposed by Colonial Secretary Joseph Chamberlain to create a Jewish national home in Uganda. Herzl had previously asked Chamberlain to permit Jewish colonisation in Egypt, near El Arish, with a view to a northward expansion into Palestine. However, the British viceroy in Egypt, Lord Cromer, rejected Herzl's proposal as likely to antagonise the Egyptians. Chamberlain had put forward the Uganda plan as a counter-proposal to Herzl in 1903, but after Herzl's death in 1904 it had been voted down by the Seventh Zionist Congress. According to Weizmann's memoirs, the conversation proceeded as follows:

> "Mr. Balfour, supposing I was to offer you Paris instead of London, would you take it?" He sat up, looked at me, and answered: "But Dr. Weizmann, we have London." "That is true," I said, "but we had Jerusalem when London was a marsh." He ... said two things which I remember vividly. The first was: "Are there many Jews who think like you?" I answered: "I believe I speak the mind of millions of Jews whom you will never see and who cannot speak for themselves" ... To this he said: "If that is so you will one day be a force."[3]

Weizmann's position as a prominent leader of the Zionist movement, and appreciation for scientific assistance he provided in the development of explosives which enabled the Allies to maintain an armaments superiority over the Central Powers throughout World War I, ensured that he was able to maintain close contact with British political leaders, positioning him to play a crucial role influencing British attitudes towards the creation of a Jewish homeland in the years leading up to the issuing of the Balfour Declaration.

World War I

On 28 July 1914, the First World War erupted in Europe between two opposing alliances: the Triple Entente consisting of the British Empire, France and the Russian Empire verses the Central Powers of Germany, Austria-Hungary and, later that year, the Ottoman Empire.

On the eve of war, the anticipated break-up of the enfeebled Ottoman Empire raised genuine nationalistic hopes among both Zionists and Arabs. The Zionists hoped to attain support from one of the world's great powers for increased Jewish immigration and eventual sovereignty in Palestine, whereas the Arab nationalists wanted an independent Arab state covering all the Ottoman Arab domains. Both Jews and Arabs could make powerful and convincing historic claims to Palestine. The Jews, on the one hand, claimed that Palestine was the homeland of their ancestors from ancient times up to 70 AD, when the Romans had destroyed the Temple in Jerusalem and driven Jews out of the region. Arabs, on the other hand, had lived in Palestine for centuries, and could point to a more recent history of living and farming in the region. Unlike with the Jews, however, there was not a distinct Arab Palestinian identity and there had never been a period of independent Arab sovereignty in Palestine.

From a purely demographic standpoint, the Zionist argument was not very strong – in 1914 they comprised only twelve percent of the total population of Palestine. However, they had a major asset in the positioning of their chief spokesman, Chaim Weizmann. Widely respected in Britain as an astute statesman and as a scientist, he was well versed in European diplomacy. Following Britain's declaration of war on the Ottoman Empire, Weizmann met with the British cabinet minister Herbert Samuel, a Jew and avid Zionist, on 10 December 1914. At that meeting Samuel informed Weizmann of a memorandum he was preparing regarding the creation of a Jewish state in Palestine, and went as far as to declare a hope to rebuild the Temple of Jerusalem as a symbol of Jewish unity. Weizmann encouraged Samuel in this pursuit and, aware of Britain's imperial sensibilities, extolled the benefits that a Jewish homeland in Palestine would deliver for British interests in the Near East.

Two days later, Weizmann used social contacts with the influential Rothschild family to secure meetings with Balfour, his first for eight years, and later, on 15 January 1915, with Chancellor of the Exchequer and pro-Zionist David Lloyd George in Downing Street. During his meeting with Balfour, Weizmann complained about the slowdown that the war appeared to have imposed on Zionist plans, to which Balfour replied, "You may get your things done much quicker after the war."[4]

Toward the end of January 1915, emboldened by Lloyd George, Herbert Samuel finally circulated an iteration of his memorandum, entitled "The Future of Palestine", among his cabinet colleagues. The memorandum stated, "Already there is a stirring among the twelve million Jews scattered throughout the countries of the world. A feeling is spreading with great rapidity that now, at last, some advance may be made, in some way, towards the fulfilment of the hope and desire, held with unshakable tenacity for eighteen hundred years, for the restoration of the Jews to the land to which they are attached by ties almost as ancient as history itself ... I am assured that the solution of the problem of Palestine which would be much the most welcome to the leaders and supporters of the Zionist movement throughout the world would be the annexation of the country to the British Empire."[5] Prime Minister Herbert Asquith was disinterested, as he considered Zionism to be an unattainable fantasy. This view was reinforced by the influential Edwin Montagu, Chancellor of the Duchy of Lancaster, who wrote to Asquith on 16 March 1915 to point out that no "Jewish race now exists as a homogeneous whole."[6] Like many other British assimilationist Jews, Montagu considered "Jews as a religious community and himself as a Jewish Englishman." Significantly, however, Samuel attracted the unconditional support of the future Prime Minister, Lloyd George. Although Samuel gained no apparent support from authoritative figures such as Asquith, Montagu and Lord Kitchener, he had succeeded in placing Zionism at the centre of Britain's political agenda.

Although Weizmann may have bemoaned the slow pace of Zionist progress during this period, his lobbying was beginning to bear rich fruit. The support of Lloyd George, Balfour, Samuel and others was secured, and history was about to thrust these men onto centre stage.

The work of Weizmann in advocating for Zionism reveals an uncanny diplomatic genius. He understood, in a way that Arab leaders of his time never grasped, that the future map of the Middle East would be determined not by the desires of its inhabitants but by the rivalries of the great powers, European strategic thinking, and domestic British politics. Britain, in possession of the Suez Canal and playing a dominant role in India and Egypt, attached tremendous strategic importance to the region. British Middle Eastern policy, however, embraced conflicting objectives, and as a result Asquith's government became embroiled in an intriguing web of distinct and contradictory negotiations over the fate of the region.

The McMahon–Hussein Correspondence

In order to obtain Arab support in the War, the British government promised Hussein bin Ali, the Sharif of Mecca, that in the event of an Allied victory, the greater part of the Arab provinces of the Turkish Empire would be granted independence.

In February 1914, Amir Abdullah, Hussein bin Ali's son, went to Cairo to lobby Lord Kitchener, British agent and Consul General in Egypt, about the possibility of British support should his father stage a revolt against Turkey. Germany and Turkey were not yet formally allied, and Germany and Britain were not yet at war; Kitchener's initial response was, therefore, non-committal. However, after the outbreak of war, Kitchener was recalled to London as Secretary of State for War, and as British military fortunes in the Middle East deteriorated, Amir Abdullah's lobbying bore fruit. Kitchener saw the usefulness of transferring the Islamic caliphate – the caliph, or successor to the Prophet Muhammad, was the traditional leader of the Islamic world – to an Arab candidate indebted to Britain, and he energetically sought Arab support for the war against Turkey.

The British High Commissioner to Egypt, Henry McMahon, exchanged letters with Hussein bin Ali between July 1915 and January 1916 in which he made ambiguous promises, on behalf of the British government, to support independent control of Arab lands subject to certain reservations and exclusions of territory not entirely Arab or concerning which Britain was not free "to act without detriment to the interests of her ally, France." McMahon specified that the exceptions covered "portions of Syria" laying to the west of "the districts of Damascus, Homs, Hama and Aleppo." The Arabs understood that Palestine would be included in the sphere of Arab independence, though it was not explicitly mentioned. Although the McMahon–Hussein correspondence was not legally binding on either side, on the basis of McMahon's assurances, the Arab Revolt against the Ottoman Turks began on 5 June 1916, and in the October of that year, Hussein declared himself "King of the Arabs."

The Sykes–Picot Agreement

While McMahon and Hussein were corresponding over the fate of the Middle East, the British were secretly negotiating with the French and Russians over the same territory. In the aftermath of the British defeat in the Dardanelles campaign of 1915, the Foreign Office decided to launch a new offensive in the Middle East, which it believed could only be carried out by reassuring the French of Britain's intentions in the region.

In May 1916 the governments of the United Kingdom, France and Russia signed the Sykes–Picot Agreement, named after its chief negotiators Mark Sykes, Baron of Kedleston, and the French Ambassador, François Picot, which defined their proposed spheres of influence and control in Western Asia should the Triple Entente succeed in defeating the Ottoman Empire. Contrary to the contents of the McMahon–Hussein correspondence, the agreement effectively partitioned the Arab provinces of the Ottoman Empire outside the Arabian Peninsula into areas of future British and French control or influence with the exclusion of Hebron and the area to the "East of Jordan." This area of exclusion, which would later become Mandatory Palestine, was to be administered by an international "condominium" of the British, French, and Russians, though it was decided that the details of this administrative arrangement could be ironed out later to allow consultations with both Russia and Hussein to be completed.

Hussein only learned of the agreement in December 1917 when it was leaked by the new Soviet government but was satisfied by two duplicitous telegrams from Sir Reginald Wingate, High Commissioner of Egypt, assuring him that the British government's commitments to the Arabs were still valid and that the Sykes–Picot Agreement was not a formal treaty.

The Balfour Declaration

The underlying motive driving British policy decisions in the Middle East during the correspondence with Hussein and the Sykes–Picot negotiations was the view of the Liberal coalition government of Herbert Asquith that a Jewish entity in Palestine was detrimental to British strategic aims in the region. That was to change dramatically with the emergence of David Lloyd George as Prime Minister on 6 December 1916, and the appointment of Arthur James Balfour as Foreign Secretary four days later.

In a radical change of policy, Lloyd George was determined to ensure that Palestine came under British control in abandonment of the British–French condominium proposed in the Sykes–Picot agreement. In the context of this new strategic thinking, an alliance with the Zionists appeared to be an attractive proposition for safeguarding British interests in the region, which were securing British control of the strategically vital Suez Canal and Egyptian buffer, and securing the route to India, the jewel in the crown of the British Empire.

Almost all historical commentators who have analysed the motivations underpinning the Lloyd George government's backing for Zionism focus exclusively on the policy's political expediency, and the influences of Weizmann, Samuel and other Zionist lobbyists. These political elements are obviously important, particularly in terms of the timing of events, but they are not the whole story. There was another crucial element that explains why Lloyd George, Balfour and others in government were so receptive to the Zionist lobby which, if not factored, leaves one with an inadequate two-dimensional understanding of their intentions. We shall begin, though, with the commonly accepted political agenda:

As the war on the Western Front entered a stalemate, with the outcome impossible to predict after the disaster on the Somme and the relentless horror of trench warfare, the War Cabinet calculated that supporting a Jewish entity in Palestine would mobilise America's influential Jewish community to support United States intervention in the war and sway the large number of Jewish Bolsheviks who participated in the 1917 Russian Revolution to keep Russia in the war.

Ahead of the American entry into World War I, it became clear that Woodrow Wilson and his advisors were in favour of Zionism. Two of Wilson's closest advisors, Louis Brandeis and Felix Frankfurter, were avid Zionists. How better to shore up an uncertain ally than by endorsing Zionist aims? Balfour led a month-long Mission to Washington D.C. and New York in early summer of 1917, where he took every opportunity to discuss Zionism with Brandeis. Although Zionism in America was still in its relative infancy, the Jewish population in America amounted to three million.

The British adopted similar thinking when it came to the Russians, who were in the midst of revolution. Several of the most prominent revolutionaries, including Leon Trotsky, were of Jewish descent. Why not see if they could be persuaded to keep Russia in the war by appealing to their latent Jewishness and giving them another reason to continue the fight?

Fears were also voiced in the Foreign Office that if Britain did not come out in favour of a Jewish entity in Palestine the Germans would pre-empt them. There was much anxiety that Jewish sympathy might be inclined towards Germany as a way of paying back the Russians for their murderous pre-war pogroms. They were apparently correct, for after the publication of the Balfour Declaration, Germany reacted immediately by negotiating with Turkey to put forward counter proposals. A German–Jewish Society was formed and in January 1918 the Turkish Grand Vizier, Mehmed Talaat Pasha, issued a statement which promised legislation by which "all justifiable wishes of the Jews in Palestine would be able to find their fulfilment."[7]

Such were the political factors motivating the new policy direction. However, there was another significant component that drove Lloyd George and Balfour to make overtures to the Zionist cause. The Balfour Declaration did not originate in a cultural vacuum. Beyond the realpolitik, its spirit is deeply rooted in British Christian traditions. Both Lloyd George and Balfour were devout Evangelical Christians who attached great religious significance to the restoration of the Jews in their ancient homeland.

William the Conqueror first encouraged Jews to settle in England after his victory at Hastings in 1066 AD as a way of escaping anti-Semitism in France, but sadly the hatred followed them across the Channel. The English Church of the Middle Ages had a long and terrible history of anti-Semitism, which culminated in the expulsion of Jews from England in 1290 AD.

Christian anti-Semitism is rooted in an unbiblical doctrine known today as 'Replacement Theology' which originated from the early Church Fathers who used allegorical interpretative techniques to assert that the Church has replaced Israel as God's chosen people and that all the biblical promises concerning the people and the land of Israel have been transferred to Christians. Tertullian (155-240 AD) pronounced that because the Jews were responsible for the death of Jesus they had been totally rejected by God. In his response to the heretic Marcion, he wrote, "It would be tedious to state at length how the figurative interpretation [of Israel's promised restoration] is spiritually applicable to Christ and His church." Origen of Alexandria (184-253 AD), in his work *Against Celsus*, claimed, "We say with confidence that they [the Jews] will never be restored to their former condition ... It accordingly behoved that city where Jesus underwent those sufferings to perish utterly ... and the invitation of happiness offered them by God to pass to others – the Christians!" Cyprian (195-258 AD), Bishop of Carthage, in his *Testimonies Against the Jews,* declared, "The Jews ... had departed from God, and had lost God's favour

... while the Christians had succeeded in their place ... the Gentiles, rather than the Jew attain to the kingdom of heaven."

Towards the end of the era of the Church Fathers, the rhetoric and language became increasingly insidious. John Chrysostom (349-407 AD) described the Synagogues as brothels and theatres frequented by thieves and wild beasts. He regarded all Jews as demon possessed devil worshippers who were beyond forgiveness. Jerome (347-420 AD) spoke of Jews as serpents who wore the image of Judas, and whose prayers were nothing more than the sounds of braying donkeys. Augustine (354-430 AD) stated that Jews deserved nothing less than death. They would be scattered across the earth to bear witness to the triumph of the Church over the Synagogue. Such is the pervasive influence of the Church Fathers on the development of Christian belief and practice that the Church is confronted by an uncomfortable reality: anti-Semitism is deeply embedded in Christian thinking, and the Church is responsible for inciting many of the historical atrocities committed against Jews.

By the Middle Ages, the Jews were regarded as 'Christ-killers' and therefore guilty of deicide. Few churches spoke in defence of the Jews. Christian art routinely portrayed Jews as demonic looking figures bent on killing Christians. This was an era of 'blood libels', inquisitions, forced conversions, state persecution and expulsions.

Although the Reformation of the 16th Century brought many positive changes to the Church, particularly through the fundamental tenet that the bible, translated into the languages of the ordinary people, was the sole source of authority, anti-Jewish vitriol continued. Martin Luther, the great hero of the Reformation, turned against the Jews in a publication titled *The Jews and their Lies* in which he referred to Jews as "miserable, blind and senseless people" whose arrogance is "as solid as an iron mountain", and as "thieves and robbers who daily eat no morsel and wear no thread of clothing which they have not stolen and pilfered by means of their accursed usury ... It cannot be anything but the terrible wrath of God which permits anyone to sink into such abysmal, devilish, hellish, insane baseness, envy and arrogance."[8] He suggested that their houses should be destroyed, their money confiscated and that they be compelled into forced labour. Adolf Hitler appealed to Luther to justify his own radical brand of anti-Semitism in his book *Mein Kampf*. William Shirer, in *The Rise and Fall of the Third Reich,* wrote, "It is difficult to understand the behaviour of most German Protestants in the first Nazi years unless one is aware of two things: their history and the influence of Martin Luther. The great founder of Protestantism was both a passionate Anti-Semite and a ferocious believer in absolute obedience to political authority. He wanted a Germany rid of the Jews ... advice that was literally followed four centuries later by Hitler, Goering and Himmler ... Luther employed a coarseness of language unequalled in German history until the Nazi time ... In no other country, with the exception of Tsarist Russia, did the clergy become by tradition so completely servile to the political authority of the state."[9]

Other products of the Reformation, however, were drawn to a doctrine known as millenarianism which envisaged the perfection of the world at the end of days when the Messiah would reign from Jerusalem for one thousand years and viewed the Jews more positively as custodians of the land in which their redemption would occur. Significantly for Britain, Oliver Cromwell and the Puritan movement were drawn towards millenarianism after the English civil war. Puritan thinking fundamentally changed the relationship between Christians and Jews in Britain. As they began to re-examine the Hebrew Scriptures, they saw that the whole of scripture was about a Jewish nation, in a Jewish land with a Jewish capital – Jerusalem. Further, it was written by Jewish authors and pointed towards a Jewish Messiah, who would usher in an era of universal peace for all nations. And so they abandoned Replacement Theology and moved to a position of belief that God's covenant with his people Israel was eternal. As the covenant related to both the people and the land of Israel, they concluded that not only was Palestine the rightful home of the Jewish people, but that God would eventually ensure that they returned to their homeland. This was the beginning of what is now called Christian Zionism.

After Cromwell's time, although millenarian theology declined, the general attitude towards the Jews in Britain remained positive. In 1792, at the height of the Methodist revivals, Charles Wesley wrote what became known as the Wesley Zionist hymn which is replete with biblical references to the re-gathering of Israel to their Promised Land from all the nations to which they had been scattered. This hymn was an integral part of the song book that was declared by many thousands of ordinary British Christians in regular worship. J C Ryle, who would later become Bishop of Liverpool, was outspoken in his support for the Jews' right to return to their homeland. Speaking of biblical prophecies yet to be fulfilled, he said, "Two points appear to my mind to stand out as plainly as if written by a sunbeam. One ... is the second personal advent of our Lord Jesus Christ before the Millennium. The other ... is the future literal gathering of the Jewish nation, and their restoration in their own land ... They [the prophets] all predict the final gathering of the Jewish nation from the four quarters of the globe, and their restoration to their own land ... I ask you, then, to settle it firmly in your mind, that when God says a thing shall be done, we ought to believe it."[10]

In the mid 19th Century, Zionist theology resurfaced in the British Evangelical movement and inspired a radical growth of highly influential and zealous pro-Jewish movements. Men of calibre like Lord Shaftesbury and William Wilberforce, better known for fighting social injustice and slavery, were at the same time, in prayer, fighting for the restoration of Israel as a prelude to the second coming of Christ. Shaftsbury, responding to news of the appointment of the first British vice-consul at Jerusalem, recorded in his diary, "The ancient city of the people of God is about to resume a place among the nations, and England is the first of all the Gentile kingdoms that ceases 'to tread her down.'"[11] Wilberforce became the first Vice President of the London Jews Society, known today as the 'Church's Ministry among Jewish People'. Britain's premier preacher of the period, Charles H Spurgeon, prophesied in 1855, "Judea, so long a howling wilderness, shall once more blossom like a rose ... We do not attach sufficient importance to the restoration of the Jews. We do not think enough about it. But certainly, if there is anything promised in the bible it is this."[12] Amongst the adherents to these movements were some significant political figures such as Joseph Chamberlain, who served as Chancellor of the Exchequer and Foreign Minister.

By the turn of the 20th Century, the Evangelical movement was the only form of Christianity prevalent in British political circles. When Lloyd George formed his new coalition Cabinet, in the providence of God, the Christian Zionist dimension was strong and growing – especially Balfour and Lloyd George – but also Arthur Henderson, Jan Smuts and George Barnes. These men were deeply religious. They had grown up on the Bible and the Holy Land was their spiritual home. They felt a genuine admiration for the Jews and their history.

David Lloyd George was raised in a Welsh village by his uncle, a Baptist minister, in an environment where study of the Bible was considered one of the highest values of society. Though brought up as a devout Evangelical, Lloyd George lost his faith as a young man, but remained a regular attendee at chapel and a connoisseur of good preaching all his life. During the war, he commented that, "The place names in Palestine are more familiar to me than those of the Western Front."[13] He never wavered throughout his long political career in his commitment to the restoration of Israel.

Balfour was arguably the most committed Christian in the Cabinet. As a boy he was tutored at home by his local Presbyterian Pastor. From an early age he developed a particular fascination with "the people of the book" and his interest in the restoration of Israel stretched far beyond politics.

Jan Smuts received a rich biblical upbringing in his native South Africa. In 1917, he declared that he hoped to see a great Jewish state arise once more in Palestine and that he regarded the Balfour Declaration as an act of moral reparation to the Jewish people for centuries of Christian anti-Semitic persecution.

Labour minister Arthur Henderson converted to a personal faith in Christ at the age of 16 after attending evangelistic meetings held by the revivalist preacher Gypsy Smith. After leaving politics he became a Methodist lay preacher. Another Labour Cabinet member, the Trade Unionist George Barnes was, according to Weizmann, one of the staunchest advocates for the Zionist cause. In his autobiography, Barnes wrote that he intended to give the Jews, "a right of asylum and citizenship in the country which to them had a peculiar interest as a cradle of their race."[14]

Andrew Bonar Law was raised in the home of a Presbyterian minister in New Brunswick, Canada. Edward Carlson was a towering Protestant figure in Northern Ireland. George Curzon was the son of an Anglican minister. In Cabinet, Curzon raised objections to the Declaration. He was the only Cabinet member who had visited Palestine and was concerned about the viability of a national home due to the small size of the land and its inhospitable terrain. Despite these reservations, when it came to the vote, he threw his weight behind the Declaration.

Edwin Montague, a practicing Jew, was the only member of the Cabinet who opposed the Declaration. He represented the voice of the anti-Zionist Jews who favoured assimilation into

Western society as the solution to anti-Semitism and feared that a national homeland would become a Jewish Ghetto.

And so it is clear that the Balfour Declaration was not a knee jerk reaction from a desperate government fighting for the survival of an Empire – it was a political statement that reflected the personal faith of the majority of the Cabinet members. More than that, it represented the culmination of over 200 years of deeply ingrained Christian and political hope to see the Jewish people return to their Promised Land.

In June 1917, at Balfour's behest, Weizmann and Lord Rothschild submitted a draft statement of support for the Zionist cause for Cabinet consideration. With the British army poised on the edge of Palestine, they recognized that victory over the Ottomans would place Britain in a position to determine the political landscape of the region after the war.

The draft statement was debated in Cabinet, and passed through numerous revisions and iterations as the Cabinet prepared to release a final statement while simultaneously invading Palestine. The process of revision was in large part due to the conflicting stances of those involved. Key players were passionately contesting for the wording to reflect their own aspirations and beliefs. One such figure was Mark Sykes, co-author of the Sykes–Picot declaration, who was designated by the Cabinet to guide the drafting the Declaration. Sykes was pro-Arab and strongly favoured Cultural Zionism, whose aspirations for Palestine stretched only as far as setting up a cultural centre in Jerusalem to celebrate Jewish heritage. Sykes succeeded in persuading the drafting committee to word the Declaration in such ambiguous terms that both Political and Cultural Zionist could interpret it according to their own agendas.

On two occasions, British officials consulted with President Wilson to gain his consent for releasing the statement. It is important to note that Britain was not acting in isolation from the international community – agreements were carefully sought with the world powers to secure international legitimacy for the Declaration. On the first occasion, 3 September 1917, Wilson replied that the time was not yet ripe; but on the latter, 6 October 1917, he agreed to its release. Assurances of sympathy towards Zionist aims were also obtained from French and Italian political leaders.

On 31 October 1917, British and ANZAC troops poised on the southern border of Palestine launched an offensive at Beersheba under the command of General Allenby in an effort to capture its vital water wells and open the way to Jerusalem. This was a region that was defended relatively lightly because never before in history had an army successfully entered Palestine by way of the forbidding Negev Desert. The battle would prove to be a turning point in world history.

Significantly, according to biblical tradition, Beersheba was a city with strong associations to Abraham. Here he lived, dug wells and worshiped God, *"Abraham planted a tamarisk tree in Beersheba, and there he called on the name of the Lord, the Eternal God"* (Genesis 21:33). Here also, God spoke to Abraham's son Isaac, *"From there (Isaac) went up to Beersheba. That night the* LORD *appeared to him and said, "I am the God of your father Abraham. Do not be afraid, for I am with you; I will bless you and will increase the number of your descendants for the sake of my servant Abraham." Isaac built an altar there and called on the name of the Lord"* (Genesis 26:23-25).

As dusk descended, the ANZAC 4th light horse brigade launched a cavalry charge that broke through the Turkish frontline. Such was the speed of their advance they rode beneath the Turkish artillery whose gunners were unable to adjust their sights quickly enough to keep up with the galloping horsemen. Private Walter Keddie described the charge, "We were all at the gallop yelling like mad. Some had bayonets in their hand, others their rifle, then it was a full stretch gallop at the trenches ... those horses put on pace and next we were jumping the trenches with the Turks underneath ... when over the trenches we went straight for the town." Sergeant Charles Doherty recounted, "The enemy's fire now came from the direction of the town and a large railway viaduct to the north. The limited number of entrances to the city temporarily checked us but those in front went straight up and through the narrow streets. Falling beams from fired buildings, exploding magazines and various hidden snipers were unable to check our race through the two available streets that were wide enough for two to ride abreast."[15] By 6.00 pm, Beersheba, with its crucial water supply, was in Allied hands and the door to Palestine had been smashed opened.

On the very same day, unaware in an era of limited communications of the dramatic events unfolding at Beersheba, Lloyd George and Balfour met with the War Cabinet to discuss their options for the Middle East. At the very moment that the light horse brigade was sweeping through the Turkish lines, the final wording of the Declaration was agreed and the momentous decision was reached to publicly issue its contents to the Zionist Federation. The timing was providential. Without the victory at Beersheba, the Declaration would have been nothing but a worthless piece of paper. It is not hard to discern the hand of God orchestrating events in London and Palestine at this critical moment in history.

The Declaration reflected the world view of the Cabinet, and was delivered in a spirit of biblical belief and co-operation between Evangelical Christianity and the Jewish people. That is not to say that the political benefits were not also a factor in the timing of its release. Lloyd George later confirmed in his testimony to the Peel Commission of 1937 that: "In this critical situation it was believed that Jewish sympathy or the reverse would make a substantial difference one way or the other to the Allied cause. In particular Jewish sympathy would confirm the support of American Jewry, and would make it more difficult for Germany to reduce her military commitments and improve her economic position on the eastern front ... The Zionist leaders gave us a definite promise that, if the Allies committed themselves to giving facilities for the establishment of a national home for the Jews in Palestine, they would do their best to rally Jewish sentiment and support throughout the world to the Allied cause. They kept their word."[16]

Two days after the War Cabinet meeting, on 2 November 1917, Balfour signed the letter, addressed to Lord Rothschild, that became known as the Balfour Declaration. The document declared the British government's "sympathy with Jewish Zionist aspirations" and stated that His Majesty's government viewed "with favour the establishment in Palestine of a National Home for the Jewish People." The letter also announced the government's intention to facilitate the achievement of this objective under the provision that "nothing shall be done which may prejudice the civil and religious rights of existing non–Jewish communities in Palestine or the rights and political status enjoyed by Jews in any other country." The document was a masterpiece of intricately designed ambiguity. Favouring a national home for the Jewish people fell short of promising a Jewish State, though that was clearly the ultimate aim of the Zionist movement, while the protected rights of the existing non–Jewish communities (avoiding the use of the term Arab) did not include references to political or national rights. Leopold Amery, an under-secretary to the Cabinet who assisted with revisions to the wording, later wrote that he was proud of having quietly produced a "judicious blend" which "left the future scope of Palestine to be decided by developments."[17]

Most people are inclined to believe in the good intentions of Balfour and his colleagues, and rightly take pride in the role that Britain played in the reinstitution of Israel in her ancient homeland. In April 2017, the British Conservative government of Teresa May rejected a Palestinian request to apologize for the Balfour

Declaration. The statement they released read, "We are proud of our role in creating the State of Israel ... the Declaration was written in a world of competing imperial powers, in the midst of the First World War and in the twilight of the Ottoman Empire. In that context, establishing a homeland for the Jewish people in the land to which they had such strong historical and religious ties was the right and moral thing to do, particularly against the background of centuries of persecution."[18] Neither was the Declaration enacted in isolation from the international community. It was approved in advance by the Allied powers whose consensus then constituted the only source of international legitimacy. The scholar Martin Kramer wrote, "The Balfour Declaration anticipated a world regulated by a consortium of principal powers – the same world that, 30 years later, would pass a UN resolution legitimating the establishment of a Jewish state ... the poetic simplicity of the Balfour Declaration resides in its presumption that a home for the Jews in their land needs no justification."[19]

However, it is difficult to avoid the conclusion that the Lloyd George government, aware of the political ramifications on the ground, set out to deceive the Arabs as to their ultimate intentions. Balfour wrote to Lord Curzon on 11 August 1919: "In Palestine we do not propose even to go through the form of consulting the wishes of the present inhabitants of the country ... The Four Great Powers are committed to Zionism ... Zionism, be it right or wrong, good or bad, is rooted in age-long traditions, in present needs, in future hopes, of far profounder import than the desires and prejudices of the 700,000 Arabs who now inhabit that ancient land."[20] Three months after the Declaration was issued, Balfour privately confided, "My personal hope is that the Jews will make good in Palestine and eventually found a Jewish State. It is up to them now; we have given them their great opportunity."[21] In conversation with Weizmann in 1921, Lloyd George and Balfour declared that they both had intended the ultimate creation of a Jewish State.

For Weizmann, the Declaration was a spectacular climax to his protracted and skilful negotiations with the Foreign Office in support of the Zionist cause. Balfour had been impressed with Weizmann during their earlier meetings, and Lloyd George wrote in his War Memoirs of a meeting with Weizmann in 1916, in which Weizmann "explained his aspirations as to the repatriation of the Jews to the sacred land they had made famous." Lloyd George continued, "That was the fount and origin of the famous Declaration about the National Home for the Jews in Palestine ... As soon as I became Prime Minister I talked the whole matter over with Mr Balfour, who was then Foreign Secretary."[22]

Not all Jews in Britain subscribed to the Zionist vision; there were many progressives who, like Edwin Montagu, advocated for Jewish assimilation into society. Weizmann succeeded in convincing Lloyd George and Balfour that the Zionist movement represented the majority of Jews, and that a public commitment by Britain to establishing a Jewish homeland in Palestine, and thereby securing support of this Jewish Zionist majority across the world, would have a decisive influence on the outcome of the war. In his Memoirs, published in 1939, Lloyd George stated: "The Balfour Declaration represented the convinced policy of all parties in our country and also in America ... The Zionist Movement was exceptionally strong in Russia and America ... It was believed, also, that such a declaration would have a potent influence upon world Jewry outside Russia, and secure for the Entente the aid of Jewish financial interests. In America, their aid in this respect would have a special value when the Allies had almost exhausted the gold and marketable securities available for American purchases. Such were the chief considerations which, in 1917, impelled the British Government towards making a contract with Jewry."[23]

The Sharif of Mecca, Hussein bin Ali, and other Arab leaders responded vehemently that the Declaration was a violation of the previous agreements set out in the McMahon–Hussein correspondence. Palestine was not explicitly mentioned in that correspondence, and territories which were not purely Arab were excluded by the McMahon letters, although historically Palestine had always been regarded as part of Southern Syria. The Arabs, taking Palestine to be overwhelmingly Arab, claimed the Declaration was incompatible with the letters, which promised the Arab independence movement control of the Middle East territories "in the limits and boundaries proposed by the Sharif of Mecca" in exchange for revolting against the Ottoman Empire during World War I. In their eyes, the Balfour Declaration was a betrayal of promises made by the British after the Arabs had fulfilled their side of the bargain.

The British claimed that the McMahon letters did not apply to Palestine, and therefore the Declaration could not be a violation of the previous agreement. Five years after the Balfour Declaration, in the White Paper of 1922 that he authored, Winston Churchill stated, "It is not the case ... that during the war His Majesty's Government gave an undertaking that an independent national government should be at once established in Palestine. This representation mainly rests upon a letter ... from Sir Henry McMahon ... to the Sharif of Mecca ... That letter is quoted as conveying the promise to the Sharif of Mecca to recognize and support the independence of the Arabs within the territories proposed by him. But this promise was given subject to a reservation made in the same letter, which excluded from its scope ... the portions of Syria lying to the west of the District of Damascus. This reservation has always been regarded by His Majesty's Government as covering the vilayet of Beirut and the independent Sanjak of Jerusalem. The whole of Palestine west of the Jordan was thus excluded from Sir Henry McMahon's pledge."[24]

However, this claim was later brought into question. Lord Grey, the Foreign Secretary during the McMahon–Hussein negotiations, made it clear in a speech to the House of Lords on 27 March 1923 that he entertained serious doubts as to the validity of the British government's interpretation of the pledges which he, as Foreign Secretary, had caused to be given to Hussein in 1915. He called for all of the secret engagements regarding Palestine to be made public. Many of the relevant documents in the National Archives were later declassified and published. Among them were the minutes of a Cabinet Committee meeting, chaired by Lord Curzon, which was held on 5 December 1918. The minutes revealed that in laying out the government's position Lord Curzon had explained that, "The Palestine position is this. If we deal with our commitments, there is first the general pledge to Hussein in October 1915, under which Palestine *was included* in the areas as to which Great Britain pledged itself that they should be Arab and independent in the future."[25] The obvious ambiguity over Britain's promise to Hussein in relation to Palestine can be understood, perhaps, when it is remembered that this was a promise delivered during the confusion of war and at a time when other Allied governments were vying for influence in the region.

The British government dispatched Commander David George Hogarth to meet with Hussein in January 1918 bearing the message that the "political and economic freedom" of the Palestinian population was not in question. Hogarth reported back that Hussein "would not accept an independent Jewish State in Palestine, nor was I instructed to warn him that such a state was contemplated by Great Britain."[26]

Continuing Arab disquiet over the course of 1918 regarding Allied intentions also led to the British 'Declaration to the Seven' which was a response to an anonymous memorandum issued by seven Syrian notables calling for a "guarantee of the ultimate independence of Arabia." The Declaration promised that the future governance of regions liberated from the Ottoman Empire should be determined by the principle of self-determination. This was followed by the 'Anglo-French Declaration' which promised "the complete and final liberation of the peoples who have for so long been oppressed by the Turks, and the setting up of national governments and administrations deriving their authority from the free exercise of the initiative and choice of the indigenous populations."[27]

Arab fears would not be easy to allay. Out of necessity, Britain had made promises to both the Arabs and the Zionists in order to gain support for war objectives. Could she now negotiate a way to reconcile these two promises when it was clear that the two parties in receipt regarded them as mutually incompatible?

The wording of the Balfour Declaration reflected a belief that the two groups vying for power in Palestine, the native Arabs, primarily farmers and small-scale traders, and Zionist Jews, many of whom were recent immigrants whose mission was to build up an independent Jewish state, could live alongside one another. Therefore, the Declaration stated that Britain would favour "the establishment in Palestine of a national home for the Jewish people" while at the same time specifying that "nothing shall be done which may prejudice the civil and religious rights of the existing non-Jewish communities in Palestine." It was a dual promise that proved impossible to keep. The incompatibility sharpened over the succeeding years and became irreconcilable. The foundational stone for modern Israel had been laid, but the prediction that this would lay the groundwork for harmonious Arab–Jewish cooperation would prove to be wishful thinking.

Endnotes

1. Jonathan Schneer, *The Balfour Declaration: The Origins of the Arab-Israeli Conflict* (London: Bloomsbury, 2010), p. 305.
2. Herzl, *Our Hope*, 1904.
3. Geoffrey Lewis, *Balfour and Weizmann* (London: Continuum, 2009), p. 63.
4. Lorenzo Kamel, *Imperial Perceptions of Palestine: British Influence and Power in Late Ottoman Times* (London: British Academic Press, 2015), p. 106.
5. Ibid., p. 106.
6. Ibid., p. 108.
7. Israel Cohen, *The Zionist Movement Revised* (Zionist Organisation of America, 1946), p. 120.
8. Cited from Jewish Virtual Library, *www.jewishvirtuallibrary.org/martin-luther-quot-the-jews-and-their-lies-quote*.
9. William Shirer, *The Rise and Fall of the Third Reich* (New York: Simon and Schuster, 1990), p. 91, 236.
10. J C Ryle, "Are You Ready for the End of Time?" 1867.
11. Cited from Yaron Perry, *British Mission to the Jews in Nineteenth-Century Palestine* (London: Frank Cass, 2003), p. 28.
12. Charles Spurgeon, *Spurgeon's Sermons Volume 1:1855*, Delivered 3 June 1855.
13. Cited from David Schmidt, "The War Cabinet of Believers", *Partners in this Great Enterprise* (Nottingham: New Life Publishing, 2017), p. 26.
14. Ibid., p. 27.
15. The accounts of Private Keddie and Sergeant Doherty are cited from The Australian War Memorial, *https://www.awm.gov.au/articles/blog/the-charge-of-the-4th-light-horse-brigade-at-beersheba*.
16. Peel Report: *Palestine Royal Commission Report Presented by the Secretary of State for the Colonies to Parliament by Command of His Majesty, July 1937*. His Majesty's Stationery Office, London, 1937, p. 22-23.

[17] Leopold Amery, *My Political Life, Vol. 11* (London: Hutchinson, 1953), p. 116-117. Cited by Kathy Durkin, "The Ambiguous Wording of the Balfour Declaration", *Partners in this Great Enterprise* (Nottingham: New Life Publishing, 2017), p. 24.

[18] Cited from *https://www.timesofisrael.com/uk-tells-palestinains-there-will-be-no-no-apology-for-balfour-declaration/*. 25 April 2017.

[19] Martin Kramer, "The Forgotten Truth about the Balfour Declaration," *Mosaic* (5 June 2017).

[20] Doreen Ingrams, *Palestine Papers 1917-1922, Seeds of Conflict* (London: John Murray, 1972), p. 17.

[21] Cited from Michael Makovsky, *Churchill's Promised Land: Zionism and Statecraft* (New Haven: Yale University Press, 2007), p. 77. The remark was made at a private dinner, and was a response to a question posed by Colonel Meinertzhagen who recorded the conversation in his diary, "Do you regard this declaration as a charter for ultimate sovereignty in Palestine or are you trying to graft a Jewish population on to an Arab Palestine?"

[22] David Lloyd George, *War Memoirs of David Lloyd George: 1915-1916* (AMS Press, 1933), p. 50.

[23] David Lloyd George, *Memoirs of the Peace Conference* (Yale University Press, 1939), p. 724-734.

[24] Churchill White Paper: *Correspondence with the Palestine Arab Delegation and the Zionist Organisation, June 1922, Cmd 1700*. His Majesty's Stationery Office, London, 1922

[25] UK Archives PRO. CAB 27/24.

[26] Peter Mansfield, *A History of the Middle East: 3rd Ed.* (London: Penguin Books, 2010), p. 130.

[27] Translation by Sir Abdur Rahman presented before UNSCOP, 3 September 1947 (doc.nr. A/364 Add. 1).

CHAPTER 2

BRITISH MANDATE: CONTRADICTION & BETRAYAL

> *The effect of the Balfour Declaration was to leave the Moslems and Christians dumbfounded ... It is impossible to minimise the bitterness of the awakening. They considered that they were to be handed over to an oppression which they hated far more than the Turk's and were aghast at the thought of this domination ... Prominent people openly talk of betrayal and that England has sold the country and received the price."*
>
> –EXTRACT FROM THE PALIN COMMISSION OF INQUIRY

The Balfour Declaration was a game-changer for the Zionist movement, which had finally obtained the official recognition from one of the great world powers that Theodor Herzl had identified as a necessary step towards a Jewish state. At a stroke, Zionism had been transformed by the British pledge from an impracticable utopian dream into a legitimate and achievable undertaking.

In the ongoing Allied campaign against the Ottoman Turks in Sinai and Palestine, both Gaza and Jaffa fell within days of the capture of Beersheba. Then, on the first day of the Jewish feast of Chanukah, 9 December 1917, five weeks after the Balfour Declaration was issued, British troops led by General Sir Edmund Allenby captured Jerusalem. In preparation for the assault, leaflets signed by Allenby calling for the defenders to surrender were translated into Arabic and dropped on the city by the Royal Flying Corps. The Arabic form of Allenby's name, al-Nabi, literally means 'the prophet'. The intensely superstitious Turks were suitably alarmed and, after fierce fighting in the surrounding suburbs, the Old City was surrendered without a shot being fired. On 11 December, Allenby entered Jerusalem to an enthusiastic welcome. Though an accomplished horseman who could have ridden triumphantly into the Old City astride his mount, he dismounted at the Jaffa Gate and entered on foot because, he said, only the Messiah should ride into the Holy City. He was also without doubt intentionally drawing a contrast to Kaiser Wilhelm II who, on a visit in 1898, insisted on entering the City seated on a white stallion. Allenby wanted to be viewed as a liberator, not a conqueror. The city was placed under martial law, and Allenby posted guards to protect sites held sacred by the Christian, Muslim and Jewish religions.

The British victory brought an end to the Ottoman Empire's rule over Jerusalem, which had stretched for exactly 400 years from the Ottoman victory over the Mamluks in 1517 AD. Turkish forces in Syria were subsequently defeated and an armistice was concluded with Turkey on 31 October 1918. At the end of the war the British and French set up a joint "Occupied Enemy Territory Administration" (OETA) in what had been Ottoman Syria. All of Palestine came under British military rule.

As British civil servants began formulating new policies for the Arab lands of the moribund Ottoman Empire, the critical factors by which they were guided were the pressing needs for reducing military commitments and expenditure in the aftermath of a costly war, preventing a renewal of Turkish dominance in the region, and safeguarding Britain's strategic interests in the Suez Canal, Iraq and the Indian subcontinent. However, in their efforts to secure victory in the war, Britain had complicated the political landscape by making conflicting promises to the Arabs, via the McMahon correspondence, to the Zionists by issuing the Balfour Declaration, and to their Allies by signing the Sykes–Picot agreement. The shift in policy between the Asquith government, which opposed the concept of a Jewish national home, and the Lloyd George government who adopted a pro-Zionist position, had created confusion, contradiction and the appearance of Britain spinning an intricate web of deceit. Now that the war was over, managing the peace would be a delicate matter requiring diplomatic finesse.

It did not take long for issues to surface. The British Military administration established Muslim-Christian Associations in all the major towns in Palestine. On 2 November 1918, just two days after the armistice was signed with Turkey, the Zionists held a parade marking the first anniversary of the Balfour Declaration. The following day a delegation from the Muslim-Christian Associations handed a petition to Colonel Ronald Henry Amherst Storrs who was, in his own words, "the first military governor of Jerusalem since Pontius Pilate."[1] The petition protested, "We have noticed yesterday a large crowd of Jews carrying banners and over-running the streets shouting words which hurt the feeling and wound the soul. They pretend with open voice that Palestine, which is the Holy Land of our fathers and the graveyard of our ancestors, which has been inhabited by the Arabs for long ages, who loved it and died in defending it, is now a national home for them … We Arabs, Muslim and Christian, have always sympathized profoundly with the persecuted Jews and their misfortunes in other countries ... but there is wide difference between such sympathy and the acceptance of such a nation ruling over us and disposing of our affairs."[2]

On 27 January 1919, the Associations joined together to hold the first Palestine Arab Congress in Jerusalem. Its main platforms were a call for Palestine to be part of an independent Syrian state and opposition to the Balfour Declaration.

The British government had made a commitment to facilitate a Jewish national home in Palestine, but the British military administration controlled many Arab areas across the Middle East and were not inclined towards sympathy for Zionist aspirations. They did not consider themselves obligated to the promotion of political aims. In June 1919, Lieutenant General Sir Louis Jean Bols, who served as Allenby's Third Army Chief of Staff during World War I, was appointed as the Chief Administrator of Palestine, a post he held until June 1920 when he signed over power to Herbert Samuel, the first British High Commissioner of Palestine. Bols was a fervent anti-Semite who was determined to leave no stone unturned in his efforts to prevent the establishment of the Jewish national home in Palestine, an attitude that filtered down to his subordinates. Support for Arab calls to unite Palestine with Syria was out of the question because of French imperial interests in Syria, but Arab opposition to the Balfour Declaration found many sympathetic ears among the higher ranks of the British military.

Encouraged by the Balfour Declaration, The Zionist Commission, later to become the Jewish Agency for Palestine, was founded by Chaim Weizmann in March 1918 to actively promote Zionist objectives in Palestine. The Palestinian Office, created in 1908 to aid Jewish immigration and land purchase for settlement, was merged into it. Under British military occupation, large transfers of funds were possible, and a major effort was launched to drain the mosquito infested marsh land of the Jezreel Valley, whose redemption as the breadbasket of Palestine became the priority of the Jewish settlers. The Zionist movement soon began organising large scale Jewish immigration into Palestine, and the construction of new settlements, much to the consternation of alarmed Arabs who feared the worst.

The London and San Remo Conferences

The Allied powers met in London in February 1920 to discuss, among other things, the future of Palestine and other territories formerly occupied by the Ottoman Turks. At the conference, the Arabs were represented by Emir Faisal, son of Sherif Hussein who had led the Arab revolt against the Turks, whilst the Zionists were represented by Chaim Weizmann. The conferees faced the almost impossible task of finding a compromise between the generally accepted idea of self-determination, ambiguous and seemingly conflicting wartime promises, and plans for a division of the spoils. It was ultimately decided to place Palestine, on both the East and West sides of the Jordan River, under British Mandatory rule.

Weizmann and Faisal had previously reached a separate agreement on 3 January 1919, at a peace conference held in Paris, pledging to work together in cordial cooperation. This agreement stated that both parties were, "Mindful of the racial kinship and ancient bonds existing between the Arabs and the Jewish people," and acknowledged that, "the surest means of working out the consummation of their national aspirations is through the closest possible collaboration in the development of the Arab states and Palestine." The important point to emphasize here is that the agreement distinguished the 'Arab states' from 'Palestine' which in context is understood to mean the 'Jewish state.' There were no general Arab objections to the creation of a Jewish state in Palestine, despite the protests of Arabs living in Palestine. Furthermore, the agreement looked to the fulfilment of the Balfour Declaration and called for all necessary measures "to encourage and stimulate immigration of Jews into Palestine on a large scale, and as quickly as possible to settle Jewish immigrants upon the land through closer settlement and intensive cultivation of the soil."[3]

Faisal, however, added a condition to his acceptance of the Balfour Declaration. He wrote a proviso in Arabic on the Paris agreement document that his signature was tied to the fulfilment of Allied war pledges concerning Arab independence. Since these pledges were not kept to Arab satisfaction after the war, the Weizmann-Faisal agreement was never enacted. Nevertheless, the fact that the leaders of the Arab nationalist movement and the Zionist movement could reach such an understanding demonstrates that had British and French imperial interests not muddied the waters, Jewish and Arab aspirations were not necessarily mutually exclusive.

The details of the British Mandate for Palestine, which had been agreed in London, were thrashed out at San Remo on the Italian Riviera during a conference convened in April 1920 to determine the precise boundaries for territories captured by the Allies during the war. The conference, attended by the Prime Ministers of Great Britain, France and Italy, and representatives of Japan, Greece and Belgium, with the United States as a neutral observer, confirmed the pledge contained in the Balfour Declaration for the establishment of a Jewish national home in Palestine.

The British delegation at San Remo was headed by Prime Minister David Lloyd George and Lord Curzon, who had replaced Lord Balfour as Foreign Secretary in October 1919. Balfour, however, was also present at the conference as a consultant for final settlement issues. The French delegation expressed many reservations about the inclusion of the Balfour Declaration in the Mandate for Palestine, and it was only after the exertion of British pressure that they were persuaded to agree to it.

BRITISH MANDATE: CONTRADICTION & BETRAYAL

The Mandate's terms recognized the "historical connection of the Jewish people with Palestine" and the moral validity of "reconstituting their national home in that country." The use of the term *"reconstituting"* is interesting in that it shows recognition of the fact that Palestine had been the Jews' historical home. Britain was made legally responsible as the mandatory power "for putting into effect the declaration made on the 8 [sic] November 1917 by the British Government and adopted by the other Allied Powers, in favour of the establishment in Palestine of a national home for the Jewish people." The incorporation of the Balfour Declaration into the Mandate for Palestine effectively raised it to the status of a legally binding foundational document under international law. Jewish immigration was to be facilitated and settlement on the land encouraged, while ensuring that the "rights and position of other sections of the population are not prejudiced." English, Arabic and Hebrew were all to be official languages.

The San Remo Conference also assured the French of a Mandate over Syria and Lebanon. Britain was awarded a Mandate over Mesopotamia, which would later become Iraq. Syria and Mesopotamia were provisionally recognized as states, but the agreement omitted any reference to recognition of Palestine as an independent state. Prior to San Remo, Palestinian Arab nationalists had worked for Palestine to be included as part of a greater Syria under Emir Faisal. After the armistice agreement with Turkey, they were encouraged in their pursuit of this aim when the British military occupation authority, fearing an Arab rebellion, published an Anglo-French Declaration in November 1918 which called for self-determination for the indigenous people of the region. By the end of 1919, the British had withdrawn from Syria, and in March 1920, a General Syrian Congress meeting in Damascus elected Faisal king of a united Syria, which included Palestine. This raised the hopes of the Palestinian Arab population that the Balfour Declaration would be rescinded, setting off a feverish series of demonstrations in Palestine in the spring of 1920. During the Passover feast in April, Arab rioters attacked the Jewish quarter of Jerusalem.

After the French Mandate over Syria was confirmed at San Remo, bringing to an abrupt end any hopes the Arabs held for a united Syria that included Palestine, Faisal was driven out of Damascus by the French authorities. The large number of Palestinian Arabs who had been with Faisal returned to Palestine determined to fight against the establishment of a Jewish nation, fuelling further rioting in Jaffa.

Arab Riots in Jerusalem

The pre-eminent Arab clan in Jerusalem throughout the Mandate period, the al-Husseinis, were fervent in their anti-British rhetoric and determined to pursue a nationalist agenda. To that end, they resolved to resist the encroachment of Jewish immigrants into Palestine at all costs. During 1919, one of the clan's leading figures, Haj Amin al-Husseini, began organising small suicide squads, known as fedayeen (literally "one who sacrifices himself"), to terrorize Jews in the hope of driving them out of Palestine. They found support amongst British military officials who encouraged the Arabs to attack the Jews.

Colonel Richard Meinertzhagen, a former head of British military intelligence in Cairo, was appointed by the government as Chief Political Officer for Palestine and charged with ensuring government policy was implemented. Meinertzhagen had been a self-confessed anti-Semite until his posting to the Near East in 1917 where he encountered Aaron Aaronsohn, a Palestinian Jew who was heading a spy network. Meinertzhagen had many talks with Aaronsohn about Palestine, and was so impressed by his courage and intelligence that he completely changed his mind and thereafter championed the Zionist cause with the evangelical zeal typical of a convert. During his time in Palestine, he recorded in his diary, which was later published, that British military officials, contrary to the policy of the government in London, "incline towards the exclusion of Zionism in Palestine."[4]

According to Meinertzhagen's diary notes, Brigadier General Waters Taylor, financial adviser to the Military Administration in Palestine from 1919 to 1923, met with Haj Amin al-Husseini in March 1920, just as the General Syrian Congress were electing Faisal as king over Syria and Palestine, and told him "he had a great opportunity at Easter to show the world ... that Zionism was unpopular not only with the Palestine Administration but in Whitehall (which was not true) and if disturbances of sufficient violence occurred in Jerusalem at Easter, both General Bols and General Allenby would advocate the abandonment of the Jewish Home. Waters-Taylor explained that freedom could only be attained through violence."[5]

Al-Husseini took the advice of Waters Taylor and instigated a riot in the Jewish quarter of Jerusalem during the Passover festival of April 1920, ostensibly as a reaction to the events unfolding at the San Remo Conference. The British military administration was fully complicit. Having first disarmed the Jews by order of the Administration, leaving them defenceless, they withdrew their troops and cordoned off the city to prevent intervention as Arab agitators encouraged the mob to "drink the blood of the Jews." Jews were attacked with impunity and their shops looted.

The Jewish community had anticipated the Arab reaction and was ready to meet it. Jewish affairs in Palestine were at that time being administered from Jerusalem by the Vaad Hatzirim (Council of Delegates), appointed by the World Zionist Organization. The Vaad Hatzirim charged Ze'ev Jabotinsky, co-founder of the Jewish Legion of the British Army during World War I, with the task of organizing Jewish self-defence. Jabotinsky had fought with distinction during the conquest of Palestine. Now, acting under the auspices of the Vaad Hatzirim, he put his experience to good use, forming the Haganah (self-defence) organization in Jerusalem which succeeded in repelling the Arab attack. Six Jews were killed and some 200 injured during the 1920 riots. Had it not been for the preliminary organization of Jewish defence, the number of victims would have undoubtedly been much greater.

After the riots, the British arrested both Arabs and Jews. Due to al-Husseini's overt role in instigating the pogrom, he was among those arrested by the British. Somehow, al-Husseini escaped to Jordan before his trial in mysterious circumstances; it is tempting to think that his many friends among the military may have lent a helping hand. He was sentenced to 10 years imprisonment in absentia.

Among the Jews arrested was Jabotinsky, together with 19 of his associates, on charges of illegal possession of weapons. Jabotinsky was sentenced to a disproportionate 15 years imprisonment with hard labour and deportation from the country after completion of his sentence. Though he had acted legitimately to defend intended victims of the riots, his sentence was harsher that that imposed on the instigator of the riots. Jabotinsky's treatment was vigorously protested in the House of Commons; Lord Robert Cecil disapproved in particular that the sentence was the same as that for two Arabs who had raped Jewish women. The Times called the verdict an "apparently vindictive punishment", while the Manchester Guardian, in an editorial, commented, "If Mr. Jabotinsky was in possession of firearms, if he organized a Defense Corps and even used it (which, however, he is stated not to have done), there is *prima facie* evidence that he may have been perfectly justified, owing to the failure of the military authorities to discharge their proper duties."[6] Protests over the sentence rumbled on for some time, and attained international coverage.

As a formal response to the riots, the British Foreign Office appointed a Commission of Inquiry, which was composed of three military officers and headed by Major General P. C. Palin, to investigate the causes. As this was a military court, it hardly offered a guarantee of independence and impartiality considering that military culpability and pro-Arab (and indeed anti-Zionist) bias amongst British military officials were under scrutiny. It was the first in a long line of Royal Commissions on the question of Palestine during the Mandate period. In its report, which was filed on 1 July 1920, it was noted that, "The Balfour Declaration ... is undoubtedly the starting point of the whole trouble."[7]

The report's substantive findings paralleled the anti-Zionist views of General Bols and the military administration, not surprising since this was a military Commission. The report's conclusion argued there were three significant causes for "the alienation and exasperation of the feelings of the population of Palestine" which had led to the disturbances. These were (1) an inability to reconcile the Allies' declared policy of self-determination for the Arabs with the Balfour Declaration, giving rise to a sense of betrayal and intense anxiety for their future; (2) misapprehension of the true meaning of the Balfour Declaration, which implied the denial of their own right of self-determination, and forgetfulness of the guarantees determined therein, due to the loose rhetoric of politicians and the exaggerated statements and writings of interested persons, chiefly Zionists; (3) Zionist indiscretion and aggression since the Balfour Declaration aggravating such fears. The report called the Zionist Commission "arrogant, insolent and provocative" and said its members could "easily precipitate a catastrophe."

Even as an ardent supporter of Israel, it is impossible not to feel sympathy with the predicament the Arab Palestinian population was placed in at this time. The Balfour Declaration was an important landmark in the fulfilment of God's purposes to restore Israel as a nation in their Promised Land, but some aspects of the political process by which it was delivered were murky to say the least. British politicians had given mendacious assurances about self-determination that hoodwinked the Palestinian Arabs and disguised their true aims. Some in Whitehall who supported Zionism did so not for altruistic or ideological reasons but because it suited an imperial strategy.

Summarising the testimony of Palestinian Arabs who were interviewed by the Commission, the report said, "The effect of the Balfour Declaration was to leave the Moslems and Christians dumbfounded ... It is impossible to minimise the bitterness of the awakening. They considered that they were to be handed over to an oppression which they hated far more than the Turk's and were aghast at the thought of this domination ... Prominent people openly talk of betrayal and that England has sold the country and received the price." Such feelings were aggravated by the proclamation of Emir Faisal as king of Syria with a potential claim to Palestine too.

The report largely rejected allegations that pro-Arab sentiments were held by military officials. Bizarrely, the primary witness in support of the allegation, Colonel Meinertzhagen, was attacked for holding an alleged Zionist bias, although the wording of the report actually confirmed that there were some British officials who held an anti-Zionist bias: "What he (Meinertzhagen) demands is not this equal holding of the scales, but a definite bias in favour of the Zionists. He is wholly unable to appreciate the justice of the native case, which he dismisses contemptuously as "superficially justifiable" ... It is fairly clear that, just as in one or two unfortunate cases certain individual officials have betrayed anti-Zionist bias, so Colonel Meinertzhagen arrived with a definite anti-Arab bias and a prejudice in favour of Zionism ... A careful examination of Colonel Meinertzhagen's reckless championship of the Zionist cause fails to convince the Court that he has added materially to the proof of general bias charged against the O.E.T.A.(S) officials."

The report criticised of the actions of the military command, particularly the withdrawal of troops from inside Jerusalem and that, once martial law had been proclaimed, it was slow to regain control. Exasperation was also expressed that the Haganah was formed by Jabotinsky under the noses of the British, "It seems scarcely credible that the fact that these men had been got together and were openly drilling at the back of Lemel School and on Mount Scopus ... and yet no word of it reached either the Governorate or the Administration until after the riots."

Although the riots were clearly instigated by the Arabs, with encouragement from a pro-Arab British military administration, the Palin report insidiously attempted to transfer culpability for the riots to 'aggressive' Zionism, to exonerate the military administration from accusations of harbouring pro-Arab bias, and to undermine the favourable position granted to the Jews by the Balfour Declaration. But it must be remembered that the Jewish community were the victims of this disturbance. It is a classic trait of racism that persecuted minorities are blamed for their own persecution.

In truth, the Palin report was an attempt to deflect culpability from British military administrators who were engaging in imperial gamesmanship under a thin veneer of noble guardianship. Policy makers in London favoured Zionism, a policy endorsed by the international community and established as resting on historic and morally valid claims. Yet the sympathies of the military on the ground and some civil servants in Whitehall were firmly behind the Arabs. Zionism prevailed in Parliament, but the tensions between the two sides resulted in contradictory statements that left both Arabs and Jews feeling betrayed.

Allenby pushed for the Palin report to be officially published, but in anticipation of Zionist objections it was decided only to convey the gist of the report verbally to a 'responsible' Zionist leader. Meanwhile, Meinertzhagen reported back to the British government that the military had been complicit in the riots and were unsupportive of government objectives. The government in London responded by swiftly transferring governance from the military, who wanted to reduce the authority of the Zionist Commission, to a civil administration that would be guided in its policy by the Balfour Declaration.

Herbert Samuel, First High Commissioner

In June 1920, the British military government in Palestine was replaced by a civilian administration as Bols signed over power to Herbert Samuel, the first British High Commissioner of Palestine. Bols insisted that Samuel sign a receipt, the wording of which is often quoted: "Received from Major-General Sir Louis J. Bols K.C.B. - One Palestine, complete."[8]

Samuel was raised in an Orthodox Jewish home and from 1909 served in various cabinet posts, being first appointed by Prime Minister Herbert Asquith as Chancellor of the Duchy of Lancaster, and then later as Postmaster General, President of the Local Government Board, and eventually Home Secretary. When Lloyd George succeeded Asquith as Prime Minister in 1916, Samuel resigned his cabinet post out of loyalty to Asquith.

Though he had renounced all religious belief as a young man while studying at Oxford, Samuel remained a member of the Jewish community and was intensely interested in Jewish communal affairs. In his memorandum to Prime Minister Asquith in 1915, Samuel put forward the idea of establishing a British Protectorate over Palestine which would allow for increased Jewish settlement. In time, he argued, the future Jewish majority would flourish spiritually and intellectually, creating a Jewish centre that would positively shape the future for Jews worldwide. Although Asquith was not interested in pursuing such an option, Samuel's ideas had helped prepare the groundwork for the Balfour Declaration. It was, therefore, no surprise that Samuel was appointed first High Commissioner of Palestine, making him the first Jew to govern in the land of Israel for nearly 2,000 years.

Samuel arrived in Palestine on 20 June 1920, to take up his appointment from 1 July. When he entered Jerusalem, he was greeted by a seventeen gun salute and given an overwhelmingly enthusiastic welcome. He served as High Commissioner for a period of five years. His appointment was viewed by many Jews as affirmation, despite the hostility of the British military administration, of the sincerity of the British promise to facilitate a Jewish national home in Palestine. Samuel himself was deeply moved by the outpouring of emotion with which he was greeted.

The new administration swiftly proceeded to implement the Balfour Declaration, announcing in August a quota of 16,500 Jewish immigrants for the first year. As a gesture toward the civilian population, he proclaimed a general amnesty for both Jews and Arabs who had been involved in the Jerusalem riots. Jabotinsky and his comrades were released from prison to an enthusiastic welcome by the Jewish community. Jabotinsky was not satisfied, however, insisting that the sentences passed against them be overturned entirely on the basis that the defender should not be placed on trial with the aggressor. After months of struggle, the British War Office agreed to revoke the sentences.

Samuel made it clear that his policy was to unite all dissenting groups under the British flag. One of his first actions was to grant Pinhas Rutenberg, a Russian born engineer and entrepreneur, concessions for the production and distribution of wired electricity. Rutenberg had played an active role in the Russian revolution of 1917. During World War I, he was among the founders of the Jewish Legion and also participated, alongside Jabotinsky, in the establishment of the Haganah. He obtained financial support from the Rothschild family to establish the Palestine Electric Company, known today as the Israel Electric Corporation, whose shareholders included Zionist organizations, investors, and philanthropists. Although the British administration claimed that electrification would enhance the economic development of the country as a whole, while at the same time demonstrating their commitment to facilitate a Jewish national home through economic rather than political means, the Arabs saw it as proof that the British intended to favour Zionism.

In an attempt to prove his impartiality and allay Arab anxieties, Samuel slowed the pace of Jewish immigration to Palestine, much to the distress of the Zionists. Then, after the death of the Grand Mufti of Jerusalem Kamil al-Husseini in March 1921, Samuel issued a pardon to his half-brother Haj Amin al-Husseini, the Arab national extremist sentenced for his role in the Jerusalem riots, and appointed him as the new Mufti of Jerusalem.

By making these concessions, many Zionists believed that Samuel had gone too far, and had damaged the Zionist cause. Their fears were to prove well founded when, after his appointment, al-Husseini began to organize larger scale fedayeen to terrorize Jews. Samuel met with al-Husseini on 11 April 1921 and was assured by the Mufti "that the influences of his family and himself would be devoted to tranquility."[9] Just three weeks later 47 Jews were slaughtered during riots in Jaffa and Petah Tikva.

Trouble started when fighting broke out between two rival Jewish socialist groups who clashed with each other during May Day parades held close to Jaffa. When the police attempted to disperse them, some local Arabs intervened to assist the police. Hearing of the fighting and believing that Arabs were being attacked by Jews, Arabs from Jaffa launched retaliatory attacks against Jewish pedestrians and began breaking into Jewish buildings, looting and beating to death any occupants they found, including children. The violence was inflamed by the presence in Jaffa of Arab nationalists who had supported Emir Faisal in

Syria. Though some Arabs bravely defended Jews and offered them refuge in their homes, many Jewish witnesses identified the assailants as their Arab neighbours.

The worst violence broke out at an immigrant hostel managed by the Zionist Commission. Terrified residents tried desperately to barricade the entrance gate, but the Arab rioters rammed their way through and poured in. When the police arrived, rather than shooting to disperse the crowd, they took aim at the building. In the courtyard one Jewish immigrant was killed by a policeman's bullet at short range, while others were slashed with knives and beaten with sticks by the Arab mob. One Arab policeman cornered two women and attempted to rape them, but they managed to escape. Others were not so fortunate. Several Jewish men and a young girl attempted to flee from the building, but each was chased down by the mob and beaten to death.

Samuel declared a state of emergency and called for reinforcements from Egypt. General Allenby obliged by dispatching two Royal Navy destroyers to Jaffa and one to Haifa. In an attempt to restore calm, Samuel met with Arab representatives. Musa Kazim al-Husseini, dismissed as the Mayor of Jerusalem the previous year because of his involvement in the riots, demanded the suspension of Jewish immigration. Samuel duly obliged, and two small boats holding 300 Jewish immigrants were forced to return to Istanbul.

Once a measure of calm had been restored, the British government created a Royal Commission headed by Sir Thomas Haycraft, Chief Justice of the Supreme Court in Palestine, to investigate the cause of the Jaffa riots. The Haycraft Commission Report blamed the Arabs for the violence, but then attempted to rationalize this by identifying a series of Arab grievances concerning the way their interests were being subsumed to the interests of the Jewish immigrants, who at the time comprised no more than ten percent of the population. Thus, while the appendix of the Commission's

Report acknowledged that "the Arab majority, who were generally the aggressors, inflicted most of the casualties", it concluded: "The fundamental cause of the Jaffa riots and the subsequent acts of violence was a feeling among the Arabs of discontent with, and hostility to, the Jews, due to political and economic causes, and connected with Jewish immigration, and with their conception of Zionist policy as derived from Jewish exponents"[10] This conclusion set a precedent that would be followed by future reports which would invariably assign blame for violence to the Arabs but then mitigate by suggesting that the Arabs were in some way being unfairly disadvantaged by Zionist policy.

Following the Jaffa riots, Samuel established a Supreme Muslim Council to create an advisory body with whom the High Commissioner could consult. It became the highest body overseeing Muslim community affairs in Mandatory Palestine. On 9 January 1922, Haj Amin al-Husseini consolidated his power when he was elected as the first President of the Supreme Muslim Council, enabling him to take control of all Muslim religious funds in Palestine. He used his authority to gain control over the mosques, the schools and the sharia courts. No Arab could reach a position of influence without being loyal to the Mufti. As the "Palestinian" spokesman, al-Husseini wrote to Winston Churchill, then the Colonial Secretary, demanding that restrictions be placed on Jewish immigration and that Palestine be reunited with Syria.

Back in Britain, the pressure being exerted on Churchill by al-Husseini was compounded by swings in public and governmental opinion which were increasingly becoming less favourable to the commitment that had been made to Zionist policy. In February 1922, Churchill telegraphed Herbert Samuel asking for cuts in expenditure, noting: "In both Houses of Parliament there is a growing movement of hostility against Zionist policy in Palestine ... I do not attach undue importance to this movement, but it is increasingly difficult to meet the argument that it is unfair to ask the British taxpayer, already overwhelmed with taxation, to bear the cost of imposing on Palestine an unpopular policy."[11]

Alarmed by the extent of Arab opposition, Churchill attempted to calm British reservations and Arab fears about the Balfour Declaration by issuing a White Paper which was published on 3 June 1922. The White Paper declared that Britain did "not contemplate that Palestine as a whole should be converted into a Jewish National Home, but that such a Home should be founded in Palestine."[12] The Paper concluded that the violence in Jaffa of 1921 was sparked by Arab resentment towards Jewish Zionists and the perception of British favouritism towards them, as well as Arab fears of subjugation. In response, although acknowledging the need for Jewish immigration to enable the Jewish community to grow, the Paper called for a limitation on Jewish immigration according to "the economic capacity of the country to absorb new arrivals." Thus, although Churchill was a staunch supporter of Zionism, he followed the precedent set by Samuel of appeasing the Arabs over immigration in order to reduce tensions, in effect rewarding the Arabs for their aggression against the Jews. The paper emphasized that the Balfour Declaration did not support "the disappearance or the subordination of the Arabic population, language, or culture in Palestine", and reaffirmed that Britain intended to "foster the establishment of a full measure of self-government in Palestine."

Although Churchill's diplomatic Paper was considered a great setback by many in the Zionist movement, he did encourage the Jewish community to "know that it is in Palestine as of right and not on sufferance" and acknowledged that the Jewish national home "should be formally recognized to rest upon ancient historic connection." This was a conviction that stayed with Churchill throughout his lengthy political career. Later, in his submissions to the Royal Commission of 1937, he denied that he had imported a 'foreign race' to Palestine. On the contrary, he claimed it was the Arabs who were the conquerors. Churchill pointed out that at the time of Christ the population of Palestine was mainly Jewish, but that all changed in the 7th Century AD, "when the Mohammedan upset occurred in world history, and the hordes of Islam swept over these places (and) smashed it all up."[13] The Jews reluctantly accepted Churchill's paper; the Arabs, however, rejected it outright.

Back in London, Lord Islington submitted a motion before the House of Lords calling for a rejection of a Palestine Mandate which incorporated the Balfour Declaration. The motion was passed by 60 votes to 25. However, the vote proved to be purely symbolic as it was subsequently overruled by a vote in the House of Commons, but only after Churchill had delivered a typically pugnacious defense of the Jewish homeland policy in a speech that succeeded in swaying opinion in his favour.

Lord Curzon, the successor to Balfour as Foreign Secretary, had opposed the Declaration prior to its publication and was therefore determined to pursue a policy that was "narrower and more prudent rather than the wider interpretation."[14] When the Conservative leader Andrew Bonar Law was appointment as Prime Minister in succession to Lloyd George in late 1922, Curzon wrote to Bonar Law stating that he regarded the Balfour Declaration as "the worst" of Britain's Middle East commitments and "a striking contradiction of our publicly declared principles."[15]

Despite this sea change in British political opinion, stirred by the removal of the pro-Zionists Lloyd George and Balfour from the key positions of power in government, Britain achieved international legitimacy for their continued control of Palestine by obtaining a civil mandate from the 52 governments that comprised the League of Nations. The use of the term 'mandate', which carries the sense of approval or endorsement for a directive to carry out a commission, was a compromise term for what was in essence a colony or protectorate. The intention behind the mandate system was to benefit the peoples of territories whose 'well-being and development' was referred to as 'a sacred trust of civilisation'. The mandated nation was obliged to act as a kind of trustee, representing the conscience of the civilised world. The Mandate was approved by the League of Nations Council on 24 July 1922, although technically it was not made official until 29 September 1923. The United States was not a member of the League of Nations, but a joint resolution of the United States Congress on 30 June 1922 endorsed the concept of the Jewish national home.

The Zionist Commission, founded by Weizmann, was appointed as the Jewish agency for Palestine for the purpose of Article 4 of the Mandate, which provided for "the recognition of an appropriate Jewish agency as a public body for the purpose of advising and co-operating with the Administration of Palestine in such economic, social and other matters as may affect the establishment of the Jewish National Home and the interests of the Jewish population of Palestine."[16]

The British Mandate for Palestine, now formalised with the League of Nations' consent, covered two administrative areas: The land west of the Jordan River, known as Palestine, and the land east of the Jordan, a semi-autonomous region known as Transjordan. Even the naming of these administrative areas revealed the divergent tendencies in the region. According to minutes recorded at a session of the League of Nations' Permanent Mandate Commission: "The country was described as "Palestine" by Europeans and as "Falestin" by the Arabs. The Hebrew name for the country was the designation "Eretz (Land of) Israel", and the Government, to meet Jewish wishes, had agreed that the word "Palestine" in Hebrew characters should be followed in all official documents by the initials which stood for that designation. As a set-off to this, certain of the Arab politicians suggested that the country should be called "Southern Syria" in order to emphasise its close relation with another Arab State."[17]

Arab spokesmen opposed the Mandate's terms because they regarded it as a breach of the Covenant of the League of Nations which endorsed popular determination. Therefore, they maintained that the League of Nations was bound by its own Covenant to support the cause of the Arab majority in Palestine. Arab leaders particularly objected to the Mandate's numerous references to the "Jewish community", whereas the Arab people, then constituting about eighty-eight percent of the Palestinian population, were acknowledged only as "the other sections."

Throughout his tenure as High Commissioner, Samuel was tireless in his attempts to establish self-governing institutions in Palestine, as required by the Mandate, but was frustrated by the refusal of the Arab leadership to co-operate with any institution which included Jewish participation.

The Palestinian Arabs believed that participation in institutions sanctioned by the Mandatory power would signify their acquiescence to the Mandate and thereby to the Balfour Declaration, and so they refused to participate. Consequently, Samuel's proposals for a legislative council, an advisory council, and an Arab agency similar to the Jewish agency, were all rejected by the Arabs. The collapse of his doomed bid to create representative institutions sounded the death knell to any possibility of joint consultation between the Jewish and Arabic communities.

From the perspective of the British authorities, burdened with heavy commitments after World War I, the objective of the Mandate administration was peaceful accommodation and the development of Palestine under British control by both Arabs and Jews. Samuel endeavoured to maintain some semblance of order between the two antagonistic communities, but in pursuit of this goal he made a fatal error by attempting to adhere by two contradictory principles:

On the one hand, Samuel called for open Jewish immigration and land acquisition, which enabled thousands of highly committed Zionists to enter Palestine from 1919 to 1923. The Third Aliyah, as it was called, made important contributions to the development of Jewish agriculture, especially collective farming. On the other hand, however, he also promised representative institutions which, if they had emerged in the 1920s, would have had as their primary objective the curtailment of Jewish immigration.

Samuel's failure to create a unified political structure embracing both Arabs and Jews in constitutional government resulted in an internal institutional partition in which the Jewish Agency exercised a degree of autonomous control over the Jewish settlement and the Supreme Muslim Council performed a comparable role for Muslims. Thus, well before the Peel Commission proposed territorial partition in 1937, and later the United Nations Commission in 1947, the groundwork for territorial partition had already been laid.

Endnotes

1. Cited from Michael Korda, *Hero: The Life and Legend of Lawrence of Arabia* (New York: Harper Perennial, 2011), p. 353.
2. Colonel Storrs communication to OETA Headquarters, 4 Nov 1918 (ISA 2/140/4A).
3. Cited by Howard Sachar, *A History of Israel from the Rise of Zionism to Our Time*, 2nd Ed (New York: Knopf, 1996), p. 121.
4. Richard Meinertzhagen, *Middle East Diary: 1917-1956* (London: Cresset Press, 1959), p. 81-82.
5. Meinertzhagen, *Middle East Diary*, p. 81-2.
6. Joseph B. Schechtman, *The Life and Times of Vladimir Jabotinsky: Rebel and Statesman* (Silver Springs, MD: Eshel Books, 1986), p. 350-351.
7. Palin Commission, *Report of the Court of Inquiry Convened by Order of His Excellency the High Commissioner and Commander in Chief*. His Majesty's Stationery Office, London, 1920.
8. Owen, C. V., "Bols, Sir Louis Jean (1867-1930)", *Oxford Dictionary of National Biography* – Online Edition.
9. Zvi Elpeleg, *The Grand Mufti Haj Amin Al-Hussaini* (London: Frank Cass, 1993), p. 9.
10. Haycraft Commission Report, *Palestine: Disturbances in May, 1921. Report of the Commission of Inquiry with Correspondence Relating Thereto*, Cmd 1540, His Majesty's Stationery Office, London, October 1921, Appendix A, p. 59.
11. Churchill to Samuel Telegram, Private & Personal, CO 733/18, 25 February 1922.
12. Churchill White Paper: *Correspondence with the Palestine Arab Delegation and the Zionist Organisation*, June 1922, Cmd 1700. His Majesty's Stationery Office, London, 1922.
13. *Palestine Royal Commission*, Minutes of Evidence, 12 March 1937, CHAR/2/317/8666, 8728, p. 507.
14. Curzon to Allenby, 16 July 1920, CP 112/799.

15 Curzon to Bonar Law, 14 December 1922, Bonar Law Papers, 111/12/46.
16 See Appendix 2 for the full text of the Mandate.
17 League of Nations, Permanent Mandate Commission, Minutes of the Ninth Session (Arab Grievances), Held at Geneva from 8-25 June 1926.

CHAPTER 3

POGROMS, PREJUDICE & APPEASEMENT

> *They dare not try to kill Zionism directly, but they try to put it in a refrigerator with the door just ajar"*
>
> –DAVID LLOYD GEORGE

Despite the riots in Jerusalem and Jaffa of 1920-21, there were periods of relative peace and cooperation during which the Jewish community in Palestine, under Britain's aegis, began to flourish. However, efforts to establish the Jewish homeland were punctuated throughout the next decade by occasional outbreaks of bloody violence, and restrictions on Jewish immigration imposed by the British government that were in clear contravention of the terms of the British Mandate.

Both the Zionists and the Palestinian Arabs realized that by the end of the Mandate period the region's future would be determined by size of population and ownership of land. Thus the central issues throughout the Mandate period were Jewish immigration and land purchases, with the Jews attempting to increase both and the Arabs seeking to slow down or halt both. Conflict over these issues often escalated into violence, and the British were forced to take action – a lesson not lost on either side.

Herbert Samuel justified placing restrictions on Jewish immigration as being in the 'interests of the present population' and the 'absorptive capacity' of the country. The concept of economic 'absorptive capacity' was essentially a political tool, a useful slogan purporting to show the government's concern for the protection of Arab interests. The influx of Jewish settlers was said to be forcing the Arab fellahin (native peasants) from their land. It was an entirely specious argument, for Arab landowners were not compelled to sell and were tough negotiators and the region was chronically under populated with large tracts of cultivatable land laid waste. And much of the land was not actually owned by Arabs. In truth, Samuel was appeasing Arab disquiet about the implications of Jewish immigration, establishing a pattern that would become the norm throughout the Mandatory period.

All the while, Arab immigration into Palestine continued unabated. While the British were imposing quotas that restricted Jewish immigration, in 1920 they specifically requested for the French authorities to stop monitoring illegal Arab immigration along the border of Lebanon and Syria, allowing unrestricted immigration of Arabs into Western Palestine.[1]

During World War I, the Jewish population had actually declined because of the war, famine, disease and expulsion. In 1915, approximately 83,000 Jews lived in Palestine among 590,000 Muslim and Christian Arabs. According to the 1922 census, the Jewish population had only risen to 84,000 despite the immigration facilitated under the Mandate, while the Arab population, subject to the same harsh conditions, had increased to 643,000. Thus, the Arab population continued to grow exponentially during the early years of the British civil administration while that of the Jews stagnated. What's more, although Samuel referenced the 'absorptive capacity' of Palestine as a limiting factor on Jewish immigration, Britain contributed to this by partitioning off swathes of the country and designating them exclusively for Arab settlement.

In March 1921, a Conference was held in Cairo to discuss the problems of the Middle East. Of particular concern to the Conference were the three conflicting policies defined by the McMahon–Hussein letters, the Sykes–Picot agreement and the Balfour Declaration. The Conference decided that Lebanon and Syria should remain under French control and that Britain should maintain the Mandate over Palestine and continue to support the establishment of a Jewish homeland there. After meetings with Abdullah bin Hussein, it was agreed that he would administer the territory east of the Jordan River, Transjordan, under the auspices of the British Mandate for Palestine with a fully autonomous governing system. It was also decided that Emir Faisal, recently ousted from Syria by the French, should become king of a newly created Kingdom of Iraq.

The appointment of Abdullah bin Hussein was a reward for his contribution to the war against the Turks. But in effect, by the stroke of a pen, the Colonial Secretary Winston Churchill severed nearly four-fifths of Palestine – some 35,000 square miles – to create a brand new Arab emirate, Transjordan. This area was now closed to Jewish immigration. It was, in reality, a state for the Palestinian Arabs. As such a 'two-state solution', the model later adopted by the United Nations as a solution to the Arab-Israeli conflict, already existed. Transjordan eventually gained its independence in 1946 as "The Hashemite Kingdom of Transjordan."

A further erosion of the Mandatory lands available for Jewish settlement occurred in 1923 when the Golan Heights were formally ceded by Britain to the French Mandate of Syria, in exchange for a smaller adjacent region on what was to become the Lebanese border. Without consideration of Jewish interests or recognition that the Golan, since the times of Joshua, had belonged to the Jewish tribes of Dan and Manasseh, it was transferred to the Syrian Druze and Arabs. This was despite the fact that Jewish benefactors, acting through the Jewish National Fund, had already purchased large tracts of land on the Golan in anticipation of settling Jews there.

The British administration went even further by placing restrictions on Jewish land purchases in what remained of Palestine, contravening the provision of the League of Nations Mandate (Article 6 – refer to Appendix) that stated: "The Administration of Palestine ... shall encourage, in cooperation with the Jewish Agency ... close settlement by Jews on the land, including State lands and waste lands not acquired for public purposes."

In total, during the period from 1919-23, approximately 40,000 Jews, mainly from Eastern Europe, arrived in Palestine. Many had been trained in agriculture in the European Zionist movements and established settlements on land purchased with funds raised by Jewish communities throughout the world. Socialism was the dominant ideology among these settlers, and this found expression in the development of unique social and economic enterprises, such as the Kibbutzim, communal agricultural settlements based on pure socialist principles (to each according to need; from each according to capacity).

The pace of Jewish immigration accelerated dramatically during the mid 1920s driven by anti-Jewish economic legislation in Eastern Europe and the imposition of restrictive quotas on Jewish immigration by the United States. During the years 1924-26, approximately 82,000 Jews flooded into Palestine, mainly as a result of anti-Semitic outbreaks in Poland and Hungary. In contrast to the earlier agriculturalist settlers, this group, known collectively as the Fourth Aliyah, contained many middle-class families who moved to the growing towns, establishing small businesses and light industry. Many would later leave the country to escape the harsh economic conditions.

Financial difficulties were by far the greatest concern for the Jewish community as the decade drew to a close. The negative impact of the global economic crisis of 1926-28 on financial support for Jewish migration led many to believe that the Zionist enterprise would fail completely due to a lack of funds. Zionist leaders attempted to rectify the situation by expanding the Jewish Agency to incorporate non–Zionists who were willing to contribute to the practical settlement of Palestine.

Arab Riots of 1929

A series of demonstrations and riots, unprecedented in terms of duration, geographical scope and direct damage to life and property, broke out in late August 1929 when a long-running dispute over access to the Western Wall in Jerusalem escalated into violence.

Tensions had been simmering at the Western Wall for a long time. The site is sacred to Jews because it is believed to be a remnant of the ancient wall that once supported the podium upon which the Jewish Second Temple sat. For centuries, the Jews had accessed the Wall for devotional purposes. However, as part of the Temple Mount, the Western Wall was under the control of the Muslim religious trust, the Waqf. Muslims consider the wall to be part of the Al-Aqsa Mosque, the third holiest site in Islam which, according to Islamic tradition, was the place where Muhammad tied his horse, Buraq, the night before his journey to heaven.

As a result of an incident which occurred in September 1925, a ruling was made which forbade the Jews to bring seats and benches to the Wall even though these were intended for worshippers who were aged and infirm. The Muslims linked any adaptations to the site with "the Zionist project", fearing that they would be the first step in taking over the Temple Mount.

In September 1928, Jews praying at the Wall during Yom Kippur placed a screen at the site, constructed from a few wooden frames covered with cloth, to separate the men from the women. Jerusalem's British Commissioner, Edward Keith-Roach, pointed out the screen while visiting the Muslim religious court overlooking the prayer area, mentioning that he had never seen it at the Wall before. This precipitated vociferous protests from the assembled sheiks who demanded that it be removed. Keith-Roach acceded to their demands and ordered ten armed men into the prayer area to tear it down, urged on by Arab residents who were shouting, "Death to the Jewish dogs!" A violent clash with worshipers took place, and the screen was destroyed. The intervention later drew censure from senior officials who judged that excessive force had been exercised without good judgment, although the British government issued a statement defending the action.

On the back of this incident, at the instigation of Haj Amin al-Husseini, rumours of a Jewish plot to seize control of Muslim holy places began to spread. A memorandum issued by the Muslim Supreme Council stated, "Having realized by bitter experience the unlimited greedy aspirations of the Jews in this respect, Moslems believe that the Jews' aim is to take possession of the Mosque of Al-Aqsa gradually on the pretence that it is the Temple", and it advised the Jews "to stop this hostile propaganda which will naturally engender a parallel action in the whole Moslem world, the responsibility for which will rest with the Jews."[2]

Haj Amin al-Husseini continued to provoke tensions by organising new constructions next to and above the Wall in October 1928. Mules were routinely driven through the praying area, often dropping excrement, and waste water was thrown on Jews from above. A muezzin was appointed to perform the Islamic call to prayer directly next to the Wall, creating noise exactly when the

Jews were conducting their prayers. The Jews protested at these provocations and tensions continued to escalate. Zionists began making demands for control over the wall; some went as far as to openly call for the rebuilding of the Temple, increasing Muslim fears over Zionist intentions.

On Thursday, 15 August 1929, during the Jewish fast of Tisha B'Av, several hundred members of the Jewish Committee for the Western Wall marched to the Wall shouting, "The Wall is ours." Once at the Wall they raised the Jewish national flag and sang Hatikvah, the Jewish anthem. The authorities had been notified of the march in advance and provided a heavy police escort in a bid to prevent any incidents. Though the march passed off peacefully, rumours spread that the Jews had attacked local residents and had cursed the name of the Prophet Muhammad.

The following day the Supreme Muslim Council organised a counter demonstration with the intention of marching to the Wall. The High Commissioner summoned al-Husseini and informed him that he had never heard of such a demonstration being held at the Western Wall, and that it would be a terrible shock to the Jews who regarded the Wall as a place of special sanctity. Nevertheless, the march went ahead and once at the Wall, the crowd burnt prayer books, liturgical fixtures and notes of supplication left in the Wall's cracks.

Inflammatory articles calculated to incite disorder began appearing in the Arab media and one flyer, signed by "the Committee of the Holy Warriors in Palestine", stated that the Jews had violated the honour of Islam, declaring: "Hearts are in tumult because of these barbaric deeds, and the people began to break out in shouts of 'war, Jihad ... rebellion' ... O Arab nation, the eyes of your brothers in Palestine are upon you ... and they awaken your religious feelings and national zealotry to rise up against the enemy who violated the honour of Islam and raped the women and murdered widows and babies."[3]

On 19 August, following the fatal stabbing of a young Jew named Abraham Mizrachi in a personal quarrel with an Arab, a Jewish crowd attacked and severely wounded the policeman who arrived to arrest the Arab responsible, and then attacked neighbouring Arab houses and wounded their occupants. The funeral of Mizrachi became the occasion for a serious anti-Arab demonstration. Though it was suppressed by force, over the next four days the Jerusalem police reported twelve separate attacks by Jews on Arabs and seven attacks by Arabs on Jews. The city was at boiling point.

A violent eruption was inevitable. On Friday 23 August, thousands of Arab villagers streamed into Jerusalem from the surrounding countryside to pray on the Temple Mount, many armed with sticks and knives. Jewish storekeepers began closing shop and gunshots were heard on the Temple Mount, apparently intended to work the crowd into a frenzy. By mid-day friction had spread to the Jewish neighbourhood of Mea She'arim where two or three Arabs were killed. Then in the early afternoon, reacting to rumours of Arabs being murdered by Jews, the Arabs began a massacre of the Jews in Jerusalem's Old City. While several Jews were being killed at the Jaffa Gate, British policemen did not open fire. They reasoned that if they had shot into the Arab crowd, the mob would have turned their anger on the police.

Most of Jerusalem's Jews had no weapons with which to defend themselves. Late on 23 August, however, with the British authorities rapidly losing control of the situation, they armed 41 Jewish special constables and 18 Jewish ex-soldiers to assist in the defence of the Jewish quarters. The following day, Arab notables issued a statement that "many rumours and reports of various kinds have spread to the effect that Government had enlisted and armed certain Jews, that they had enrolled Jewish ex-soldiers who had served in the Great War; and the Government forces were firing at Arabs exclusively."[4] Al-Husseini informed the authorities that a large crowd of excited Arabs in the Haram area were also demanding arms and calling the retention of Jews as special constables carrying arms a breach of faith by the Government. The Government initially denied the rumours, but by 27 August they were forced to disarm and disband the special constables.

Violence quickly spread to other parts of Palestine, with rampant rioting and widespread looting causing extensive damage. Law enforcement agencies were overwhelmed by the scale of the disturbances. Although the Palestine Police force could muster 1,500 officers, the majority were Arab, with only a small number of Jews and 175 British officers. In Hebron there was only one British policeman, with around two-dozen Arab constables under his command, guarding the entire city.

There were many isolated attacks on Jewish villages, and in some cases, entire villages were destroyed. The kibbutz of Mishmar Ha-Emek was attacked on 26 August by an Arab mob, which was dispersed by the locals and British police. The following day the members of the kibbutz were evacuated for their safety by order of the British authorities. Two days later, the empty kibbutz was attacked again by an Arab mob which burned its barn, uprooted trees and vandalised its cemetery. However, the most horrific atrocities committed during the 1929 Arab riots were unleashed against the Jewish communities in the ancient cities of Hebron and Safed.

The Hebron and Safed Massacres

For many years, the small Jewish community in Hebron had lived in peace with their tens of thousands of Arab neighbours. Anticipating trouble with the whole of Palestine at boiling point, Haganah leaders offered to organise the community's defence or to help them evacuate several days before violence flared in

Jerusalem. The leaders of the Hebron community declined these offers, insisting that they trusted the *A'yan* (Arab notables), with whom they had established friendships and business relationships, to protect them. However, serious tensions were simmering just below the surface and the outward appearance of tranquility in the city was about to be shattered by the worst pogrom of the entire British Mandate.

Aharon Reuven Bernzweig, who was visiting Hebron and survived the massacre, later described the mood of the city in a letter to his family: "We had forebodings that something terrible was about to happen – but what, exactly, we did not know. I was fearful and kept questioning the local people, who had lived there for generations. They assured me that in Hebron there could never be a pogrom ... The local population had always lived very peacefully with the Arabs."[5]

Hebron is a place of special significance for both Judaism and Islam because it is the site of the Tomb of the Patriarchs where Abraham is believed to have been buried. The city's Jewish population was comprised of a Sephardi Jewish community (Jews originally from Spain, North Africa and Arab countries) who spoke Arabic, wore Arab dress and had cultural connections with the Arabs of Hebron, and Ashkenazi (native European) Jews who, in 1925, opened the Slobodka Yeshiva in the city.

The Yeshiva students lived separately from the Sephardi Jewish community; the two communities maintained separate schools, worshipped in separate synagogues, and did not intermarry. They also lived in relative isolation from the Arab population, which created a sense among the Arabs that these European "Zionist immigrants" were not to be trusted. Despite the general suspicion, however, one Yeshiva student, Dov Cohen, still recalled being on "very good" terms with his Arab neighbours.

But suddenly, on the night of Friday 23 August 1929, the tension simmering within this cauldron of nationalities bubbled over after false rumours reached Hebron that Jews were carrying out "wholesale killings of Arabs" in Jerusalem. For a period of three days, Hebron turned into a city of terror and murder as the Arab residents led a rampaging massacre against the bewildered and helpless Jewish community. By the conclusion of the massacre, 67 Jews lay dead, their homes and synagogues destroyed, and the few hundred survivors were forced to relocate to Jerusalem. The aftermath left Hebron barren of Jews for the first time in hundreds of years.

The Arab mobs inflicted unspeakable atrocities upon the Jewish community, killing and raping men, women and children and looting Jewish property. Many of the victims were tortured, or mutilated – children in front of their parents, women in front of their husbands. Today, a small museum in Hebron, established by the Jewish historian Noam Arnon, displays photographic evidence of the massacre – a girl struck over the head by a sword with her brains spilling out, people with their eyes gouged out.

Sir John Chancellor, the British High Commissioner, visited Hebron in the aftermath and later wrote to his son, "The horror of it is beyond words. In one house I visited not less than twenty-five Jews, men and women, were murdered in cold blood."[6] Describing the attacks, the subsequent Shaw Report stated, "Arabs in Hebron made a most ferocious attack on the Jewish ghetto and on isolated Jewish houses lying outside the crowded quarters of the town. More than 60 Jews – including many women and children – were murdered and more than 50 were wounded. This savage attack, of which no condemnation could be too severe, was accompanied by wanton destruction and looting. Jewish synagogues were desecrated, a Jewish hospital, which had provided treatment for Arabs, was attacked and ransacked, and only the exceptional personal courage displayed by Mr. Cafferata – the one British Police Officer in the town – prevented the outbreak from developing into a general massacre of the Jews in Hebron."[7]

Arab youths began the riots on the Friday night by hurling rocks at the Yeshiva students as they walked by and stabbing a young boy to death. The following morning, on the Jewish Sabbath, Arab mobs gathered around the Jewish community armed with clubs, knives and axes. While the women and children hurled stones that smashed windows, the men ransacked the insides of Jewish houses and destroyed Jewish property. According to the testimony of Aharon Reuven Bernzweig, "right after eight o'clock in the morning we heard screams. Arabs had begun breaking into Jewish homes. The screams pierced the heart of the heavens. We didn't know what to do … They were going from door to door, slaughtering everyone who was inside. The screams and the moans were terrible. People were crying "Help! Help!" But what could we do?"[8]

A crippled clinical pharmacist, Gershon Ben-Zion, who had served both Jews and Arabs for four decades, was killed in front of his family. His daughter was raped and then murdered, and his wife's hands were cut off.

The lone British policeman, Raymond Cafferata, was hopelessly overwhelmed, and the reinforcements he desperately called for did not arrive for two days, a delay that became a cause of bitter resentment towards the British. In a vain attempt to calm the growing mob he ordered his mounted constables, who were themselves Arabs, to disperse the crowds but they were woefully undermanned and ultimately unsuccessful. In his own testimony, Cafferata recounted how he had personally shot dead two of the attacking Arabs, one of whom was one of his own constables: "On hearing screams in a room, I went up a sort of tunnel passage and saw an Arab in the act of cutting off a child's head with a sword. He had already hit him and was having another cut, but on seeing me he tried to aim the stroke at me, but missed; he was practically on the muzzle of my rifle. I shot him low in the groin. Behind him was a Jewish woman smothered in blood with a man

I recognized as a police constable named Issa Sheriff from Jaffa. He was standing over the woman with a dagger in his hand. He saw me and bolted into a room close by and tried to shut me out shouting in Arabic, "Your Honour, I am a policeman" ... I got into the room and shot him."[9]

Hundreds of Jews were saved by their more benevolent Arab neighbours, who offered them sanctuary from the mob by hiding them in their own houses. Bernzweig told how an Arab called Haj Eissa El Kourdieh saved a group of Jews by hiding them in his cellar. There they waited with a "deadly fear" for the trouble to pass, worrying that the "murderers outside would hear [the little children who kept crying]."[10] Zmira Mani wrote about an Arab named Abu Id Zaitoun who brought his brother and son to rescue her family. The Arab family protected the Manis with their swords, hid them in a cellar along with other Jews they had saved, and eventually found a policeman to escort them safely to the police station at Beit Romano on the outskirts of the city.

The police station became a shelter for the terrified Jews, but was soon besieged by thousands of Arabs who descended from Hebron, shouting "kill the Jews!" Though the rampaging mob tried to break down the doors, the station held secure. Each night, a few men were allowed to leave the station to conduct funerals for murdered Jews at Hebron's ancient Jewish cemetery.

The most disturbing atrocities were committed at the Yeshiva. On Friday, 23 August, an Arab mob hurled stones through the windows and grabbed the sole student inside as he tried to escape the building, stabbing him to death. The next day, a crowd armed with staves and axes attacked and killed two Jewish boys, one stoned to death and the other stabbed. Many Jews, including the Yeshiva students, sought refuge in the house of Eliezer Dan Slonim, the son of the Rabbi of Hebron. He had excellent relations with the Arabs and those sheltering at his house were confident they would come to no harm. Rabbi Slonim was offered a deal by the rioters: If he surrendered all the Ashkenazi Yeshiva students over to the Arabs, the lives of the Sephardi community would be spared. When the Rabbi refused to hand over the students the Arabs killed him on the spot and began a massacre of those in his house. Survivors recounted the carnage that ensued. Moses Harbater, an 18-year-old student, was stabbed and two of his fingers were severed. He described at a later trial of some Arab rioters how a fellow student had been mutilated and killed. In total, forty-two teachers and students from the Yeshiva were murdered.

Dutch-Canadian journalist Pierre Van Passen wrote a harrowing account of the scene he witnessed in the Slonim house after the massacre which reveals an attempted cover-up by British officials:

"What occurred in the upper chambers of Slonim's house could be seen when we found the twelve-foot-high ceiling splashed with blood. The rooms looked like a slaughterhouse … the blood stood in a huge pool on the slightly sagging stone floor of the house. Clocks, crockery, tables and windows had been smashed to smithereens. Of the unlooted articles, not a single item had been left intact except a large black-and-white photograph of Dr. Theodore Herzl, the founder of political Zionism. Around the picture's frame the murderers had draped the blood-drenched underwear of a woman."

"We stood silently contemplating the scene of slaughter when the door was flung open by a British soldier with fixed bayonet. In strolled Mr. Keith-Roach, governor of the Jaffa district, followed by a colonel of the Green Howards battalion of the King's African Rifles. They took a hasty glance around that awful room, and Mr. Roach remarked to his companion, "Shall we have lunch now or drive to Jerusalem first?" In Jerusalem the Government published a refutation of the rumours that the dead Jews of Hebron had been tortured before they had their throats slit. This made me rush back to that city … I intended to gather up the severed sexual organs and the cut-off women's breasts we had seen lying scattered over the floor and in the beds. But when we came to Hebron a telephone call from Jerusalem had ordered our access barred to the Slonim house."[11]

Violence spread to the holy city of Safed in northern Galilee on 29 August. Arab rioters murdered Jewish residents and the main Jewish street was looted and burned. The Shaw Report stated: "At about 5:15 pm, on the 29 August, Arab mobs attacked the Jewish ghetto in Safed ... in the course of which some 45 Jews were killed or wounded, several Jewish houses and shops were set on fire, and there was a repetition of the wanton destruction which had been so prominent a feature of the attack at Hebron."

Eyewitness accounts describe how Arabs from Safed and nearby villages, armed with weapons and kerosene tins, perpetrated the violence. Victims were mutilated and the burnt body of a woman was hung from a window. Other victims, including women, were cut to pieces with knives. But the darkest horror occurred when rioters broke into an orphanage, smashed the children's heads with clubs and cut off their hands. The following testimony was submitted by David Hacohen, who later served in the Israeli Knesset from 1949-69:

"One Friday morning we heard that there had been a pogrom in Safed. We read the official announcement: 'On August 29, at 6:15, disturbances broke out in Safed. The army arrived on the scene at 8:35 and immediately restored order. There were some fatal casualties and many houses were burnt. The Jewish inhabitants were at once transferred to safety. Since then calm has prevailed in Safed' ... We had enough experience not to trust the reassuring official announcement."

"We set out on Saturday morning. When at noon we entered the town through the main road, I could not believe my eyes ... I met some of the town's Jewish elders, who fell on my neck weeping bitterly ... Inside the houses I saw the mutilated and burned bodies of the victims of the massacre, and the burned body of a woman tied to the grille of a window. Going from house to house, I counted ten bodies that had not yet been collected. I saw the destruction and the signs of fire. Even in my grimmest thoughts I had not imagined that this was how I would find Safed where 'calm prevailed.'"

"The local Jews gave me a detailed description of how the tragedy had started. Advancing on the street of the Sephardi Jews from Kfar Meron and Ein Zeitim, they looted and set fire to houses, urging each other on to continue with the killing. They slaughtered the schoolteacher, Aphriat, together with his wife and mother, and cut the lawyer, Toledano, to pieces with their knives. Bursting into the orphanages, they smashed the children's heads and cut off their hands. I myself saw the victims. Yitshak Mammon, a native of Safed who lived with an Arab family, was murdered with indescribable brutality: he was stabbed again and again, until his body became a bloody sieve, and then he was trampled to death. Throughout the whole pogrom the police did not fire a single shot ... While the looting and killing were still going on, the police were searching the Jews for arms."[12]

After six days of extreme violence, the British administration finally deployed troops to bring an end to the riots. Of the 139 Jews killed during the troubles, half lived in Hebron, making this the worst massacre of Jews in Palestine since the Crusades. The events at Hebron, together with those in Safed, created shock waves that rocked the Jewish communities in Palestine and around the world, becoming propaganda symbols of Jewish persecution at the hands of bloodthirsty Arabs. It must be acknowledged, of course, that the scale of pogroms in Eastern Europe dwarfed the massacres at Hebron and Safed, and the European pogroms did not provide examples to match the stories of Arabs acting to save their Jewish neighbours.

Despite the fact that Jews had been living in Gaza and Hebron for centuries, the British shamefully forced the Jews, who were the victims of the violence, to leave their homes and prohibited Jews from living in the Gaza strip and Hebron in an effort to appease Arabs and to prevent further violence. It was, in effect, an ethnic cleansing of Jews living in Hebron, one of the oldest Jewish communities in the world. It was an injustice that was contrary to both the spirit and the letter of the Mandate.

Richard Meinertzhagen, the pro-Zionist British intelligence officer, wrote in his diary, "The Jews have been granted a home in their old country after 2,000 years of deplorable exile. We have assumed trustee-ship and have accepted the responsibility of assisting them in establishing themselves in their home. We have undertaken to see that they get fair play, and, as I read the mandate, the Jews are placed in a position of "most favoured nation" in Palestine, always providing that the Arab civil and religious rights are not prejudiced … There has never, to my knowledge, been a single instance of Zionist progress at the expense of Arab religious rights, though many instances have from time to time been trumped up by Arabs and supported by their British sympathisers, and it is this latter factor which is at the root of the evil in Palestine."[13]

The British Reaction

The now familiar response of the British was to set up a Commission of Inquiry, which was headed by Sir Walter Shaw, to determine the causes of the riots. The so called Shaw Commission heard public evidence for several weeks, and issued its report in March 1930 which concluded that the fundamental cause of the violence was, "the Arab feeling of animosity and hostility towards the Jews consequent upon the disappointment of their political and national aspirations and fear for their economic future." It also noted Arab fears of Jewish immigrants, who appeared to have unlimited funds from abroad, "not only as a menace to their livelihood but as a possible overlord of the future." The report also found that the "outbreak in Jerusalem on August 23 was from the beginning an attack by Arabs on Jews for which no excuse in the form of earlier murders by Jews has been established."

The Commission acknowledged the ambiguity of previous British statements regarding Palestine which had contributed to differing interpretations of British promises to both Arabs and Jews. It therefore recommended that the Government clearly define its intentions for Palestine. It also recommended that the issue of further Jewish immigration and land sales to the Jews be carefully reconsidered to avoid "a repetition of the excessive immigration of 1925 and 1926." The issue of land tenure would only be eligible for review if new methods of cultivation stimulated considerable growth of the agricultural sector.

Henry Snell, one of the Commission members, signed the report but added a note of reservation. Although he was satisfied that Haj Amin al-Husseini was not directly responsible for the violence, he believed the Mufti was aware of the nature of the anti-Zionist campaign and the danger of disturbances. He therefore attributed to the Mufti a greater share of the blame than the official report had. Snell also disagreed with the Commission on matters of Jewish immigration and did not support restrictions on Jewish land purchases.

The Shaw Commission's recommendations led directly to a subsequent Commission headed by Sir John Hope Simpson. Its report, published on 21 October 1930, recommended the cessation of Jewish immigration due to the lack of agricultural land to support it. The report completely misrepresented the economic capacity of Palestine, casting doubt on the prospects for industrialisation and asserting that no more than 20,000 families could be accommodated by the land. The report concluded that the Arabs were being "displaced" by Jews even though its own pages revealed that there was an uncontrolled influx of Arabs from neighbouring states.

In a letter accompanying the report, Hope Simpson noted that "All British officials tend to become pro-Arab, or perhaps more accurately *anti-Jew* ... Personally I can quite well understand this trait. The helplessness of the Fellah (peasant) appeals to the British official [with] whom he comes in touch. The offensive self-assertion of the Jewish immigrant is, on the other hand, repellent."[14] This comment is indicative of the general bias towards supporting Arab opposition to Jewish immigration held by officials in both the Colonial and the Foreign Offices. Some of the British bias was rooted in anti-Semitism; some of it merely reflected disdain for Zionism. In Hope Simpson's case, it was rooted in both.

While the British constantly made efforts to restrict and curtail Jewish immigration, Arab immigration remained unrestricted throughout the Mandatory period. It is simply impossible to reconcile the reasons for controlling Jewish immigration with the incongruous British practice of ignoring the uncontrolled illegal immigration of the Arabs. Major Claude Scudamore Jarvis, the British Governor of the Sinai from 1922-36, observed, "This illegal immigration was not only going on from the Sinai, but also from Transjordan and Syria, and it is very difficult to make a case out for the misery of the Arabs if at the same time their compatriots from adjoining states could not be kept from going in to share that misery."[15] Winston Churchill, a veteran of the first days of the British Mandate, said in 1939, "So far from being persecuted, the Arabs have crowded into the country and multiplied till their population has increased more than even all world Jewry could lift up the Jewish population."[16]

Ultimately, the British administration was forced to admit that the argument about the absorptive capacity of the country was ostensibly false. The 1937 Peel Commission concluded: "The heavy immigration in the years 1933-36 would seem to show that the Jews have been able to enlarge the absorptive capacity of the country for Jews."

While the Hope Simpson report dismayed the Jewish community, it was overshadowed by the simultaneous release of the insidious White Paper of Colonial Secretary Lord Passfield, published in October 1930, which reflected his deep-seated prejudice against Zionism. This report strongly asserted the strength of Britain's obligations to the Arabs and argued that they should not be overlooked to satisfy Jewish interests.

The White Paper was an attempt to frame a formal statement of British policy in Palestine, as recommended by the Hope Simpson Report, in the hope of clarifying unresolved questions concerning the British Mandate for Palestine and the Balfour Declaration. The Paper was considered highly favourable towards the Arabs.

The Paper stated that the development of a Jewish national home in Palestine was not considered central to the Mandate. Although the Paper did assert an intention to fulfil obligations to both Arabs and Jews, the tone was unmistakably anti-Jewish. Jewish institutions were heavily criticised for promoting labour policies that were deemed damaging to the economic development of the Arab population. The Paper also repeated the findings of Hope Simpson that there was insufficient cultivable land to support any new immigrants. Jews who had already purchased tracts of land would be allowed to continue developing them, but thereafter would need to secure permission from the British authorities before acquiring additional land. When determining whether to grant particular requests for land, the British would take into consideration the unemployment levels among both Arabs and Jews.

The Passfield Paper was gleefully seized upon by opponents of the Zionist cause because they interpreted it as overturning the

Balfour Declaration. Jewish organisations worldwide protested furiously, and rigorous objections were raised on both sides of the British Parliament. An appalled David Lloyd George commented, "They dare not try to kill Zionism directly, but they try to put it in a refrigerator with the door just ajar."[17] Many British government representatives distanced themselves from the White Paper, causing an uncomfortable atmosphere of dissent for Prime Minister Ramsay MacDonald.

Chaim Weizmann resigned as president of the Jewish Agency, stating that the British had betrayed their promises. To clear the air, Ramsey MacDonald was forced to write a letter to Weizmann reaffirming the government's commitment to encouraging further Jewish settlement. His letter stated, "The obligation to facilitate Jewish immigration and make possible dense settlement of Jews on the land is still a positive obligation of the Mandate, and it can be fulfilled without jeopardizing the rights and conditions of the other part of the Palestine population."[18]

Despite the restrictions placed on its growth, the Jewish population increased to more than 160,000 by the start of the 1930s, and the community became solidly entrenched in Palestine. Unfortunately, as the Jewish presence grew stronger, so did the Arab opposition. And to compound the problems caused by this opposition, the standard British responses to Arab riots had established a cycle that only served to encourage further outbreaks of violence.

During each riot, the British administration would make little effort to protect the Jews from Arab attacks. Then, once calm was restored, the British government would establish a Commission of Inquiry to identify the cause of the riot. The Commission would issue a report identifying Arab aggression as the cause, but then conclude that this aggression stemmed from fear that they were being displaced by Jewish immigrants. Therefore, to prevent further disturbances, each Commission followed a precedent of appeasing the Arabs by recommending that restrictions be placed on Jewish immigration. Rioting thus became a learned behaviour for the Arabs as they recognized that staging a riot against the Jews was an effective tool for stopping Jewish immigration. Rather than preventing trouble, the British method of resolving conflicts actually encouraged outbreaks of violence. At the same time, Arabs were allowed to enter Palestine freely and the increases in Arab population figures were never considered when estimating the country's absorptive capacity.

The findings of successive reports encouraged the Arabs to believe that they had been disadvantaged by Jewish settlement, but this ignored evidence to the contrary contained in their own pages. The Shaw Commission report, for example, acknowledged that, "Jewish activities have increased the prosperity of Palestine, have raised the standard of life for the Arab workers and have laid the foundations on which may be based the future progress of the two communities and their development into one state." Yet still the subsequent Passfield White Paper imposed restrictions on Jewish immigration and land purchase in direct contravention of Britain's legally binding obligation under the Mandate to give every assistance to Jewish immigration. Although the Balfour Declaration, which was incorporated into the Mandate, spoke of favouring the establishment of a national home for the Jews, it became British policy to promote Arab interests in equality with Jewish interest. But because Britain failed to regulate Arab migration after 1922, the Jews were insidiously placed in a disadvantaged position.

In December 1931, Ze'ev Jabotinsky delivered a speech in Warsaw, the report of which in the Times attributed to him the statement, "Jews might become the dynamite which would blow up the British Empire."[19] Eager not to create the impression that he was suggesting that the Jews might harm the British Empire, Jabotinsky responded with a clarification of his meaning in a letter to the Times: "It was England, not the Jews, whom I accused of playing with 'dynamite' ... Our experience with England as Mandatory for Palestine has resulted in making 15,000,000 people lose faith in a nation whose name, to every Jew, has always stood for straightforward moral earnestness. The Mandatory has become an unmitigated hindrance to any progress of Zionism ... England acts as though she wished to set ablaze 15,000,000 torches of despair scattered in every corner of the world."[20]

Throughout 1933, and for the following decade, British Foreign Office and Colonial Office officials received a growing tsunami of daily and weekly reports about the increasingly horrific conditions of Jews in Romania, Poland and Germany. Moreover, Weizmann and his Zionist colleagues were extremely energetic in their constant lobbying to keep the government in London, of whatever political persuasion, to its Mandatory promise to develop a Jewish homeland, and ultimately a sovereign Jewish State.

A fresh wave of Arab riots erupted in 1933, instigated by the Arab Executive Committee. The riots were sparked by an influx of 37,000 Jewish immigrants fleeing persecution in Nazi Germany. Many of these new arrivals were highly educated, and some brought considerable wealth into the Jewish community, which contributed to developments in the fields of agriculture, industry, medicine, science and education.

The Arab population perceived this influx to be a serious threat. On 5 October 1933, the Arab Executive Committee, established in December 1920 by the Palestinian Arabs at a congress in Haifa to act as the representative of the Arabs but never formally recognized by the British, called for a general strike to show the anger of the Arab people and announced that a protest rally would take place on 13 October at the Temple Mount in Jerusalem. The British authorities, fearing a riot, issued a prohibition order against the demonstration, and stationed police officers at the gates of the Old City to prevent the Arab rally from accessing the

Temple Mount area. A crowd gathered at noon on the appointed day, led by members of the Arab Executive Committee, but the police succeeded in dispersing them with the use of clubs.

On 29 October demonstrations were held in Jaffa, Haifa and Nablus. Despite promises that the demonstrations would be peaceful, they quickly escalated into violence. Roy Spicer, the Police Commissioner in Palestine, once more suppressed the riots by sending in police officers on horseback armed with clubs. The 1933 Palestinian riots, as they came to be known, were a prelude to a more sustained and violent Arab revolt that broke out in Palestine during the years 1936–39.

Endnotes

1. Public Record Office, Kew Gardens, Foreign Office, Great Britain 371/20819.
2. Cited by the Shaw Commission Report, *Report of the Commission on the Palestine Disturbances of August 1929, Cmd. 3530.* His Majesty's Stationery Office, London, 1930, p. 31.
3. Cited by the Shaw Commission Report, p. 30.
4. Cited by the Shaw Commission Report, p. 66-67.
5. Cited from *www.hebron1929.info/Hebronletter*.
6. Cited from Jerold S. Auerbach, *Hebron Jews: Memory and Conflict in the Land of Israel* (Plymouth: Rowman & Littlefield, 2009), p. 72.
7. Shaw Commission Report, p. 64.
8. Cited from *www.hebron1929.info/Hebronletter*.
9. Cited from Benny Morris, *Righteous Victims: A History of the Zionist–Arab Conflict, 1881–1999* (New York: Alfred A. Knopf, 2001), p. 114.
10. Citied from *www.hebron1929.info/Hebronletter*.
11. From the autobiography of Pierre Van Passen, *Days of our Years* (1939), cited by en.hebron.org.il/history.
12. David Hacohen, *Time to Tell: An Israeli Life 1898-1984* (New York: Cornwall Books, 1985), cited from *www.camera.org*.
13. Richard Meinertzhagen, *Middle East Diary: 1917-1956* (London: Cresset Press, 1959), p. 142.
14. Remarks by Sir John Hope Simpson to Lord Passfield, 18 August 1930, London. Public Record Office, Cabinet Papers 24/215.
15. Cited by the Peel Report: *Palestine Royal Commission Report Presented by the Secretary of State for the Colonies to Parliament by Command of His Majesty, July 1937.* His Majesty's Stationery Office, London, 1937.
16. Michael Makovsky, *Churchill's Promised Land: Zionism and Statecraft* (New Haven: Yale University Press, 2007), p. 167.

[17] Hansard, 17 November 1930.
[18] Cited from *www.jewishvirtuallibrary.org/the-macdonald-letter-february-1931*.
[19] Reported in *The Times* Newspaper, 2 January 1932.
[20] Letter to *The Times* Newspaper, 26 January 1932.

CHAPTER 4

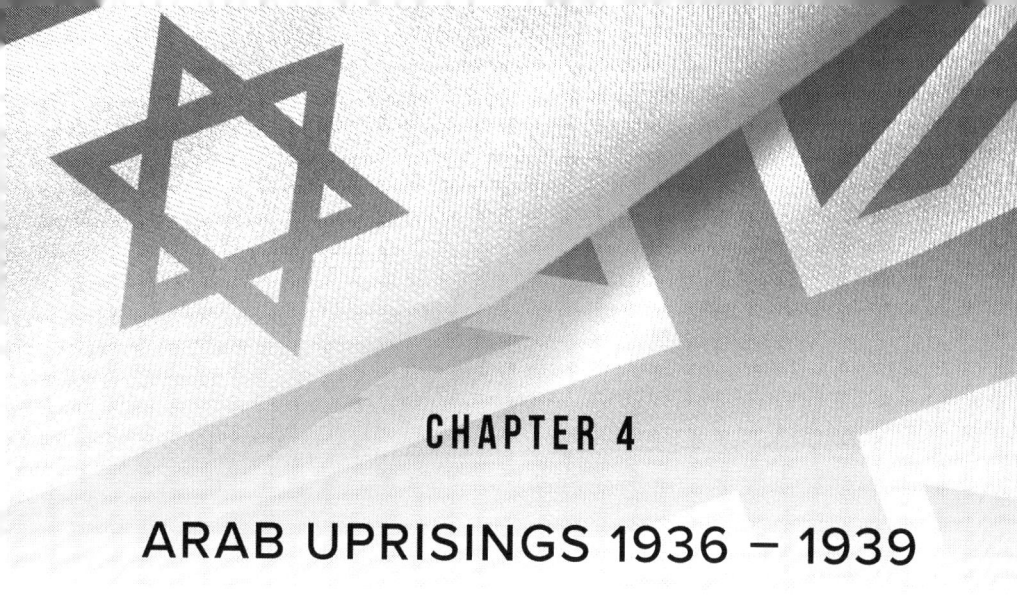

ARAB UPRISINGS 1936 – 1939

> " *The Jew murders the Arab and the Arab murders the Jew. This is what is going on in Palestine now. And it will go on for the next 50 years in all probability."*
>
> —MAJOR-GENERAL BERNARD MONTGOMERY

The menacing shadow of Nazism that was cast across Germany during the 1930s brought about an intensification of anti-Semitism throughout Europe. At the annual Nazi party rally held in Nuremberg in 1935, laws were introduced by the Reichstag which institutionalized many of the racial theories prevalent in Nazi ideology. These laws excluded German Jews from Reich citizenship and prohibited them from marrying or having sexual relations with persons of "German or related blood." A supplementary decree which outlined the definition of who was classified as Jewish was passed on 14 November 1935, and from that date the Reich Citizenship Law officially came into force.

The Nuremberg laws had a crippling social and economic impact on the Jewish community. They were labelled as parasites and many non-Jews stopped socialising with Jews or transacting with Jewish-owned businesses, many of which were forced to close because of the resulting loss of customers. Jews were no longer permitted to work in the civil service or government regulated professions such as medicine and education, forcing many middle-class business owners and professionals to take menial employment. Those with the means to do so attempted to leave the country, fearing for their survival, but this was in itself problematic; Jews were required to pay 90 per cent of their wealth as an emigration tax upon exiting the country and it was almost impossible for potential Jewish emigrants to find a country willing to take them. The Israeli novelist, Amos Oz, described how his parents came to Jerusalem running for their lives, "My parents - they tried to become American, they tried to become British, they tried to become Scandinavian - nobody wanted them, anywhere."[1] Palestine offered their only hope of sanctuary.

With the threat of another war with Germany looming, the last thing the British needed was a wide-ranging Arab revolt. Control of the Suez Canal, Iraqi oil fields, and the Iraq-Haifa oil pipeline which passed through Palestine were of vital strategic importance to the British Empire. Taking any action which might offend Arab sensibilities was out of the question. The rapidly deteriorating circumstances in Europe conspired to thwart such hopes as many of the Jews escaping from Germany, upon finding that they were not welcome in other European states, made their way to Palestine. As the troubles of the previous decade had demonstrated, any increase in Jewish immigration or land acquisition was bound to inflame Arab angst and foster resentment against the Mandate.

To the dismay of the British Administration, in April 1936, violence erupted once more in Palestine. An Arab attack on a Jewish convoy led to a series of reprisals and counter reprisals that swiftly escalated into a full-blown Arab rebellion featuring terrorist attacks against both the Jews and the British. During the summer of that year, thousands of Jewish-farmed acres and orchards were destroyed, Jewish civilians were attacked and murdered, and some Jewish communities, such as those in Beisan and Acre, were forced to evacuate for safer areas. This summer of unrest was the first stage of a far ranging "Arab Revolt" orchestrated by the Arab High Committee under the leadership of Haj Amin al-Husseini that flared for prolonged periods over the next three years, a revolt that would prove to be the decisive episode in the efforts of the Arabs to resist the British mandate's support for a Jewish national home in Palestine.

The seeds of the outbreak can be traced to the death of Sheikh Izz ad-Din al-Qassam, a radical Islamic preacher of Syrian origins, on 20 November 1935. Five years earlier, al-Qassam established the Black Hand, an anti-Zionist and anti-British militant organization. He recruited disenfranchised Arab peasants and personally led them in a sustained campaign of vandalism against orchards planted by Jewish farmers and British constructed railway lines. In November 1935, two of his men engaged in a firefight with a Palestine police patrol hunting fruit thieves in which a policeman was shot dead. In response, the police launched a manhunt and cornered al-Qassam in a cave near Ya'bad. In the ensuing battle, al-Qassam was killed. Many thousands of his supporters marched in the funeral cortege as it headed towards his grave in Haifa. In recent times, al-Qassam's legacy has been claimed by the radical Islamist movement Hamas, which has named its armed brigade after him.

Earlier in 1935, a large clandestine arms shipment destined for the Haganah was intercepted at the port of Jaffa, sparking Arab fears that the Jews were preparing for a military takeover of Palestine. Their anxiety was compounded by the rapid acceleration of Jewish immigration generated by the worsening conditions in Europe. This created a highly combustible atmosphere that was electrified by the widespread outrage at al-Qassam's death. A perfect storm was brewing.

With tensions running dangerously high, the sparks that ignited the uprising were struck in April 1936 when a convoy of trucks on the Nablus to Tulkarm road was stopped by an Arab roadblock and the assailants shot dead three Jewish drivers. The following day unidentified masked gunmen shot and killed two Arab workers sleeping in a hut near Petah Tikva in an apparent revenge attack. This in turn incited Arab rioting in Jaffa, in which a mob rampaged through a residential area indiscriminately killing Jews and destroying property. On 20 April 1936, David Ben Gurion told mourners at a funeral held for nine victims of the Jaffa riot that Jews would only be safe "in communities which are 100 per cent Jewish and built on Jewish land."[2]

As the violence flared, a political coalition of prominent Arab leaders, led by the Mufti Haj Amin al-Husseini, united to protest against Zionist advances in Palestine. The Arab Higher Committee, as the group was known, began their protest by calling for a general strike of Arab workers and a boycott of Jewish products in support of three basic demands: The immediate cessation of Jewish immigration; an end to all further land sales to the Jews; and the establishment of an Arab national government. About one month into the strike, the Arab Higher Committee called for a general non-payment of taxes in explicit opposition to Jewish immigration. One thing was clear: the Arabs were not going to acquiesce peaceably to continued Jewish immigration into Palestine.

In the countryside, armed insurrection flared sporadically, becoming more organised over time. One particular target of the rebels was the Mosul–Haifa oil pipeline of the Iraq Petroleum Company which had been constructed only a few years earlier. It was repeatedly bombed at various points along its length. Other attacks were launched against railways and civilian targets including Jewish settlements, secluded Jewish neighbourhoods in the mixed cities, and Jewish people, both as individuals and in groups.

The government responded to the crisis by rounding up Palestinian Arab leaders and detaining them in a camp at Auja al-Hafir in the Negev desert. Troop numbers were increased rapidly in an attempt to regain control. On 2 June 1936, a failed attempt by rebels to derail a train bringing reinforcements from Egypt forced the administration to place the railways under constant guard, increasing the strain on security forces that were already stretched taut.

A statement of policy issued by the Colonial Office in London on 7 September 1936 declared that the situation was a "direct challenge to the authority of the British Government in Palestine"[3] and announced the appointment of Lieutenant–General John Dill as supreme military commander. By the end of September, the size of the British military garrison in Palestine had swollen to 20,000 troops, most of whom were deployed rounding up gangs of Arab agitators.

In October 1936, the British, working in collaboration with their regional Arab allies, Amir Abdullah of Transjordan, King Ghazi of Iraq, and King Abdul Aziz ibn Saud of Saudi Arabia, mediated a temporary suspension to hostilities with the Arab Higher Committee and the violence abated. But although the revolt was seemingly over, the Arabs were seething with rage. They wanted both Britain and the Jews out of Arab territory.

The intensity of the Arab Revolt, at a time when Britain was preparing for the possibility of another war, pressurised the British into rethinking their policy in Palestine. With British strategic policy focusing increasingly on the need to foster goodwill in the Middle East to protect vital oil supplies, Jewish leverage in the Foreign Office was in decline. There were no longer pro-Zionists of the calibre of Balfour and Samuel influencing policy in the Foreign Office and the new administration was less inclined toward supporting the Zionist position. Winston Churchill, a stalwart supporter of the Zionist cause from the early days of the Mandate, was cast adrift from government and trapped in a political wilderness that would not end until he was called upon during Britain's darkest hour. Furthermore, Whitehall had calculated that the Jews would have no choice but to support Britain against Nazi Germany, and so there was no strategic imperative to court their favour. The revolt demonstrated that Arab support, on the other hand, was far from certain. Thus, Britain's commitment to a Jewish homeland in Palestine began to dissipate, and the Mandate authorities became more inclined to pursue a policy of appeasement towards the Arabs.

Such a change in policy would not, however, be easy to implement. Since the Balfour Declaration, successive British governments had endorsed the establishment of a Jewish national home in Palestine. The British Mandate itself was actually premised on that pledge. By the mid 1930s, the Jewish community in Palestine had grown to about 400,000, and Jewish economic and political structures were deeply embedded. The extent of the Jewish presence and the rapidly deteriorating fate of European Jewry meant that the British would have an extremely difficult time extricating themselves from their commitment to the Balfour Declaration. Furthermore, the existing Palestinian Arab leadership, dominated by Haj Amin al-Husseini, were unwilling to grant members of the Jewish community citizenship or to guarantee their safety if a new Arab state were to emerge. Thus, there were only three stark options open to the British: The imposition of a partition plan, a withdrawal to leave the Jews and Arabs to fight it out, or to stay and improvise.

In an effort to figure out a solution and alleviate the situation a Royal Commission of Inquiry was despatched from London to Palestine to investigate the root causes of the Arab-Jewish conflict and to propose a way forward. The Commission, headed by Lord Robert Peel (known as the Peel Commission), issued its recommendations in July 1937.

The Peel Commission identified that the same causes that brought about the Arab uprisings of 1929 and 1933 lay at the heart of the 1936 revolt, but had been intensified by two external factors: (1) The sufferings of the Jews in Germany and Poland, resulting in a great increase of Jewish immigration into Palestine; and (2) the prospect of Syria and the Lebanon soon obtaining the same independence as Iraq and Saudi Arabia. Egypt was also on the eve of independence.

The Commission found that the principle causes of the disturbance were, as in all previous outbreaks, the desire of the Arabs for national independence and their hatred and fear of the establishment of the Jewish national home. The Commission report also listed the six subsidiary factors that were considered the most important. These were: (1) The advance of Arab nationalism outside Palestine; (2) the increased immigration of Jews since 1933; (3) the opportunity enjoyed by the Jews for influencing public opinion in Britain; (4) Arab distrust in the sincerity of the British Government; (5) Arab alarm at the continued Jewish purchase of land; (6) the general uncertainty as to the ultimate intentions of the Mandatory power.

The Commission described the disturbances as "an open rebellion of the Palestinian Arabs, assisted by fellow-Arabs from other countries, against Mandatory rule" and noted two unprecedented features of the revolt: the support of all senior Arab officials in the political and technical departments of the Palestine administration and the "interest and sympathy of the neighbouring Arab peoples" which had resulted in support for the rebellion in the form of volunteers from Syria and Iraq.

The Commission concluded that the British obligations to both the Arab and Zionist positions were irreconcilable, and that the existing Mandate was unworkable. Describing the present reality, the report stated, "The contrast between the modern democratic and primarily European character of the National Home and that of the Arab world around it is striking ... There can be no question of fusion or assimilation between Jewish and Arab cultures ... The gulf between the races is already wide and will continue to widen if the present Mandate is maintained." The Commission's central recommendation was to abolish the Mandate and to partition Palestine into Jewish and Arab states, with a retained British Mandate under international supervision over Nazareth, Bethlehem, Jerusalem and a corridor from Jerusalem to Jaffa.

The proposed Jewish state included the coastal strip stretching from Mount Carmel to south of Be'er Tuvia, as well as the Jezreel Valley and the region of Galilee. The partition was based on current Jewish land ownership and population demographics, and incorporated the country's most productive agricultural land. However, the Jewish state that would have been created from this partition plan, in the north of present-day Israel, would have been astonishingly small. The land to be allotted to the Jews was less than one half of that which the United Nations would recommend ten years later.

The larger Arab state, to be linked to Transjordan, was to include the hilly regions of Judea and Samaria, and the Negev. Until the establishment of the two states, the Commission recommended that the Jews should be prohibited from purchasing land in the area allocated to the Arab state. To overcome demarcation problems, it was proposed that land exchanges be carried out concurrently with the transfer of population from one area to the other. This radical proposal would have involved the transfer of 225,000 Palestinian Arabs from the Jewish state to the Arab state and Transjordan. Demarcation of the precise borders of the states was entrusted to a technical partition committee.

The Peel Commission did not believe that Jewish immigration was detrimental to the financial well-being of the Arab population. On the contrary, it concluded that, "The Arab population ... has had some share in the increased prosperity of Palestine. Many Arab landowners have benefited from the sale of land and the profitable investment of the purchase money. The *fellaheen* are better off on the whole than they were in 1920. This Arab progress has been partly due to the import of Jewish capital into Palestine and other factors associated with the growth of the National Home. In particular, the Arabs have benefited from social services which could not have been provided on the existing scale without the revenue obtained from the Jews." However, the report also warned that, "Such economic advantage as the Arabs have gained from Jewish immigration will decrease if the political breach between the races continues to widen." And so, as with all previous Commissions of Inquiry, the report called for further limitations on Jewish immigration and land purchases.

The British government initially accepted the recommendations of the Peel Commission for the partitioning of Palestine, and the announcement was endorsed by Parliament in London. However, with war clouds looming over Europe, they realized that any attempt to implement it against the will of the Palestinian Arab majority would rouse up the entire Arab world against Britain.

The Jewish response to the Commission was mixed. The religious Zionists and sections of the Labour Zionist movement were bitterly opposed to the recommendations. However, David Ben Gurion welcomed the Commission's support for the notion of population transfer, which he believed was the foundation for national consolidation in a free homeland. As we have seen earlier in this chapter, his conviction in the aftermath of the Jaffa riots of the previous year was that Jews would only be safe "in communities which are 100 per cent Jewish and built on Jewish land." Subsequently, the two principal Jewish leaders, Chaim Weizmann and Ben Gurion, convinced the Twentieth Zionist Congress to reject the proposed boundaries but agree in principle to partition as a basis for further negotiation. Meanwhile, the Haganah began building settlements on land not previously occupied.

Palestinian Arab nationalists violently rejected any kind of partition proposal and refused to regard it as a solution. Responding to their objections, British Secretary of Foreign Affairs, Anthony Eden, suggested an alternative plan, "which would not give Jews any territory exclusively for their own use."[4] Eden's proposal is illustrative of the creeping dissipation of support for Zionism in Whitehall. A decade later, he betrayed pro-Arab leanings in a letter to his private secretary, "If we must have preferences, let me murmur in your ear that I prefer Arabs to Jews."[5]

Ultimately, the partition plan was shelved when the technical team dispatched to make detailed plans, the Woodhead Commission, reported that partition was impracticable. Reporting in 1938, the Commission rejected the Peel plan primarily on the grounds that it could not be implemented without a massive forced transfer of Arabs. The British Government accompanied the publication of the Woodhead Report with a statement of policy rejecting partition as impracticable due to "political, administrative and financial difficulties."[6]

Naturally, the British government was attempting to manoeuvre itself into the position of disinterested noble guardians stuck between two irreconcilably irrational opponents, but in reality, Palestine was critical to British interests, and they could not afford to compromise their control of the Iraqi-Haifa oil pipeline. The Arabs frequently targeted the pipeline during the revolt, and something had to be done to pacify the region. The Peel Commission findings, particularly the further limits imposed on Jewish immigration and on the transfer of land to Jewish immigrants, were clearly intended as an attempt to appease the Arabs, but the Arabs were far from placated.

The Arab revolt resumed in the autumn of 1937, shortly after the Peel Commission recommendations were released. In this second phase, clashes with British forces became much more severe, as did the attacks on Jewish settlements. The British rapidly began to lose control of the situation and were forced into deploying even more repressive measures in an effort to intimidate the Arab population and undermine popular support for the revolt. The full range of ruthless tactics developed by Britain for anti-colonial warfare and quelling rebellions were all in evidence: torture, murder, collective punishment, detention without trial, military courts, aerial bombardment and 'punitive demolition' of more than two thousand houses.

The starting pistol for the resumption of the uprising was fired with the assassination of the Acting District Commissioner of Galilee, Lewis Andrews, on 26 September 1937 by Arab gunmen in Nazareth. The British responded, on 30 September, by issuing regulations authorizing the High Commissioner to outlaw associations whose objectives he regarded as contrary to public policy. Haj Amin al-Husseini was removed from the leadership of the Supreme Muslim Council, and both the local National Committees and the Arab Higher Committee were disbanded. Five Arab leaders were arrested and deported to the Seychelles and in fear of arrest Jamal al-Husseini fled to Syria and Haj Amin al-Husseini to Lebanon. All frontiers with Palestine were closed, telephone connections to neighbouring countries were withdrawn, press censorship was introduced and a special concentration camp was opened near Acre.

As violent attacks against British forces and Jewish settlements intensified, the British authorities inaugurated military courts, which were established for the trial of offences connected with the carrying and discharge of firearms, sabotage and intimidation. The British imposed the death penalty for unauthorised possession of weapons, ammunition, and explosives, but since many Jews had permission to carry weapons and store ammunition for defence purposes this order was directed primarily against Palestinian Arabs. In total, 108 Arabs were executed in Acre prison, the majority hanged for illegal possession of arms. Despite this, however, the Arab campaign of murder and sabotage continued and in the hill country Arab gangs began to reorganize into guerrilla fighting units.

On 2 October 1938, an organized gang of Arabs massacred 21 Jews – including three women and ten children – in a coordinated assault on the Jewish Quarter of Tiberias. The Arab attackers stabbed, shot and burned to death their helpless victims. The New York Times reported on the massacre as follows: "Not since the riots of 1929, when Arabs fell on Jewish men, most of whom were rabbinical students, as well as women and children, in the ancient towns of Hebron and Safed, has there been in Palestine such a slaughter as the attack of last night. The main synagogue of the town was destroyed by fire, and the district offices, the police station and the British police billet were fired on. The attack apparently was well organized, since the Arab gang, before descending on Tiberias, cut all telephone communications. Coming in two parties from opposite directions at a given signal, which was a whistle blown from the hills surrounding the town, the firing began simultaneously in all quarters … The bandits rushed to the central synagogue and, finding there a beadle named Jacob Zaltz, killed him and then set the building afire … the Arabs broke in and stabbed and burned to death Mr. Kabin [an elderly American Jew who had recently come to Palestine] and his sister … From there the bandits went on to the house of Joshua Ben Arieh, where they stabbed and burned to death Joshua, his wife and one son, and then shot dead his infant son. In the same house three children of Shlomo Leimer, aged 8, 10, and 12, were stabbed and burned to death. Proceeding farther, the Arabs broke into the house of Shimon Mizrahi, where they killed his wife and five children, ranging in ages from 1 to 12 years, and then set fire to the house."[7]

In July 1938, when the Palestine Government seemed to have largely lost control of the situation, the garrison was further strengthened from Egypt, and in September it was reinforced from England. The police were placed under the operational control of the army commander, and military officials were empowered to supersede civil authorities in the enforcement of order. In October the Old City of Jerusalem, which had become a rebel stronghold, was re-occupied by the troops. By the end of the year a semblance of order had been restored in the towns, though terrorism continued in rural areas until the outbreak of World War II.

It took the British three years to suppress the revolt, and to do so required Britain to despatch its largest expeditionary force since the Great War – 50,000 troops – to Palestine. By the summer of 1939, when Germany was about to invade Poland, Major-General Bernard Montgomery, who arrived in 1938 to command a division, reported: "This rebellion is definitely and finally smashed. We have such a strong hold on the country that it is not possible for the rebellion to raise its head again on the scale we previously experienced."[8]

In their efforts to crush the revolt, the British sanctioned the arming of the Haganah and a British intelligence officer, Captain Charles Orde Wingate, was appointed as their commander. Wingate was a pro-Zionist Christian who believed passionately in the Bible and embraced the prophetic vision of the Jews' return to the land of Israel. He therefore embarked upon his commission with religious zeal, working tirelessly to help realize that Zionist ideal. He was also an outstanding visionary leader who fostered aspirations to become the commander of the army of any future Jewish state.

Wingate instigated the philosophy of "active defence" that is still practised today by the Israeli Defense Forces, organizing 'Special Night Squads' predominantly comprised of Haganah volunteers to combat Arab attacks. Their tactics were based on the strategic principles of surprise, mobility, and night attack.

Wingate commanded and accompanied them on patrols, frequently ambushing Arab saboteurs who were attacking the oil pipelines of the Iraq Petroleum Company, and raiding the border villages the attackers had used as bases. In these raids Wingate's men sometimes imposed severe collective punishments on the villagers which were criticised by Zionist leaders as well as Wingate's British superiors. The Colonial Administrator Sir Hugh Foot described the activities in which the Special Night Squads engaged, which included torture, whipping, abuse and execution of Arabs, as "extreme and cruel." But the brutal tactics proved effective in quelling the uprising, and Wingate was awarded the DSO in September 1938.

Wingate established and maintained strong relationships with the leaders of both the Jewish community and the Haganah, learning Hebrew and demonstrating his ardent commitment to the ideal of a Jewish homeland. He frequently returned to Kibbutz En Harod because he felt familiar with the biblical judge Gideon, who fought in this area, and used it himself as a military base. Amongst the Jewish community he was called 'ha-yedid', the friend.

Wingate's support for the Zionist cause, however, was controversial. Though the Palestinian authorities had much to be grateful for, Wingate was intensely disliked by senior elements of the Administration who were alarmed by his associations with political causes in Palestine. As with the case of Colonel Meinertzhagen before, his military superiors considered him compromised as an intelligence officer and were convinced that he was promoting his own agenda rather than that of the army or the government. And so, Wingate was rewarded for his efforts by being deported back to England in May 1939 with a stamp in his passport, "the bearer should never be allowed entry to Palestine." The efforts of the Haganah in suppressing the Arab revolts were 'rewarded' with the infamous White Paper of 1939, which is the subject of the next chapter.

Though Wingate's personal involvement with the Zionist cause was thus curtailed, many of those he trained became the future leaders of the Palmach, the elite fighting arm of the Haganah, and later, the Israeli Defense Forces. He was loved by leaders such as Zvi Brenner and Moshe Dayan who had trained under him, and who claimed that Wingate had "taught us everything we know." He served with distinction during World War II, most notably in the Burma campaign where he created the Chindits, a deep penetration unit that operated in jungle territory held by the Japanese. He died tragically in an aeroplane crash in Burma in 1944.

Impact of the Arab Riots

Despite the intervention of up to 50,000 British troops and 15,000 Haganah, the uprising continued for over three years. By the time the violence finally abated, in terms of the human cost a total of 415 Jewish deaths were recorded. The British death toll was 262. The toll on the Arabs was estimated to be roughly 5,000 dead, 15,000 wounded, and 5,600 imprisoned. In total, ten percent of the Arab community's adult male population had been killed, wounded or detained. The Arab death toll included 108 who were hanged in Acre prison, and 961 who died because of what official British reports described as "gang and terrorist activities."

Apart from the deplorable loss of life, in the overall context of the Jewish settlement's development in the 1930s the collateral losses endured during the revolt were relatively insignificant. Although hundreds were killed, plantations destroyed and property damaged, no Jewish settlement was captured or destroyed and several dozen new ones were established.

The most significant positive impact of the Arab uprising was that it spurred the Jewish economy to greater self-reliance. The development of crucial infrastructure was accelerated. For example, whereas the Jewish city of Tel Aviv had previously relied on the nearby Arab seaport of Jaffa, hostilities dictated the construction of a separate Jewish run seaport for Tel Aviv, inspiring a delighted Ben Gurion to note in his diary, "We ought to reward the Arabs for giving us the impetus for this great creation."[9] Metal works were established to produce armoured sheeting for vehicles and a rudimentary arms industry was founded. The Arab boycott, moreover, had the paradoxical effect of increasing Jewish employment – cheaper Arab labour had previously been favoured by many Jewish businesses – but now Jewish workers had replaced striking Arab labourers, employees, craftsman and farmers. Most of the important industries in Palestine were owned by Jews and in the trade and banking sectors they were much better placed than the Arabs.

From a security point of view, the revolt reinforced the Jewish community's already entrenched belief that there was a need for a strong Jewish defence network, leading to the formation and development of Jewish underground militias, primarily the Haganah, which would later prove decisive in the wars of 1947-48. As a consequence of collaboration with the British colonial authorities and security forces, many thousands of young men had their first experience of military training, which Moshe Shertok and Haganah leader Eliyahu Golomb cited as one of the most significant fruits of the Haganah's policy of restraint.

By the conclusion of the revolt, the Arabs were exhausted. The overriding emotion of the peasant population was sheer relief that it was over. Politically, they had gained nothing. Their already divided leadership was fragmented further with many in exile, and paralysed by divisions between those outside Palestine and those inside it that persisted for decades thereafter. The Arabs were simply incapable of matching the Zionists' highly sophisticated organization. Without unified leadership social cohesion was severely weakened, and their military capability relative to the Jewish community was critically degraded by the strident efforts of the British authorities to confiscate all weapons from the Arab population while simultaneously sanctioning the arming of the Haganah.

This relative decline in Arab social and military cohesion was exacerbated by imbalances between Jewish and Arab economic performance. The revolt was a disaster for the Arab economy which did not have the resources or resilience to support the hardships that befell them. Thousands of Arab houses were destroyed, and massive financial costs were incurred as a consequence of the general strike and the devastation of fields, crops and orchards. The economic boycott further damaged the fragile Arab economy through loss of sales of goods and increased unemployment.

The Palestinian Arabs were, therefore, critically weakened in advance of their ultimate confrontation with the Jewish settlement in the 1947 war of independence. Clearly, the revolt had proven to be counterproductive, although it has been credited with signifying the birth of the Arab Palestinian identity.

One significant outcome of the revolt was the involvement of the surrounding Arab states as advocates for the Palestinian Arabs. Whereas Britain had previously tended to deal with its commitments in Palestine as separate from its commitments elsewhere in the Middle East, by 1939 pan-Arab pressure carried increasing weight in London.

From the British perspective, as the inevitable war with Germany approached, policy makers feared that, while they could rely on the support of the Jewish population in Palestine who had no alternative but to support Britain, the support of Arab governments and populations in an area of great strategic importance for the British Empire was not assured. Prime Minister Neville Chamberlain concluded, "If we must offend one side, let us offend the Jews rather than the Arabs."[10]

In February 1939, Secretary of State for Dominion Affairs, Malcolm MacDonald, called together a conference of Arab and

Zionist leaders on the future of Palestine at St. James' Palace in London but the discussions ended on 27 March without agreement. British officials became resigned to the conclusion that the two communities could not be reconciled, and so support for developing an exit strategy that would enable Britain to bring the Mandate to a close while safeguarding strategic interests began gathering momentum. Perhaps the ultimate achievement of the Arab Revolt was to make the British sick of Palestine. Major-General Bernard Montgomery concluded, "The Jew murders the Arab and the Arab murders the Jew. This is what is going on in Palestine now. And it will go on for the next 50 years in all probability."[11]

Endnotes

1. Cited from *The Independent*, "Israel's voice of reason: Amos Oz on war, peace and life as an outsider", 10 March 2009.
2. From an article titled "Funeral of Nine Jewish Dead", *Palestine Post*, Tuesday 21 April 1936.
3. Cited in the Peel Report: *Palestine Royal Commission Report Presented by the Secretary of State for the Colonies to Parliament by Command of His Majesty, July 1937*. His Majesty's Stationery Office, London, 1937.
4. Public Record Office, Kew Gardens, Foreign Office, Great Britain 371/20821; Nov. 26, 1937, Eden to Lindsay, British Ambassador to the United States.
5. Eden to Harvey, 7 September 1951, BL 56402. Cited by Bernard Wasserstein, *Britain and the Jews of Europe, 1939-1945* (Oxford: Oxford Paperbacks, 1988), p. 34.
6. *Palestine: Statement by His Majesty's Government in the United Kingdom Presented by the Secretary of State for the Colonies to Parliament. Cmd 5893*, HMSO, November 1938.
7. From an article appearing in the New York Times, 4 October 1938.
8. Cited from Nick Reynold, *Britain's Unfulfilled Mandate for Palestine* (London: Lexington Books 2014), p. 231.
9. Tom Segev, *One Palestine, Complete: Jews and Arabs under the British Mandate* (London: Picador, 2001), p. 388.
10. Cabinet Meeting on Palestine, CAB 24/285, 20 April 1939.
11. Tom Segev, *One Palestine Complete*, p. 442.

CHAPTER 5

THE BROKEN PROMISE

> *After a period of five years no further Jewish immigration will be permitted unless the Arabs of Palestine are prepared to acquiesce in it. Now, there is the breach; there is the violation of the pledge; there is the abandonment of the Balfour Declaration; there is the end of the vision, of the hope, of the dream"*
>
> —WINSTON CHURCHILL

As Europe teetered on the brink of another catastrophic war, the situation in Palestine was becoming increasingly vexing for the British government. In late 1938, a Cabinet committee on the future of Palestine, attended by the Foreign Secretary Lord Halifax and the Colonial Secretary Malcolm MacDonald, was convened to consider the direction of policy in the region. Halifax warned the committee, "The government would shortly be confronted with a very difficult decision, namely, was it to be regarded as fundamental to obtain a settlement with the Arabs?" MacDonald, speaking immediately after Halifax, told his colleagues, "The government had to choose between its commitment to the world of Jewry and its commitment to the world of Islam."[1]

Against the background of impending global conflict, the committee recommended that Britain could not afford to antagonise the Muslim world which was demanding the cessation of Jewish immigration into Palestine. The final committee report stated, "The British Empire itself is to a very considerable extent a Moslem Empire. For example, some 80 millions of our fellow subjects in India are Moslems. From the defence point of view it is literally out of the question that we should antagonise either the Moslems within the Empire or the Arab kingdoms of the Near East."[2] The result was a policy compromise between the Foreign Office and the Colonial Office which would eventually lead to reneging on the Balfour Declaration.

In February 1939, the British government called a Conference at St James' Palace in London to negotiate an agreement between the Arabs and Jews about the future governance of Palestine in the hope of bringing an end to the Mandate. The Arab delegates only agreed to attend on the condition that they would not meet directly with the Jewish representatives, believing that such a meeting would legitimise Jewish claims over Palestine. So the British government was forced to hold separate meetings with the two sides. MacDonald made it clear that if no agreement was reached the government would impose a solution.

The Palestinian Arab delegation was led by Jamal al-Husseini, who presented the fundamental elements of the Arab position which were independence for Palestine, an end to the notion of a Jewish national home in Palestine, replacement of the Mandate by a treaty and a permanent cessation of Jewish immigration.

The Jewish delegation was led by Chaim Weizmann, chairman of the World Zionist Organization, although it was David Ben Gurion, who rose to prominence as the leader of the Jewish Agency in Palestine from 1935, who dominated the decision making. At a meeting on 24 February, Ben Gurion laid out the Jewish Agency's minimum terms which were the continuation of the Mandate and the rejection of anything that would imply Jewish minority status. At the same meeting MacDonald announced the preferred British policy, which was that Palestine would become an independent state allied to Britain and that the Jewish minority would have protected status. And so a yawning chasm was wrenched open between the two parties.

Three days later, newspapers in Palestine published a cable from Ben Gurion which stated, "There is a scheme afoot to liquidate the National Home and turn us over to the rule of gang leaders."[3] The Jewish delegation refused to hold any further formal sessions and reduced its involvement to informal meetings in MacDonald's office. Finally, on 17 March, Weizmann sent a letter to MacDonald which read, "The Jewish delegation, having given profound consideration to the proposals placed before it by His Majesty's Government ... regrets that it is unable to accept them as a basis for agreement, and has therefore decided to disband."[4]

The Conference, therefore, ended in abject failure without any progress made towards an agreement. In truth, the whole process was little more than a pantomime as the British government had pre-determined what it was going to do irrespective of what transpired at St James'. The result, as McDonald had threatened, was the unilateral imposition of a British solution, the terms of which were presented with the publication of his infamous White Paper on 17 May 1939, known by the Jews as the 'Black Paper.' It turned out to be even more damaging than its 1931 predecessor, the Passfield White Paper, because it directly threatened Britain's ongoing commitment to the Balfour Declaration.

The MacDonald White Paper rejected the Peel Commission's partition plan on the grounds that any attempt at implementation would not be feasible. In a staggering reversal of previous commitments, the document stated that Palestine would be neither a Jewish nor an Arab state, but an independent state, to be established within ten years, in which Jews and Arabs would share government. The notion of shared government was quite fanciful considering that the Arabs would not even share in meetings with the Jewish delegation at St James' Palace, and had refused to participate in every attempt to establish unified political structures during the entire Mandate. The document stated, "His Majesty's Government believe that the framers of the Mandate in which the Balfour Declaration was embodied could not have intended that Palestine should be converted into a Jewish State against the will of the Arab population of the country … His Majesty's Government therefore now declare unequivocally that it is not part of their policy that Palestine should become a Jewish State … The objective of His Majesty's Government is the establishment within 10 years of an independent Palestine State … The independent State should be one in which Arabs and Jews share government in such a way as to ensure that the essential interests of each community are safeguarded."[5]

The Paper restricted Jewish immigration to 75,000 over the next five years, subject to the country's "economic absorptive capacity", and decreed that any further immigration after that would depend on the agreement of the Arabs, who were not specifically mentioned in the Mandate document at all. Furthermore, the Paper decreed that a two-thirds Arab majority should be maintained in Palestine. With such an Arab majority, most of whom were bitterly hostile to any kind of Jewish presence in Palestine, the political rights of the Jewish people in their national home would have been thoroughly compromised. As was the norm with British governmental documents pertaining to Palestine, restrictions were to be imposed on any future land acquisition by Jews.

The rationale behind the stringent restrictions on Jewish immigration was the familiar appeasement of Arab anxiety: "Fear of indefinite Jewish immigration is widespread amongst the Arab population ... this fear has made possible disturbances which have ... produced a bitterness between the Arab and Jewish populations which is deplorable between citizens of the same country. If in these circumstances immigration is continued up to the economic absorptive capacity of the country, regardless of all other considerations, a fatal enmity between the two peoples will be perpetuated, and the situation in Palestine may become a permanent source of friction amongst all peoples in the Near and Middle East."

The policy reversal turned on the clause in the Balfour Declaration, reiterated in the San Remo Conference documents, which promised to guarantee the civil and religious rights of existing non-Jewish communities in Palestine. Though it is clearly a subordinate clause to the promise of a Jewish homeland and made no reference to political or national rights, British government officials exploited it to create a loophole that enabled His Majesty's Government to reject the idea of a Jewish state. They went as far as stating that they would regard it as contrary to their obligations to the Arabs under the Mandate that the Arab population of Palestine should be made the subjects of a Jewish State against their will.

The Zionist dream of an independent homeland was thus summarily ended at the stroke of a British bureaucrat's pen. All presented in the garb of legality but quite despicable. Why? Because with war looming the British were terrified of another major Arab revolt which would play into Hitler's hands. Such an outcome had to be avoided at any cost. The conclusion was reached that the Arabs, who were still engaged in the final throws of revolt against British authority, had to be appeased, but the price of that appeasement would be the blood of European Jews whose only escape route from the Holocaust had been severed and the betrayal of the Palestinian Jews who had fought alongside British forces to suppress the Arab revolt.

The White Paper was debated fiercely in Parliament on 22 – 23 May 1939. The central recommendations represented a clear reneging of the Balfour Declaration, and intense objections were hurled across the floor. A typically defiant Winston Churchill tore into the Paper: "After a period of five years no further Jewish immigration will be permitted unless the Arabs of Palestine are prepared to acquiesce in it. Now, there is the breach; there is the violation of the pledge; there is the abandonment of the Balfour Declaration; there is the end of the vision, of the hope, of the dream."[6] Fine words, but in the pre war period, the rhetoric of Churchill was marginalised as nothing more than the blustering of an obsolete Edwardian maverick by a British establishment bent on appeasement.

Leopold Amery, who like Churchill was a fierce critic of the government's policy of appeasement towards Germany, thundered against the Paper: "The watchword is 'appease the Arabs', appease the Mufti. Appease them at all costs. Appease them by abandoning the declared policy of every government for 20 years past. Appease them by breaking faith with the Jews."[7]

Amery, whose mother was a Hungarian Jew, continued, "The White Paper is a direct invitation to the Arabs to continue to make trouble. As for the Jews, they are now told that all the hopes that they have been encouraged to hold for 20 years are to be dashed to the ground, all their amazing effort wasted – in so far as it was an effort to create a National Home – all the pledges and promises that have been given to them broken."[8]

David Lloyd George denounced the White Paper as an act of perfidy, while the Liberal MP James Rothschild told parliament that "for the majority of the Jews who go to Palestine it is a question of migration or of physical extinction."[9] When it came to a vote, several Conservative Government MPs either voted against the proposals or abstained, including Winston Churchill and the illustrious Jewish Secretary of State for War, Leslie Hore-Belisha.

The following day the House of Lords accepted the new policy without a vote.

The Palestinian Arabs staged enthusiastic demonstrations before the publication of the White Paper following rumours that the British were proposing to allow Palestine independence on the same terms as Iraq. They saw this as a reward for their courageous confrontation of Britain during the Revolt of 1936-39 and it seemed obvious, when the Paper was published, that their leaders would eagerly accept it. Their excitement was premature. Celebrations were soon dampened by the concerns of the Arab Higher Committee that the independence of a future Palestine Government would prove to be illusory, as the Jews could scupper it by refusing to participate. They also felt that the limitations on Jewish immigration did not go far enough and called for a complete prohibition on immigration and a total abandonment of the Jewish national home policy. In June 1939, with the Arab Revolt still raging and believing that the British were on their knees, the Arab Higher Committee, under pressure from Haj Amin al-Husseini, rejected the White Paper outright.

Despite these reservations, and reflective of the deep divisions that routinely paralysed attempts by the Palestinian Arab leadership to show a cohesive front, the leader of the Arab delegation at the London Conference, Jamal al-Husseini, and fellow delegate Musa al-Alami agreed to the terms of the White Paper and both signed a copy of it in the presence of the Prime Minister of Iraq, Nuri as-Said.

The publication of the White Paper unleashed a storm of protests from Zionists across the world. Jews were stunned into disbelief. David Ben Gurion called it "the greatest betrayal perpetrated by the government of a civilized people in our generation ... formulated and explained with the artistry of experts at the game of trickery and pretended righteousness."[10] Chaim Weizmann decried it as "a death sentence for the Jewish people" and warned MacDonald, "You are handing over the Jews to their assassins."[11] Weizmann told MacDonald that at least in Hitler one found the virtue of an absolutely frank brutality, whereas he (MacDonald) was covering up his betrayal of the Jews under a semblance of legality. In an attempt to prevent the White Paper from passing into law, Weizmann managed to secure an audience with Chamberlain. He later described the meeting with these words: "The Prime Minister of England sat before me like a marble statue, his expressionless eyes were fixed on me, but he never said a word ... I got no response."[12]

The response issued by the Jewish Agency for Palestine was unsurprisingly scathing, reflecting a deep sense of betrayal and issuing warnings about the consequences that would follow the imposition of the White Paper. They accused the British of denying the Jewish people their rights at the "darkest hour" of Jewish history. Their response, set out in a series of five statements, is reproduced below:[13]

1 The new policy for Palestine laid down by the Mandatory in the White Paper now issued denies to the Jewish people the right to rebuild their national home in their ancestral country. It transfers the authority over Palestine to the present Arab majority and puts the Jewish population at the mercy of that majority. It decrees the stoppage of Jewish immigration as soon as the Jews form a third of the total population. It puts up a territorial ghetto for Jews in their own homeland.

2 The Jewish people regard this policy as a breach of faith and a surrender to Arab terrorism. It delivers Britain's friends into the hands of those who are biting her and must lead to a complete breach between Jews and Arabs which will banish every prospect of peace in Palestine. It is a policy in which the Jewish people will not acquiesce. The new regime now announced will be devoid of any moral basis and contrary to

international law. Such a regime can only he established and maintained by force.

3   The Royal Commission[14] invoked by the White Paper indicated the perils of such a policy, saying it was convinced that an Arab Government would mean the frustration of all their (Jews') efforts and ideals and would convert the national home into one more cramped and dangerous ghetto. It seems only too probable that the Jews would fight rather than submit to Arab rule. And repressing a Jewish rebellion against British policy would be as unpleasant a task as the repression of the Arab rebellion has been. The Government has disregarded this warning.

4   The Jewish people have no quarrel with the Arab people. Jewish work in Palestine has not had an adverse effect upon the life and progress of the Arab people. The Arabs are not landless or homeless as are the Jews. They are not in need of emigration. Jewish colonization has benefited Palestine and all its inhabitants. Insofar as the Balfour Declaration contributed to British victory in the Great War, it contributed also, as was pointed out by the Royal Commission, to the liberation of the Arab peoples. The Jewish people has shown its will to peace even during the years of disturbances. It has not riven sway to temptation and has not retaliated to Arab violence. But neither have the Jews submitted to terror nor will they submit to it even after the Mandatory has decided to reward the terrorists by surrendering the Jewish national home.

5   It is in the darkest hour of Jewish history that the British Government proposes to deprive the Jews of their last hope and to close the road back to their homeland. It is a cruel blow, doubly cruel because it comes from the government of a great nation which has extended a helping hand to the Jews, and whose position must rest on foundations of moral authority

and international good faith. This blow will not subdue the Jewish people. The historic bond between the people and the land of Israel cannot be broken. The Jews will never accept the closing to them of the gates of Palestine nor let their national home be converted into a ghetto. The Jewish pioneers who, during the past three generations, have shown their strength in the rebuilding of a derelict country, will from now on display the same strength in defending Jewish immigration, the Jewish home and Jewish freedom.

Zionist groups in Palestine, seething with resentment, launched a sustained campaign of attacks on government property and Arab civilians which lasted for several months. On 17 May, to mark the publication of the White Paper, telephone wires were cut, government offices attacked and riots broke out in Jerusalem. The next day, a general strike was called in protest. Jewish attacks on Arabs and Government property continued through the summer.

The right-wing Zionist Para-military group the Irgun, who had split from the Haganah in 1931 in protest against its defence charter and policy of restraint, began formulating radical plans for a rebellion to evict the British from Palestine and to establish an independent Jewish state. Ze'ev Jabotinsky, former Haganah leader and the founder of Irgun, proposed a plan for a revolt to take place in October 1939, which involved the Irgun occupying Government House, along with other centres of British power in Palestine, raising the Jewish national flag, and holding them at all cost for at least 24 hours. Simultaneously, Zionist leaders in Western Europe and the United States would proclaim an independent Jewish state in Palestine, and would function as a government-in-exile. The Irgun plan received serious consideration. Irgun leader Avraham Stern formulated plans to recruit and train 40,000 Jewish fighters from Europe to sail to Palestine and join the rebellion. The Polish government, in support of his plan, began training Jews and setting aside weaponry for them. Only the outbreak of World War II in September 1939 prevented these plans from being executed.

Without doubt the White Paper of 1939 is a dark stain upon the British Administration of Palestine, representing a complete moral failure in governance in so far as it was an appeasement of Arab terrorism. The Permanent Mandates Commission of the League of Nations accused Britain of a flagrant breach of the Palestinian Mandate and of imposing a virtual suspension on Jewish immigration. Four of the seven members intended to strike down the restrictive White Paper as a violation of the Mandate and scheduled a meeting for 8 September 1939, but their intervention was scuppered when war broke out just days before when German forces marched into Poland on 1 September. In reality the League of Nations was toothless; it had no power to intervene.

Leading Zionists in the United States made efforts to lobby Franklin D Roosevelt in the hope that the President might press the British to modify their policy, but to their dismay the White Paper provoked no official reaction from the American authorities. President Roosevelt made a token display of disapproval, instructing the State Department to inform London that it was hoped that no drastic changes would be implemented, but the US ambassador in London, Joseph Kennedy, was instructed to limit his criticism of the White Paper to private conversations. There would be no official US protest, no White House statements challenging the White Paper, not a single substantive step that might influence London on the Palestinian issue. The British authorities interpreted Roosevelt's minimalist response as a signal that they could proceed without fear of any real consequences.

And so, with the Nazi Holocaust descending on Europe, and the persecuted Jewish population becoming increasingly desperate for an escape route, the MacDonald White Paper became the policy of the British Government. It could not have happened at a worse time. Jews were scrambling to flee Europe but no nation would accept them. Their only hope was Palestine, and Britain had just slammed the gates shut. Palestine would remain virtually closed to the Jews for the duration of the war and beyond, leaving hundreds of thousands of Jews stranded in Europe, condemned to face the nightmare of Hitler's Final Solution. Even in the years after the defeat of Nazism, the British refused to allow the destitute and displaced Holocaust survivors sanctuary in Palestine.

The implementation of the White Paper was a treacherous, villainous act that dishonoured Britain by breaking the promise of the Balfour Declaration; it was cold, ruthless and calculating, delivered as death was closing around the Jews of Europe. Even today, many Israeli Jews consider the British morally responsible as accessories to the Holocaust. Yet scarcely have voices been raised in Britain to acknowledge any culpability. Indeed, what is promoted is a sanitized version of the events. Revisionist historians have even gone so far as to claim that the White Paper actually saved the Jewish nation. They claim that without appeasement, the Arabs would have made alliances with Hitler, handing control of the Suez Canal, Iraqi oil, and the Palestine oil pipeline to the Axis powers on a plate. Unchecked by the British administration, an Arab-Nazi alliance would have instigated a second Holocaust which would have resulted in the complete annihilation of the Jewish population in Palestine. The truth is that had the British facilitated the migration of Jews, the extended Jewish population of Palestine would have become a powerful ally commanding a formidable fighting force that could have garrisoned the region.

When the revisionist histories and sanitised accounts have been properly consigned to the waste disposal unit, the uncomfortable truth that confronts Britain today, supported by all mainstream historians, is that the White Paper policy was severely unfavourable to the Jews. More than that, the restrictions on immigration and land purchase by the Jews were, at least in part, motivated by anti-Semitic sentiments. This assertion is not merely an interpretive inference. Declassified British records from the era confirm that some senior British government officials did, indeed, harbour anti-Semitic prejudices.

The Prime Minister Neville Chamberlain wrote privately to his sister, "No doubt the Jews aren't a lovable people; I don't care about them myself, but that is not sufficient to explain the pogrom."[15] Osbert Peake, Parliamentary Under-Secretary for the Home Office, stated that if the Allies permitted Jewish immigration, they would be "relieving Hitler of an obligation to take care of these useless people."[16] H. F. Downie, the British Head of the Middle East Department of the Colonial Office, stated on 27 April 1940 that, "the Jews are enemies just as the Germans are, but in a more insidious way," and that "our two sets of enemies [Nazis and Jews] are linked together by secret and evil bonds." A year later, on 15 March 1941, he wrote, "one regret[s] that the Jews are not on the other side in this war."[17] The author of the White Paper, MacDonald, had himself caused upset to the Jewish delegation at the London Conference with remarks he was reported to have made to the Arab delegation which were taken to be anti-Semitic.

In a House of Commons debate on 20 July 1939, MacDonald admitted that a 'Division of Destroyers' was being employed to ensure that Jews who had escaped Hitler did not evade British capture as they approached Palestine. And so, on the very first day of World War II, while German dive bombers rained death on Warsaw, His Majesty's ship Lorna fired the first shot of the war by a British naval vessel on a rickety overcrowded Jewish refugee ship, *Tiger Hill*, as she approached the Palestinian coast to unload her cargo of misery. Two refugees on board, having escaped from Europe, were killed. And thus, fuelled by anti-Semitic sentiments and a misguided policy of appeasement, Britain abandoned hundreds of thousands of Europe's Jews to the slaughter of the Holocaust.

Endnotes

1. Cabinet Papers 27/651, 14 November 1938.
2. Ibid.
3. Published by Davar Newspaper, 27 February 1939.
4. Cited from Shabtai Teveth, *Ben-Gurion: The Burning Ground, 1886 – 1948* (Boston: Houghton Mifflin, 1987), p. 705.
5. White Paper of 1939: *Palestine: Statement of Policy Presented by the Secretary of State for the Colonies to Parliament by Command of His Majesty, May 1939, Cmd 6019.* His Majesty's Stationery Office, London, 1939.
6. Cited from Winston S. Churchill, *Winston Churchill Speeches: Never Give In* (London: Pimlico, 2007), p. 190.
7. Cited from David W. Schmidt, *Partners together in this Great Enterprise* (Jerusalem: Xulon Press, 2011), p. 186.
8. Ibid., p. 186.
9. House of Commons Debates, Volume 347 Column 1984 [1].
10. Cited from Walter Laqueur, *A History of Zionism* 3rd Ed. (London: Taurisparke Paperbacks, 2003), p. 528.
11. Bernhard Wasserstein, *Britain and the Jews of Europe, 1939-1945* (Oxford: Oxford Paperbacks, 1988), p. 21, citing CZA [Central Zionist Archives] S25/7563.
12. Cited from Walter Laqueur, *A History of Zionism*, p. 527.
13. Cited from *http://www.jewishvirtuallibrary.org*.
14. The Royal Commission referred to was the Peel Commission of 1937 which was cited in the MacDonald White Paper but which reached very different conclusions, calling for partition of Palestine into a Jewish state and an Arab state.
15. Chamberlain Papers, 30 July 1939.
16. Cited from David S. Wyman, *The Abandonment of the Jews: America and the Holocaust* (New York: The New Press, 2007), p. 114.
17. Cited from *www.jewishhistorytimeline.com/timeline/1940-ce-h-f-downie-england/*.

CHAPTER 6

HA'APALA

> " *What is morally wrong cannot be politically right* "
>
> —WILLIAM GLADSTONE, PRIME MINISTER

By issuing the White Paper of 1939, the British Government cruelly betrayed a friend at their hour of greatest need. Such despicable behaviour was bound to cause irreparable damage to the prospects for future cooperation. The Jews had decisively weighed in to support Britain at the pivotal point of the Great War and had fought alongside the British Mandatory authorities to crush the Arab uprisings on the eve of World War II. Their reward for this? Britain had stretched out a hand to help the Jews by protecting the Zionist beachhead in Palestine during its most vulnerable, insecure period in the 1920s and 30s. But now, as the Jews were being sucked into a whirlpool of death, that hand had been snatched away.

When the war started, Ben Gurion declared, "We will fight the war as if there were no White Paper, and we will fight the White

Paper as if there were no war."[1] These were proud words, but in reality, the Jews were powerless. One can only imagine what Ben Gurion was thinking as the war progressed and reports began filtering through of the mass murder perpetrated against European Jews, while still the British were turning Jewish refugees away from Palestine.

The British policy was executed with ruthlessly efficiency. The Arabs were placated, as was the intention. There were no major Arab revolts in Palestine during the war despite the efforts of Haj Amin al-Husseini to stir up jihad. Why should there have been? The White Paper had elevated the Arab interests over those of the Jewish community. The British had given the Palestinian Arabs almost everything they wanted, including a virtual guarantee that by the end of the war Palestine would become an Arab state by default. Meanwhile, in abrogation of the Balfour Declaration, Jewish immigration beyond a token limit was declared illegal. But there should have been nothing illegal about Jewish immigration, for that was the entire point of the British Mandate.

The British government had calculated coldly that there was no need to court favour from the Jews as they were bound to support the war against Germany. In the short term, they were correct. Despite their sense of betrayal, Jews followed the call of Ben Gurion to "fight the war as if there were no White Paper." In May 1941, the Palmach was established to defend the Jewish community in Palestine against the threat of an Axis invasion through North Africa. The British refusal to provide arms to the Jews, even when Rommel's forces were advancing through Egypt, led many of the Zionist leaders to conclude that ultimately conflict with Britain was inevitable. Despite this, the Jewish Agency called on Palestine's Jewish youth to volunteer for the British Army, and nearly thirty thousand Palestinian Jews joined the fight to stop Rommel's Africa Corps. These soldiers would become the core of the Haganah, later the Israel Defense Forces, which defeated the

Arabs in 1948. In June 1944, the British agreed to create a Jewish Brigade that fought in Italy.

The Jewish Response to Britain's Immoral Immigration Policy

While encouraging Jewish youth to enlist in the British army to fight the war, Ben Gurion had also declared his intention to "fight the White Paper as if there were no war."

The great statesman William Ewart Gladstone, Prime Minister of Great Britain on four separate occasions between 1868-94, is attributed with making the aspirational declaration, "What is morally wrong cannot be politically right."[2] By betraying the Jews for the sake of political expediency and self interest, the Chamberlain government of 1939 were guilty of breaking Gladstone's axiom. They had committed to an immoral policy which would have devastating consequences for Europe's stricken Jews. The figure set for permitted immigration, 75,000 over five years, was but a pathetic drop in the vast ocean of millions facing extermination. Had the British flung open the gates of Palestine, hundreds of thousands of Jews would have survived the Holocaust.

Before the outbreak of war, the Nazi's had declared that Jews were a sub-human race. Propaganda material compared them to disease carrying rodents. There was absolutely no room for uncertainty about the Nazis' determination to eliminate the Jews from German occupied territory. Anti-Semitism was rearing up menacingly in other parts of Europe also, and everywhere persecution had reached epidemic levels. As the doom-laden storm clouds of death closed around them, terrified Jews were desperate to escape, but where could they go? Nobody wanted them. There was no shelter in Europe. Palestine was the only hope, but her shores were guarded by stealthy iron clad destroyers bristling with guns and flying the Union Jack. Did the British government not conceive of what was coming upon the Jews?

After Germany had annexed Austria in March 1938, Roosevelt called for an international conference to promote the emigration of Austrian and German Jewish refugees and create an international organization whose purpose would be to deal with the general refugee problem. The conference was held in Evian, France, from 6-15 July 1938. Thirty-two nations were represented. Britain only attended on the condition that Palestine was not mentioned as a possible solution. With the Arabs in revolt in Palestine, Britain was only interested in the political aspects of the problem, protecting their interests in Iraqi oil and control of the Suez Canal, not the moral aspect of averting a human catastrophe.

Detailed evidence of persecution was presented to the conference. Yet nothing was done to help European Jewry, a failure all the more striking because at this stage there was no difficulty in extricating Jews from German-occupied territory because of the Nazi policy of forced emigration. Golda Meir, present as a representative of the Palestinian Jews, later recalled, "Sitting in that magnificent hall listening to the delegates of 32 countries rise and each in turn explain how they would have liked to take in substantial numbers of refugees and how unfortunate it was that they were unable to do so was a terrible experience. I felt a mixture of sorrow, rage, frustration and horror. I wanted to get up and scream at them all, don't you know that these numbers are human beings. People who may spend the rest of their lives in concentration camps or wandering around like lepers."[3]

After the Evian conference, if any doubt had remained about the fate awaiting the Jews, it was surely removed on the terrible night of 9 November 1938, as Nazi para-military forces and civilians carried out a vicious pogrom against Jews throughout Germany. The pogrom came to be known as *Kristallnacht*, the *Night of Broken Glass*, from the shards of broken glass that littered the streets after Jewish-owned stores, buildings, and synagogues had their windows smashed. Hundreds of Jews were murdered, many thousands more were thrown into Nazi concentration camps and what remained of their wealth was confiscated.

The world stood aghast but did nothing. Britain, for once, was the only nation to respond. Parliament agreed to admit to Britain 10,000 youths in an operation that came to be known informally as *Kindertransport*. In the period leading up to the outbreak of war, Jewish children were transported from Germany, Austria, Czechoslovakia, Poland and the Free City of Danzig. Once safely on British shores, the children were placed in foster homes, hostels, schools and farms. Many would be the only members of their families who survived the Holocaust. Those aged 16 were subsequently shipped overseas to Canada where they were interned for the remainder of the war, but nevertheless, on this occasion, Britain had done something good. No other country admitted that many Jews.

However, the implementation of the 1939 White Paper sealed the fate of the millions of Jews remaining in Europe. Their only possible escape route from the horror stalking them in Europe had been blocked by British bureaucrats and Royal Navy gun boats. The British government, after Evian and *Kristallnacht*, could not have been blind to the consequences. Their assiduous resolve to turn the tide of despairing Jews away from Palestine was viewed by many as real co-operation with Hitler. To make matters worse, Britain wielded her considerable influence over other countries to discourage them from providing safe haven to Jewish refugees.

The Jewish Agency could not abandon their people. Faced with such severe restrictions on immigration, they had no option but to resort to a programme of clandestine immigration. With support from the Haganah and various other underground organisations, they set about smuggling Jewish men, women and children, people the world seemingly viewed as worthless debris and refuse, into Palestine by all and any means possible.

The operation was signified by the code name Aliyah Bet ('bet' being the second letter of the Hebrew alphabet), to distinguish it from Aliyah Aleph ('aleph' being the first letter of the Hebrew alphabet) which referred to the limited Jewish immigration permitted by British authorities. Aliyah means 'to go up to the land', and is taken from the last word of the final book of the Hebrew Bible, 2 Chronicles 36:23: *"Thus saith Cyrus king of Persia, 'All the kingdoms of the earth hath the LORD God of heaven given me; and he hath charged me to build him a house in Jerusalem, which is in Judah. Who is there among you of all his people? The LORD his God be with him, let him go up.'"* Today in Israel, the clandestine immigration of Jews is also designated by the Hebrew word Ha'apala, which means 'ascension', and the refugees who participated in Ha'apala are called "Ma'apilim." Ma'apilim is a classic term in the Zionist lexicon: "Ha'apilu, ha'apilu, el rosh ha-har ha'apilu", which means "Charge audaciously up the mountain", is the refrain of a classic song about the immigrants who ran the British blockade of Palestine. The name originates from the obscure story of the ma'apilim, on the margins of the great saga of the spies, who defiantly marched toward the crest of the hill country expressing the strong will of the people to enter the land of Israel immediately (Numbers 14:39-45). The descriptor 'clandestine' was used because the Jews refused to consider the immigration illegal.

Ha'apala commenced in July 1934 and continued until May 1948, ending with the declaration of independence by the State of Israel. There were two distinct phases. The first, which covered the period from 1934-42, was initially an operation to facilitate immigration beyond the quotas established under the British administration but, as the persecution of Jews intensified in Europe, became a desperate attempt to rescue Jews from Nazi terror. The second, from 1945-48, was an attempt to find homes for

Jewish Holocaust survivors who were among the millions of displaced persons languishing in refugee camps in occupied Germany. In total, 150,000 immigrants were brought into Palestine, the overwhelming majority arriving by sea. Most ended their journey behind barbed wire fences in British detention camps.

Prior to implementing the Final Solution to exterminate all Jews in Europe, the policy of Nazi Germany allowed for the reduction of Jewish numbers by emigration. The Nazi authorities understood that encouraging operations that were attempting to take Jews from Europe to Palestine in violation of the immigration policy of the British government presented an opportunity not only to remove their unwanted Jews, but also to make trouble for Britain by stirring Arab unrest. The Nazis were quite willing, for a price, to facilitate the transportation of Jews to Mediterranean ports for shipment overseas. In 1938, Hitler goaded the world to take action, "I can only hope and expect that the other world, which has such deep sympathy for these criminals [the Jews], will at least be generous enough to convert this sympathy into practical aid. We, on our part, are ready to put all these criminals at the disposal of these countries, for all I care, even on luxury ships."[4]

The first major obstacle the ma'apilim had to overcome was the Royal Navy blockade. Of the 141 Ha'apala voyages attempted over the entire period, mostly in dilapidated unseaworthy ships, dubbed as "coffin ships", that were crammed beyond capacity with refugees, over half were intercepted at sea by British naval patrols. Over 1,600 refugees drowned at sea. Of those who managed to stay afloat and evade the Royal Navy to make landfall on the shores of Palestine, most knew no Hebrew apart from a phrase they had learned for the journey, "I am a Jew of Israel." Thousands were caught by the British authorities waiting on the beaches before they could be absorbed into the Jewish community and were interned at detention camps awaiting deportation. Others were placed on board ships to be sent away to internment camps in Cyprus or Mauritius having never set foot on the land of Israel. Some of these unfortunate souls committed suicide believing that their last embers of hope had been extinguished.

After the implementation of the 1939 White Paper, with the Nazi terror spreading across Europe, the battle for survival off the shores of Palestine became increasingly desperate. The British government was ruthlessly determined to send a clear signal to the Jews that the gates of Palestine were closed, but the Jews had nowhere else to go and faced unspeakable horrors if they remained in Europe. There were many harrowing stories, but two terrible incidents in particular came to define the narrative of the first phase of Ha'apala: These were the sinkings of the *SS Patria* and the *SS Struma*.

The Sinking of the *Patria*

In September 1940 the Central Office for Jewish Emigration chartered three ships, the *SS Pacific*, *SS Milos* and *SS Atlantic*, to take Jewish refugees from the Romanian port of Tulcea to Palestine. A month later, a large exodus of refugees was allowed to leave Vienna in an operation organized by Berthold Storfer, a Jewish businessman working under the supervision of Adolf Eichmann. The refugees were transported down the Danube on four river boats to Tulcea, where they boarded the waiting vessels.

The *SS Pacific* arrived off Haifa on 1 November, followed a few days later by the *SS Milos*. Both ships were intercepted by the Royal Navy and escorted into Haifa harbour, where the British authorities detained the 1,770 refugees aboard the ships. Having been warned of the ships' arrival, the British Colonial Office was determined to refuse entry to the immigrants, concluding that provoking Jewish anger was preferable to inflaming an Arab revolt, and that an example needed to be made to dissuade other potential immigrants from attempting illegal entry into Palestine. The British High Commissioner, Sir Harold MacMichael, issued a deportation order on 20 November, ordering that the refugees be taken to the British Indian Ocean territory of Mauritius. The refugees were transferred to a requisitioned French ocean liner, the *SS Patria*, for transportation.

The *SS Atlantic* arrived off Haifa, carrying a further 1,634 refugees, on 24 November. She too was escorted by the Royal Navy into the harbour, and the following day, the authorities began transferring her refugees to the *SS Patria*.

The *SS Patria* was an 11,885-ton ocean liner launched in 1913. She had reached the Port of Haifa shortly before Italy declared war on France and Britain, and had remained in port for safety. After the French surrendered to Nazi Germany the British authorities seized the *Patria* for use as a troop ship. As a civilian liner she was permitted to carry 805 people, but after being requisitioned she was authorised to carry 1,800 troops (excluding the crew). She still only had enough lifeboats for the original 805 passengers and crew, so these were supplemented with life rafts.

At 9.00 am on 25 November, an explosion ripped through *Patria's* hull, creating a gaping hole in her side that stretched below the waterline. As sea water gushed through the breech, she turned on her side and sank in only 16 minutes. She was carrying the 1,770 refugees transferred from the *Pacific* and *Milos* and had boarded 134 passengers from *Atlantic*. Most were rescued by British and Arab boats that rushed to aid the stricken ship. However, 267 people were declared missing, mainly Jewish refugees though the toll included members of the ship's crew and some British soldiers. Many of those lost were trapped in *Patria's* hold as she rolled on her side and were unable to escape. Eventually, 209 bodies were recovered and buried in Haifa.

Controversy raged for many years over who was responsible for sinking the *Patria* and causing such a tragic loss of life. The

British authorities believed it an act of sabotage by the Irgun. Other rumours circulated that the refugees on board, out of despair, had caused the explosion in an attempt to disable the ship and prevent her from sailing. It was not until 1957 that the mystery was finally resolved when Munya Mardor published a book in which he admitted to planting a bomb onboard the ship. He claimed that he was acting under orders from the Haganah to disable *Patria*. There was never any intention to cause loss of life or to sink the *Patria*, only to force her to remain in Haifa for repairs and thus gain time to press the British to rescind the deportation order, but the Haganah had catastrophically miscalculated the effects of the explosives used. As Mardor recounted, "There was never any intent to cause the ship to sink. The British would have used this against the Jewish population and show it as an act of sabotage against the war effort."[5] On the contrary, he claimed that the primary objectives of the Haganah during Aliyah Bet were to fight the sanctions imposed by the British White Paper of 1939 and to avoid casualties. Mardor continued to work at the port after the *Patria* sinking in order to remove suspicion from himself.

The Haganah established an investigative body to examine how a relatively small amount of explosives could have created such a large hole in the ship. They concluded that the ship's superstructure was in such poor condition that it was unable to withstand the pressure of the explosion.

The surviving refugees from *Patria*, together with the remaining 1,560 passengers on board the *Atlantic*, were taken to the Atlit detention camp. The British authorities were still determined to make an example by deporting them. However, following an international campaign, the survivors of *Patria* were given immigration certificates to stay in Palestine on the direct intervention of Winston Churchill, who wrote, "Personally, I hold it would be an act of inhumanity unworthy of the British name to force them to re-embark on ships bound for Mauritius."[6]

The remaining 1,560 *Atlantic* passengers who had not boarded the *Patria* were deported to Mauritius on 9 December. On arrival, they were placed in detention camps enclosed by barbed-wire fences overlooked by watch towers. The men and women were segregated, even husbands from wives. Any who were caught violating this rule were punished with cruel beatings administered by British soldiers. By the end of the war, a shocking one in ten had died on the Island from a combination of poor diet, disease, and harsh treatment by British guards. It was a desperately tragic epilogue to the story of the *Patria*.

The Final Solution was not the first solution proposed in Nazi Germany to resolve the 'Jewish Problem'. Initially, it was hoped that the Jewish population of Germany could be 'encouraged' to emigrate. As efforts to accomplish this objective prior to World War II were only partially successful, largely because no other countries were willing to open their borders to the Jews, Franz Rademacher, head of the Jewish Department of the Ministry of Foreign Affairs for the German government, proposed a plan in June 1940 to relocate the Jewish population of Europe to the island of Madagascar. With Adolf Hitler's approval, Adolf Eichmann released a memorandum on 15 August 1940 calling for the resettlement of a million Jews per year for four years to Madagascar, with the island to be governed as a police state under the SS. It was assumed that many Jews would succumb to its harsh conditions should the plan be implemented. Executing the plan, however, was not feasible as long as the British naval blockade of Germany persisted. It was postponed after the Axis powers lost the Battle of Britain in September 1940, and permanently shelved in 1942 after the commencement of the Final Solution.

The Madagascar plan may have been fanciful, but the fact that it carried traction in the highest echelons of Nazi government indicates that had a viable destination for Jewish emigration been identified, the Final Solution may have been avoided. Hitler, however, took notice of the *Patria* incident and saw the strength of Britain's resolve to close Palestine at all costs to Jewish immigration. As the war progressed, it became increasingly difficult for Jews to escape Europe. The British government showed no compassion, excluding immigrants from Palestine so as to maintain the two-thirds Arab majority prescribed by the 1939 White Paper. Hitler concluded that forcing Jews to leave German occupied territories was no longer a viable option due in part to Britain's unbreakable resolve to prevent Palestine becoming a safe haven. And thus, by narrowing Hitler's options, Britain inadvertently contributed towards his decision to resort to the Final Solution.

The *Struma* Disaster

On 12 December 1941, the *MV Struma* sailed from the Romania port of Constanta on the Black Sea with an estimated 781 Jewish refugees, survivors of the massacre of Jews in the regions of Bessarabia and Bukovinia, crammed on board hoping for sanctuary in Palestine.

Earlier that year, Nazi SS *Einsatzgruppen* mobile killing units had entered Bessarabia, hunting down and murdering tens of thousands of Jews. As an accompaniment to the slaughter, Mihai Antonescu, Romania's ruler at the time, made this chilling declaration in front of the Romanian Council of Ministers on 8 July 1941: "With the risk of not being understood by some traditionalists which may be among you, I am in favour of the forced migration of the entire Jew element from Bessarabia and Bukovina, which must be thrown over the border … There has never been a more suitable moment. If necessary, shoot with the machine gun."[7]

The *Struma* was an old ship, launched in 1867 as a steam powered luxury yacht. But by now she was a dilapidated barge powered by an unreliable second-hand diesel engine and relegated to carrying cattle on the River Danube. She was only 45 metres long, with a beam of 6 metres and a draught of 3 metres.

As terrified Jewish refugees from Bessarabia began to arrive in Constanta desperate to escape the Nazi killing squads, they were forced to pay extortionate prices for passage to Palestine on the *Struma*. They had no choice but to comply, for the only alternative was probable death. Passengers were informed they would be sailing on a renovated ship with a short stop-over in Istanbul to collect Palestinian immigration visas. It was a cruel deception, for there were no visas waiting to be collected. They were not permitted to see the *Struma* until the day of the voyage. What they found was not a renovated ship, but a wreck with only two lifeboats. Below deck, *Struma* had dormitories with berths for up to 120 people in each. Passengers were to sleep on bunks four abreast, with 2 foot width for each person. There was only one bathroom facility, and no kitchen. But the refugees had staked all they possessed on this final chance for freedom, so there could be no turning back. As they boarded, Romanian customs officers confiscated any remaining valuables and food they were carrying.

And so, the old rusting cattle barge departed, crammed with 781 Jews, including 269 women, some of whom were pregnant, and 103 young children. *Struma's* diesel engine failed several times between her departure from Constanta and her arrival in Istanbul on 15 December 1941. The crew of a Romanian tug boat that answered a distress call after one failure refused to repair the engine unless they were paid. The refugees had spent all their money purchasing tickets for the voyage so they had no option other than to hand over all their wedding rings to pay for the repairs. *Struma* got under way, but when the engines failed again she had to be towed into Istanbul.

There she remained at anchor while British diplomats and the Turkish government of Refik Saydam negotiated over the fate of the passengers. In a vicious three way stand-off, British diplomats urged Turkish officials to prevent the *Struma* from continuing her voyage; Turkey refused to allow the passengers to disembark unless the British authorities allowed them immigration certificates to enter Palestine; The Romanian government adamantly refused to countenance any suggestion of towing the dilapidated wreck with her wretched cargo back to Constanta. In an attempt to resolve the impasse, the head of the Jewish Agency flew to London to implore the British government to issue the certificates.

Britain could have issued certificates to all on board, for there were enough available within the permitted limits on immigration. But Harold MacMichael, the British High Commissioner for Palestine, thought it might encourage other Jews to attempt illegal entry if they were issued, so he cruelly delayed notifying the Turkish Authorities, an action that would only serve to prolong the suffering of *Struma's* Jews.

Finally, on 12 February, British officials informed the Turkish authorities that any children onboard the *Struma* would be given Palestinian entry visas, but Turkey took the view that all the refugees should receive certificates, or none of them. Further disputes then arose over how the children would be transported to Palestine. Britain declined to send a ship, while Turkey refused to allow them to travel overland.

By now, while diplomats were arguing over the fate of the refugees, the *Struma* had been quarantined in Istanbul for more than two months. The refugees were running critically short of food, and the squalor and suffering on board the cramped ship were unbearable. The boat deck was so small that passengers had to take turns to escape the stifling quarters below deck to breathe fresh air. The only passengers allowed to disembark during the entire stay in harbour were a heavily pregnant woman who suffered a miscarriage and four others with connections to Turkey.

After 71 days of fruitless negotiations between Turkey and Britain, and thoroughly fed up with the situation, the Turkish police force was ordered to board the ship on 23 February. After swiftly overcoming resistance from the beleaguered refugees, the police cut her anchor and had her towed through the Bosporus and out into the Black Sea. Despite weeks of work by Turkish engineers, the engines would not start so the Turkish authorities abandoned the *Struma* to drift helplessly without a working engine, with no fuel, radio or anchor, with inadequate food and water provisions, six miles off the coast of Istanbul with nowhere to go and absolutely no way of getting there.

Within hours, on the morning of 24 February, the Shchuka-class Soviet submarine Shch-213 torpedoed the *Struma*, taking her to be an enemy vessel, killing all but one of those on board. It was the greatest exclusively civilian loss of life on the Black Sea during World War II.

The *Struma* sank quickly with many of those who survived the torpedo blast trapped below deck and condemned to death by drowning. Those who survived the sinking clung to pieces of wreckage, but for hours no rescue came and one by one they died from drowning or hypothermia. Of the estimated 781 people killed, more than 100 were children. David Stoliar, a 19 year old refugee, clung to a cabin door that was floating in the sea. Turks in a rowing boat rescued him the next day. He was the sole survivor. Turkey held Stoliar in custody but he was eventually released after Britain agreed to grant him papers to enter Palestine.

The *Struma* disaster sparked outrage against Britain and Turkey from the Jewish community throughout the world. In Palestine, the High Commissioner, Harold MacMichael, was branded a murderer. On 9 June 1942, Lord Wedgwood opened a debate on the *Struma* affair in the House of Lords by alleging that Britain had blatantly reneged on its commitments to the Jews and he urged the League of Nations to transfer the Mandate for Palestine to the USA. He bitterly condemned officials of his own government with these words: "I hope yet to live to see those who sent the *Struma* cargo back to the Nazis hung as high as Haman cheek by jowl with their prototype and Fuehrer, Adolf Hitler."[8]

The *Struma* disaster is still referred to in Israel as a symbol of British culpability for the deaths of so many Jews in World War II. On 26 January 2005, Israeli Prime Minister Ariel Sharon told the Knesset, "The leadership of the British Mandate displayed ... obtuseness and insensitivity by locking the gates to Israel to Jewish refugees who sought a haven in the land of Israel. Thus were rejected the requests of the 769 [sic] passengers of the ship *Struma* who escaped from Europe – and all but one found their death at sea. Throughout the war, nothing was done to stop the annihilation [of the Jewish people]."[9] On 31 March 2013, Likud Knesset Member Moshe Feiglin demanded an apology from Turkey for the *Struma* affair. He wrote a Facebook post titled "Demand for an apology from the Turks," in which he detailed the *Struma* sinking. Feiglin concluded his post by saying, "The truth is that we don't need an apology! And also not financial compensation. The Jewish people have a special skill. They know how to remember!"[10]

The *Struma* disaster, along with the sinking of the refugee laden *Patria* 15 months earlier, became symbolic rallying points for the militant Irgun and Lehi Zionist groups, encouraging them to launch a violent revolt against the British presence in Palestine. Anger in Palestine at the terrible loss of life on the *Struma* and *Patria* was compounded at the end of the war when official figures revealed that of the 75,000 immigration certificates permitted for Jewish immigration by the 1939 White Paper, over 30,000 were unused! According to their own quota policy, the British authorities had needlessly turned away thousands of despairing refugees, wasting Jewish lives that could have been saved because of their bloody-minded determination to appease Arab sensitivities over Jewish immigration.

Endnotes

[1] As quoted by James William Parks, *A History of Israel* (1949), p. 342. Variants include, "We must support the army as though there is no White Paper, and fight the White paper a though there is no war", Shabtai Teveth, *Ben-Gurion: The Burning Ground, 1886 – 1948* (Boston: Houghton Mifflin, 1987), p. 717.

[2] This attribution has been disputed. The phrase has also been attributed to other political figures including Abraham Lincoln and Mahatma Ghandi. The concept appears to have originated with Hannah Moore, *The Works of Hannah Moore, Volume 4*, 1873, p. 179, "Nothing, that is morally wrong, can be politically right."

[3] Golda Meir, *My Life* (New York: G. P. Putnam's & Sons, 1975), p. 158.

[4] Speech at Konigsberg, April 1938. Cited from Ehud Avriel, *Open the Gates! A Personal Story of "Illegal" Immigration* (Worthing: Littlehampton Book Services Ltd, 1975), p. 21.

[5] Cited from Eva Feld, "The Story of the SS Patria", *Jewish Magazine*, August 2001.

[6] Cited from Michael Makovsky, *Churchill's Promised Land: Zionism & Statecraft* (New Haven: Yale University Press, 2007), p. 186.

[7] Cited from "The Stenograms of the Ministers' Council, Ion Antonescu's Government", Vol. IV, July-September 1941, Bucharest, 2000, p. 57.

[8] Cited from Martin Sicker, *Pangs of the Messiah: The Troubled Birth of the Jewish State* (Westport CT: Greenwood Publishing Group, 2000), p. 161.

[9] Ariel Sharon, "PM Sharon's Speech at Special Knesset Session Marking the Struggle Against Anti-Semitism", Israel Ministry of Foreign Affairs, 26 January 2005.

[10] Cited from *The Jerusalem Post*, "Turkey owes us an Apology over the 'Struma'", 3 April 2013.

CHAPTER 7

THE FINAL SOLUTION AND BRITAIN'S SIN OF OMISSION

> "We at this moment have upon us a tremendous responsibility. We stand at the bar of history, of humanity and of God"
>
> —ARCH BISHOP WILLIAM TEMPLE, MARCH 1943

Hitler attempted to deport Jews to Palestine in the early stages of World War II, not motivated by any sense of good will or generosity, but in the dual hopes of ridding Germany of its Jewish population and triggering a widespread Arab revolt against the British. After the *SS Patria* disaster, where Britain had demonstrated granite resolve in preventing Jews from entering Palestine, Hitler took note of British attitudes towards the Jews. If deportation of Jews was not feasible due to the refusal of others to take them, what options were left to him to rid Germany of their hated Jewish pestilence?

The Holocaust may not have been Hitler's first choice for resolving the Jewish Problem, but since he could not dump them elsewhere, with even Palestine closed, why not exterminate the Jews? By narrowing the options, Britain's closure of the gates of Palestine contributed to the damning of European Jewry to the gas chambers.

The Final Solution was the Nazi plan for the systematic genocide of all Jews across German occupied Europe. The policy was formulated in procedural terms by the Nazi leadership at the Wannsee Conference near Berlin in January 1942, and culminated in the Holocaust in which Jews from all over Europe were deported to six annihilation camps established in former Polish territory: Chelmno, Belzec, Sobibor, Treblinka, Auschwitz-Birkenau, and Majdanek. The death camps were killing centres designed to carry out genocide on a mass scale. In its entirety, the Final Solution consisted of gassings, shootings, random acts of terror, disease, and starvation that accounted for the deaths of about six million Jews, two-thirds of the Jewish population of Europe. Approximately half were killed in the six annihilation camps, while many others were murdered in the network of transit and forced labour camps where Jews were concentrated across Europe.

The precise origin of the Final Solution is shrouded in uncertainty, and may not be attributable to a single decision. What is clear is that the genocide of the Jews was the culmination of a decade of Nazi policy. After the Nazi party's rise to power, state-enforced racism resulted in anti-Jewish legislation, boycotts, "Aryanization," and finally the *Kristallnacht* pogrom, all of which aimed to remove the Jews from German society.

The programme evolved incrementally during the early years of the war into an attempt to murder every last Jew in Germany's grasp. In 1940, following the fall of France, the Madagascar Plan was devised by Adolf Eichmann to relocate Europe's Jewish population to the French colony. The plan, however, was not possible while the British naval blockade of Germany persisted. It was postponed after the Axis powers lost the Battle of Britain in

September 1940, and was permanently shelved in 1942. Instead, western European Jews were deported to Jewish ghettos which had been established in occupied Poland. During the German invasion of the Soviet Union in June 1941 mobile killing squads, the SS paramilitary *Einsatzgruppen*, began destroying entire Jewish communities. The methods used, shooting or gassing victims inside mobile vans, were soon regarded as being too inefficient and psychologically traumatic for the killers. To overcome these problems, a more efficient mechanism for disposing of people on an industrial scale was implemented across all of German occupied Europe. On 31 July 1941, Reinhard Heydrich of the SS received a directive to prepare "the total solution of the Jewish question." The construction of the annihilation camps in Poland had already begun, and Heydrich had already sent out invitations for the Wannsee Conference. Shortly after this Conference, the Nazi's began clearing the ghettos by herding Jewish victims onto death trains bound for the camps, which were mainly guarded by soldiers from occupied eastern European countries so as to spare German soldiers from psychological distress. The camps were specifically designed for the purpose of implementing the Final Solution on an industrial scale.

Hitler and the Mufti

In the period between the wars, Arab nationalists bore Germany no ill-will, surprising perhaps considering Germany's support for the Ottoman Empire. However, like many Arab countries, Germany was perceived as a victim of the post-World War I settlement. Hitler himself often spoke of the "infamy of Versailles." Unlike France and Great Britain it had not exercised imperial designs on the Middle East, and its past policy of non-intervention was interpreted as a token of good will.

Although, to the relief of the British, there was no general Arab revolt against the Allies during World War II, in the summer of 1940, and again in February 1941, Haj Amin al-Husseini submitted a draft declaration of German-Arab cooperation to the Nazi government for approval. The proposed declaration included the chilling clause: "Germany and Italy recognize the right of the Arab countries to solve the question of the Jewish elements, which exist in Palestine and in the other Arab countries, as required by the national and ethnic interests of the Arabs, and as the Jewish question was solved in Germany and Italy."[1]

Al-Husseini leveraged his influence with the Nazis to promote Arab nationalism in Iraq where he supported an attempted coup d'état by Rashid Ali in April 1941. The situation of Iraq's Jewish community rapidly deteriorated, with extortion and murder commonplace. When the coup failed, al-Husseini escaped to Persia where he was granted diplomatic asylum first by Japan, and then by Italy.

Al-Husseini travelled to Rome in October 1941 to lobby for Italian support for the Arab cause, outlining proposals to the Italian Foreign Ministry to support the war against Britain on condition that the Axis powers "recognize in principle the unity, independence, and sovereignty, of an Arab state, including Iraq, Syria, Palestine, and Transjordan."[2] Al-Husseini met with Benito Mussolini on 27 October. According to al-Husseini's account, it was an amicable meeting in which Mussolini expressed his hostility to the Jews and Zionism.

In November 1941, al-Husseini travelled to Germany and met with Adolf Hitler, Heinrich Himmler and Joachim Von Ribbentrop in an attempt to persuade them to extend the Nazis' anti-Jewish programme to the Arab world. He asked Hitler for a public declaration that recognized and sympathized with the Arab struggles for independence and liberation, and that would support the elimination of the Jewish national homeland. Hitler rebuffed the Mufti's requests, however, telling him the time was not right. Hitler did not want an Arab revolt, at least not yet, as he did not expect one to succeed but asked al-Husseini "to lock ... deep in his heart" that once Germany had defeated Russia and broken through the Caucasus into the Middle East, it would have no further imperial goals of its own and would support Arab liberation. Hitler outlined how, "Germany's objective would then be solely the destruction of the Jewish element residing in the Arab sphere under the protection of British power."[3] In other words, Jews were not simply to be driven out of the German sphere but would be hunted down and destroyed even beyond it. Al-Husseini assured Hitler that, "The Arabs were Germany's natural friends because they had the same enemies ... namely the English, the Jews, and the Communists."[4]

Some historical apologists sympathetic to Arab nationalistic aims in Palestine have questioned whether al-Husseini knew of the Holocaust while it was in progress. However, in his memoirs al-Husseini recalled a meeting with Himmler in the summer of 1943, where Himmler inveighed against Jewish "war guilt" and revealed the ongoing extermination of the Jews. Himmler told him that the Germans had already exterminated more than three million Jews. Al-Husseini wrote, "I was astonished by this figure, as I had known nothing about the matter until then."[5] Clearly, the Mufti knew from this time about the genocide. His memoir continues, "Himmler asked me on the occasion: 'How do you propose to settle the Jewish question in your country?' I replied: 'All we want from them is that they return to their countries of origin.' He replied, 'We shall never authorise their return to Germany.'"[6]

Despite knowing of the scale of the genocide, numerous letters from al-Husseini to various governmental authorities have been published that provide overwhelming evidence of his support for the Nazi genocide and his determination to prevent Jewish refugees from escaping to Palestine. On 13 May 1943, he lobbied the

German Foreign Office to block a proposal to transfer Jews from Bulgaria, Hungary and Romania to Palestine. A month later, on 14 June 1943, he recommended that Hungarian Jews be transported to concentration camps in Poland rather than be allowed to find asylum in Palestine. In September 1943, he blocked negotiations to rescue 500 Jewish children from the Rab Concentration camp in Italy.

In November 1943, al-Husseini declared that, "It is the duty of Muhammadans in general and Arabs in particular to ... drive all Jews from Arab and Muhammadan countries ... Germany is also struggling against the common foe who oppressed Arabs and Muhammadans in their different countries. It has very clearly recognized the Jews for what they are and resolved to find a definitive solution for the Jewish danger that will eliminate the scourge that Jews represent in the world."[7] Al-Husseini made this remark in full knowledge of what the Nazi's "definitive solution for the Jewish danger" entailed.

Throughout the remainder of World War II, al-Husseini worked for the Axis Powers broadcasting propaganda messages that targeted Arab public opinion, one might say an Arabic version of "Lord Haw Haw." On 1 March 1944, while speaking on Radio Berlin, al-Husseini exhorted the Arab world: "Arabs, rise as one man and fight for your sacred rights. Kill the Jews wherever you find them. This pleases God, history, and religion. This saves your honour. God is with you."[8]

Towards the end of the war, as defeat for the Axis powers became inevitable, al-Husseini requested asylum in neutral Switzerland but this was denied. On 5 May 1945, he was taken into custody by the French occupation forces at Konstanz and transferred to Paris where he was held under house arrest. Yugoslavia sought to indict the Mufti as a war criminal for his role in recruiting 20,000 Muslim volunteers for the SS who had participated in the killing of Jews in Croatia and Hungary. However, in

1946, he escaped from French detention and continued his fight against the Jews from Cairo.

It would be an injustice to Arabic people in general to assume that they supported Nazism on the basis of al-Husseini's associations with Hitler, but as the nominal leader of the Arab nationalists in Palestine, by making common cause with the Nazis he grievously discredited the nationalist movement.

The British Response to the Holocaust

The Simon Wiesenthal Centre, named after a death camp survivor who became a Nazi-hunter, is scathingly critical of the Allies for their failure to take practical steps that could have helped many of Hitler's victims. It is, therefore, apposite to examine the responses of British authorities to the horror they knew was being unleashed upon the Jewish community during the Holocaust. It must first be acknowledged that there are many documented acts of selfless bravery by the 'Righteous among the Nations' who risked their own lives to save Jews, including some by individual Britons, but apart from the admirable efforts of the *Kindertransport*, what of British officials? As the Mandatory power in Palestine, Britain was duty bound to consider carefully her obligations towards the suffering of the Jews. What ought, or could, the British government have done to help?

Senior British officials were not ignorant of the scale and horror of atrocities committed against Jews, even from the earliest stages of the Holocaust. Code-breakers at the highly secretive Bletchley Park began to learn of mass shootings of Jews as early as July 1941, immediately after the invasion of the Soviet Union. Their sources were decrypts of German signals which continued into 1943 in a "low grade" cipher, describing the massacres and detailing numbers murdered. Such knowledge, one would feel, should have motivated the select group of informed officials, very few in number because of the cloak of secrecy thrown over Bletchley, to warn the Jews in occupied Europe of the fate awaiting them and to mobilise rescue schemes. The galling truth, however, is that since the messages often repeated material sent via Enigma, and Bletchley could recognize the similarities, the easily broken cipher provided vital "cribs" to Enigma in "real time." It was decided that nothing should be done that might tip off the German's that the cipher was being intercepted, and thereby risk losing the cribs. No warnings were issued because cracking the Enigma code was deemed a higher priority than saving the lives of Jews. This disturbing link between Bletchley and the Holocaust only came to light when secret documents were declassified 50 years after the events.

By mid 1942, as the Nazis started emptying the ghettos, news of the atrocities being committed against the Jews were emerging through less secretive sources. On 29 May 1942, Richard Lichtheim sent a telegram from the Jewish Agency's office in Geneva to its London office, in which he wrote, "It is certainly no exaggeration to predict that at the end of this war two or three million Jews in Europe will be physically destroyed while of the remaining a similar number will be destitute refugees."[9] On 29 August 1942, Gerhart Riegner, the Geneva-based World Jewish Congress representative, sent a telegraph message to his New York and London offices which corroborated Lichteim's report. Riegner had been informed indirectly about the plans for the final solution by German industrialist Eduard Schulte.[10] His cable, sent to his contacts in the British Foreign Office and the State Department in Washington, stated, "Received alarming report stating that, in the Fuehrer's Headquarters, a plan has been discussed, and is under consideration, according to which all Jews in countries occupied or controlled by Germany numbering 3.5 to 4 million should, after deportation and concentration in the East, be at one blow exterminated, in order to resolve once and for all the Jewish question in Europe." Both British and US officials received the telegram with disbelief. The US State Department dismissed the message as "a wild rumour, fuelled by Jewish anxieties."[11]

Regular reports of atrocities were reaching the BBC, but they were not broadcast. Sceptical controllers at the BBC did not believe the reports and refused to give any credence to what they thought were exaggerated anti-Nazi propaganda stories. The claims, they argued, were too ridiculous to be true. The government too was silent, choosing not to publicise evidence of the horrors they knew to be unfolding in the death camps.

In October 1942, David Ben Gurion, leader of the Jewish Agency in Palestine, implored the world to break out of its collective state of denial and remove their blinkers: "Anyone who does not see what Jewry is facing is blind and is neither a Jew nor a human being. First of all, the Jews are not in their place. After the war, every last Jewish collective in every [European] country will have been displaced. True, this has also happened to other peoples, to a small extent. Poles and Czechs have been displaced, and so now have the French. But it has not happened to them to the same extent. [The Nazis] have not displaced the entire French people. However, it is possible to displace the Jewish people; all of French Jewry, all of Dutch and Romanian Jewry can be displaced. They can also murder them all. I do not know if Jews will survive after Hitler. But if the world war ends, [members of other peoples] will return to their places and towns, and the Jews will have nowhere to return. Not a memory will remain of their homes, shops, and property."[12]

Finally, towards the end of 1942, the BBC relented and began issuing broadcasts that acknowledged the gravity of crimes being executed as part of a plan for the extermination of Jews after receiving independent confirmation from Jewish representatives on the London based Polish National Council of the monstrous events unfolding in occupied Europe. The atrocities being committed were becoming common knowledge, yet still the British government did nothing to intervene. While the evidence of industrial scale murder of Jews continued to mount, British politicians procrastinated and policies remained unchanged. In a letter to the Times newspaper on 5 December 1942, William Temple, Arch Bishop of Canterbury, railed against the hesitant attitude of the politicians, "Sir – You rightly give prominence in your issue for today to the appalling facts now coming to light with regards to Hitler's project for the extermination of the Jews. It is a horror beyond what imagination can grasp. I am assured by free Church friends that I may write in their name as well as in that of members of the Church of England, to express our burning indignation at this atrocity, to which the records of barbarous ages scarcely supply a parallel … In comparison with the monstrous evil confronting us the reasons for hesitation usually advanced by officials have an air of irrelevance."[13]

In Parliament, a series of fierce debates raged over the Jewish problem in Europe and what, if anything, the British should be doing about it. Eleanor Rathbone, an independent Member of Parliament who had pressurised the government throughout 1942 to publicise the evidence of the Holocaust, implored Members during the debates to take urgent action: "If the blood of those who have perished unnecessarily during the war were to flow down Whitehall, the flood would rise so high that it would drown everyone within those gloomy buildings which house our rulers. What is past is past but the future is still within our control … Let no one say, 'We are not responsible.' We are responsible if a single man, woman or child perishes whom we could and should have saved."[14]

By late 1942, direct testimony from eyewitnesses in Poland, most notably that of the heroic Polish resistance fighter, Jan Karski, had provided a wealth of information to Washington and London about the location of the main extermination camps, of the scale of the slaughter and of systematic massacres outside the camps in which groups of Jews including infants were shot, and buried, some still alive, in pre-prepared trenches. At the height of the destruction of Polish Jewry, Karski was ordered to travel clandestinely to London to deliver a report on the situation of occupied Poland to the Polish government-in-exile. Shortly before his departure, Karski met with two Jewish leaders who pressed him to inform the world's statesmen of the desperate plight of Polish Jewry and of the hopelessness of their situation. Their message was: "Our entire people will be destroyed." The Jewish leaders' appeals so touched Karski that he decided to see things with his own eyes. At great risk to his own life, he was smuggled into the Warsaw ghetto and into a transit camp in the Lublin area where he witnessed transports of Jews en route to the Belzec annihilation camp. The horrors he witnessed affected him deeply and propelled him to become a voice for the suffering of the dying Jews.

In November 1942, Karski reached London, delivered his report to the Polish government-in-exile, and then set out energetically for a series of meetings with politicians, including Winston Churchill and Foreign Minister Anthony Eden, journalists and public figures, pleading for action. He was greeted with a wall of disbelief and indifference. After completing his mission, Karski travelled on to Washington, where he met with President Roosevelt and other dignitaries, and tried once more in vain to stir up public opinion against the massacre of the Jews.

While government officials were equivocating about their responses to the Holocaust, highly sensitive papers which were stored in the National Archives until they were made public in 2018 have revealed that the wartime Ministry of Information repeatedly warned of a rising tide of anti-Semitism on the home front, but these reports were either belittled or ignored by officials who claimed that Jews themselves were entirely to blame for any increase in prejudice. The papers suggest that tensions were being stoked by resentment against Jewish evacuees escaping the heavy German bombing of London's East End, citing the Jews' "lack of pleasant standards of conduct as evacuees."[15] Another allegation laid against Jews was that they demonstrated "an inordinate attention to the possibilities of the 'black market.'"[16] When, on 3 March 1943, a stampede at a bomb shelter in the East End's Bethnal Green Underground station caused the deaths of 173 people, some rabble-rousing individuals were putting about a baseless canard that the tragedy was caused by panicking Jews.

Despite the presence of this simmering anti-Semitism in British society, the redoubtable Arch Bishop William Temple, for long an advocate for opening the shores of Britain and Palestine to Jewish refugees and of Britain offering whatever assistance was necessary to help Jews escape Hitler's Final Solution, reminded the House of Lords on 23 March 1943 of the parable of the Good Samaritan. He asserted that the Priest and Levite who passed by and did nothing represent those who are condemned for neglecting the opportunity to show mercy: "The Jews are being slaughtered at the rate of tens of thousands a day … We cannot rest as long as there is any sense among us that we are not doing all that might be done. We have discussed the matter on the footing that we are not responsible for this great evil, and that the burdens lie on others, but it is always true that the obligations of decent men are decided for them by contingencies that they did not themselves create and very largely by the action of wicked men. The Priest and the Levite in the parable were not in the least responsible for the traveller's wounds as he lay there by the roadside, and no doubt they had many other pressing things to attend to, but they stand as the picture of those who are condemned for neglecting the opportunity of showing mercy. We at this moment have upon us a tremendous responsibility. We stand at the bar of history, of humanity and of God."[17]

The bar that William Temple referred to is the place where the accused person stands in a court of law to hear the charges read out against them. He was declaring before the House of Lords that Britain was standing in the place where the charges of history, of humanity and of God were being brought against her for refusing to help the Jews during their darkest hour. Britain would be held to account for her inactivity.

Historical consensus holds that the passionate and moving protests of campaigners like Rathbone and Temple went unheeded. They precipitated no change in the British government's policy of restricting entry for Jewish refugees to Palestine, and all other British territories. Campaigners on behalf of the Jews faced a brick wall of government intransigence, procrastination and a complete lack of any sense of urgency. Like the Priest and the Levite in the parable of the Good Samaritan, Britain passed by on the other side of the road. And all the while, the pace of the killings in the death camps was accelerating.

The British government took the view that no change in immigration policy could be considered unilaterally, so under growing pressure to respond they convened a joint conference with the US to discuss the possibility of humanitarian action to aid Jewish refugees. The conference commenced on 19 April 1943 in Bermuda, the same day as the outbreak of the Warsaw Ghetto revolt. The British privately made it clear to the US administration in advance that the purpose of the conference was actually to ensure that no change in policy was necessary. They refused to even discuss Palestine as a possible refuge because of what Nahum Goldmann, founder of the World Jewish Congress, called "[their] policy, both foolish and immoral, of appeasing Arab Nazis."[18] The British shut down any thought of negotiating with the Nazis for the release of Jews on the grounds that "many of the potential refugees are empty mouths for which Hitler has no use" (one Jewish activist commented bitterly, "'Potential corpses' would be a more appropriate term than 'potential refugees'").[19] The delegates also rejected the idea of making food shipments to starving Jews because it would violate the Allied blockade of Axis Europe, even though they had previously made an exception for German-occupied Greece. All of these limitations left the delegates at Bermuda spending an inordinate amount of time on relatively small-scale steps, principally the evacuation of 5,000 Jewish refugees from Spain to the Libyan region of Cyrenaica. The New York Times reported on the conference under the headline, "To 5,000,000 Jews in the Nazi Death-Trap Bermuda was a Cruel Mockery."[20]

The cruel indifference of British attitudes towards the plight of the Jews was bitterly exposed by Henry Morgenthau, United States Secretary for the Treasury, who wrote to President Roosevelt on 16 January 1944, "The British were apparently prepared to accept the probable death of thousands of Jews in enemy territory because of the difficulties of disposing of any considerable number of Jews should they be rescued."[21] But apart from opening borders to Jewish immigrants, what else could Britain have done to help the Jews?

From early 1944, impassioned pleas were being made for the Royal Air Force to undertake bombing missions against the railway lines leading to the death camps and even against the gas chambers themselves. The RAF maintained that precision strikes against the camps were militarily impossible, but such protestations carried the air of desultory excuse. No thorough feasibility study of the issue was made, and the "dismissive tone" in some of the documents of the time give the sense that no-one was bothered enough to make bombing the camps a priority. Such raids would have been extremely dangerous for the air crews, and risked killing Jews concentrated in the camps, but they were possible. Reconnaissance images published after the war demonstrate that the RAF photographed the camps from the air, suggesting that they had the capability of reaching the camps with bombers.

Indeed, bombs did fall on Auschwitz on one occasion from a misdirected American bombing raid that was targeting nearby factories. Many, including survivors from the death camps, believe the Allies should have acted whatever the mission's chances of success.

What was lacking was the will to undertake such missions at a time when it was argued that limited resources had to be prioritised towards other objectives. However, the lack of proper consideration given to bombing the camps leads to wider questions of why more was not done to save the Jews from Nazi persecution. If British prisoners of war were being exterminated can anyone seriously doubt that the RAF wouldn't have done all they could to stop it? By refusing to disrupt the operation of the death camps, the RAF unwittingly, if not deliberately, co-operated with Hitler in the extermination of the Jews.

We have highlighted how Britain did not aid those seeking an escape route through immigration and refused the opportunity to disrupt the operation of the death camps through bombing raids. How else could Britain have intervened?

In September 1944, Ben Gurion delivered a withering denunciation of the Allies for their failure to act during the Holocaust. His moving words eloquently answer the question of how Britain could have chosen to help: "What have you done to us, you freedom-loving peoples, guardians of justice, defenders of the high principles of democracy and of the brotherhood of man? What have you allowed to be perpetrated against a defenceless people while you stood aside and let it bleed to death, without offering help or succour, without calling on the fiends to stop, in the language of retribution which alone they would understand? Why do you profane our pain and wrath with empty expressions of sympathy which ring like a mockery in the ears of millions of the damned in the torture house of Nazi Europe? Why have you not even supplied arms to our ghetto rebels, as you have done for the partisans and underground fighters of other nations? Why did you not help us establish contacts with them, as you have done in the case of the partisans in Greece and Yugoslavia and the underground movements elsewhere? If, instead of Jews, thousands of English, American or Russian women, children and aged had been tortured every day, burnt to death, asphyxiated in gas chambers would you have acted in the same way?"[22]

Such was the anger felt towards Britain for her failure to respond to the Holocaust that from February 1944, hard line militant Jewish groups in Palestine, such as the Irgun, under the leadership of Menachem Begin, and a small terrorist splinter group, Lehi (Fighters for the Freedom of Israel), known for its founder as the Stern Gang, embarked on a widespread campaign of terror against British officials. The High Commissioner of Palestine Harold MacMichael, blamed for sending the Jewish refugees aboard *MV Struma* to their deaths, narrowly escaped assassination in an ambush Lehi mounted on 8 August 1944 on the eve of his replacement as High Commissioner.

On 6 November 1944, Lord Moyne, the British Minister of State in the Middle East, was assassinated outside his home in Cairo by two Lehi operatives, Eliyahu Hakim and Eliyahu Bet Zuri. Both men were quickly captured, and at the conclusion of their trial for the murder, Eliyahu Hakim rose to his feet and declared, "We accuse Lord Moyne and the government he represents, with murdering hundreds and thousands of our brethren; we accuse him of seizing our country and looting our possessions. We were forced to do justice and to fight."[23] Revulsion at the assassination is said by some to have turned British Prime Minister Winston Churchill against the Zionist cause.

Why was Lord Moyne specifically targeted by the Lehi? The answer lies with the peculiar story of Joel Brand, a member of the Jewish-Hungarian Aid and Rescue Committee, who had approached the British in April 1944 with a proposal from Adolf

Eichmann, the SS officer in charge of deporting Hungary's Jews to Auschwitz. Eichmann's proposal, the so-called "blood for trucks" plan, was that the Nazis would release up to one million Jews in exchange for 10,000 trucks and other goods from the Western Allies. The Allies, while sceptical, did initially give some consideration to discussing the offer with the Germans, but changed their minds when intelligence assessments concluded that it was a German trap to embarrass the US government and damage the alliance with the Soviets.

Brand was interrogated in Cairo for several months. In his testimony to the Eichmann trial of 1961, he recalled that during one conversation at the Anglo-Egyptian club a tall gentleman in civilian attire who he did not know had asked him about Eichmann's proposal and replied to Brand's explanations with a dismissive, "What shall I do with those million Jews? Where can I put them?"[24] When Brand left shortly afterwards, feeling unwell, his military escort told him that the man who had made that remark was Lord Moyne. Some years after the event Brand admitted, "I later learnt that Lord Moyne had often deplored the tragic fate of the Jews. The policy which he had to follow, however, was one dictated by a cold and impersonal administration in London. It may be that he paid with his life for the guilt of others."[25]

The truth as to whether it was Moyne who spoke with Brand may never be known with certainty, but Brand believed it so and his report almost certainly cost Moyne his life. On the basis of Brand's account of that conversation, Moyne was unjustly held responsible for the deaths of the one million Hungarian Jews who might have been saved. When the British finally released Brand in October 1944, he joined the Lehi group that would carry out Moyne's assassination one month later.

From the outset of the Irgun and Lehi campaign of terror, it was opposed by Ben Gurion and the Jewish Agency who launched a public campaign to force a cessation to their insurrection against the British. The Jewish Agency were still committed to a policy of restraint and cooperation with the British administration, at least until the war was over, in the hope that Churchill, as a supporter of the Zionist cause, would press for a resumption of Jewish immigration. After the assassination of Moyne, the Haganah were ordered to suppress the Irgun's insurgency in a campaign known as 'the Hunting Season'. During this campaign, which lasted until February 1945, many Irgun members were kidnapped, interrogated, and turned over to the British. Obedience to the order to hand Irgun members to the British was purely voluntary, and some Haganah members were relieved of their duties for refusing to go along with the campaign altogether. The Irgun ordered its members not to resist the Haganah, or retaliate with violence, so as to prevent a civil war.

Britain's ruthless enforcement of stringent immigration quotas had cut off from the European Jews their only hope of escape from the horrors of the ghettos and concentration camps. Consequently, the Jewish militant groups condemned Britain for being guilty as accessories to the Holocaust, and there were many among the Jewish community who, though they deplored their methods, were sympathetic to their aims.

Throughout 1945, as Allied forces liberated the death camps, the full horror of the Holocaust was exposed for all to see. It was worse than had been imagined. Six million Jews had been slaughtered. The Jewish community was stunned. Many blamed Britain, at least in part, for the appalling loss of life. The sense of betrayal felt towards Britain for implementing the policy of the 1939 White Paper cut savagely into the Jewish soul. By the end of the war, an overwhelming majority of the Jewish community in Palestine wanted Britain out of the land.

Winston Churchill, as an avowed supporter of Zionism, has often been criticised because he neither abrogated nor amended the 1939 White Paper as Prime Minister. However, Churchill knew he was isolated within the government on this issue. Not for the first time, Churchill was standing alone on the right side of history. Even a cursory review of British government documents exposes an almost neurotic fear, common to many officials, that he was about to wreck British interests in the Arab world by his support for the Zionists. There are an abundance of documented examples of Churchill clashing with officials, whom he often held to be anti-Semites using spurious anti-Zionist arguments to dignify their hostility and indifference towards the plight of the Jews. Throughout the war, Churchill explored many avenues to provide refuge for Jews fleeing the Nazis, including in Palestine, and in the teeth of sustained opposition from virtually all his officials. Indeed, such was the perception of Churchill's solicitude for Jews among them that, on occasions, callous members of his own inner staff withheld from him Jewish requests out of fear that he would respond positively to them. When the Palestine government approved the policy of deporting illegal Jewish immigrants to the British Island of Mauritius, Churchill only approved it retrospectively on the proviso that they not be sent back to Europe. Lord Lloyd, the Colonial Secretary, deliberately left him unaware of the fact that the policy precluded any future return of the deportees to Palestine.

William Temple had warned that Britain was standing at the bar – the place where the accused stands to face the judgment of a court – and she had been found wanting. Confronted with the opportunity to show mercy, British politicians fiddled while the Jews burned. They refused to sanction bombing raids against the death camps that would have slowed the rate of slaughter. They offered no support to the many agencies that were attempting to rescue Jews. They provided no arms to equip resistance movements in the ghettos. They did not even publicise the Holocaust, raise a voice of protest, or warn of retribution for evils committed.

Most damnably of all, Britain had ruthlessly closed the gates of Palestine to the Jews in an act of appeasement towards the

Arabs, cutting off their only escape route, and had continued to enforce that policy with cold hearted rigour throughout the war even as the murder of Jews escalated. Any Jews caught attempting clandestine immigration to Palestine were rounded up and incarcerated in detention camps where they were treated harshly to discourage others from making the attempt. One in every ten Jews held in Mauritius died while in captivity. Incredibly, Britain continued to prevent displaced Holocaust survivors from entering Palestine even after the conclusion of the war.

Britain considered herself to be a country governed by Christian values, but how would the God that she claimed to serve, who was the God of Abraham, Isaac and Israel, judge Britain both for her actions towards His chosen people and for the assistance and succour she chose not to supply? Britain had stood at the bar where the charge sheet was read out and had been found wanting. What consequences would she now reap?

Endnotes

1. Cited from Bernard Lewis, *The Jews of Islam* (Westport CT: Greenwood Publishing Group, 2002), p. 190.
2. Cited from Zvi Elpeleg, *The Grand Mufti: Haj Amin Al-Hussaini, Founder of the Palestinian National Movement* (London: Routledge, 1993), p. 65.
3. Cited from David Yisraeli, *The Palestinian Problem in German Politics 1889-1945* (Ramat Gan: Bar Ilan University, 1974), p. 310.
4. Cited from Walter Laqueur, *The Israel-Arab Reader: A Documentary History of the Middle East Conflict* (London: Penguin, 1979), p. 106.
5. Cited from Achcar, "Blame the Grand Mufti", Le Monde Diplomatique, 2010, p. 151-152.
6. Cited from Laurens, *Une Mission Sacree de Civilisation. La Question de Palestine. 2* (Paris: Fayard, 2002), p. 469.
7. Achcar, p. 152.
8. Cited from Howard Sacher, *Aliyah: The People of Israel* (New York: World Publishing Company, 1961), p. 231.
9. Lichtheim to Lauterbach (copies to Montor, Linton and Lourie), May 29, 1942, USHMMA RG-68.127M (CZA L22/188), 235.
10. Raul Hilberg, *The Destruction of the European Jews, 3rd Ed* (New Haven, CT: Yale University Press, 2003), p. 1201. Schulte informed Isidor Koppelmann (business associate), who informed Benjamin Sagalowitz (head of the press agency of the Union of Jewish Communities in Switzerland), who in turn informed Riegner.
11. Yehuda Bauer, *Rethinking the Holocaust* (New Haven, CT: Yale University Press, 2001), p. 219.
12. Cited from *www.jewishvirtuallibrary.org/select-quotations-of-david-ben-gurion*.
13. Archbishop William Temple, open letter to *The Times* newspaper, 5 December 1942.
14. Cited from Martin Gilbert, *Auschwitz and the Allies* (London: Pimlico, 1981), p. 139.

15. Cited from an article by the *Times of Israel*, 25 August 2918, *https://www.timesofisrael.com/as-holocaust-raged-uk-officials-blamed-jews-for-rising-wartime-anti-semitism*.
16. Ibid.
17. Hansard, 23 March 1943, "German Atrocities: Aid for Refugees."
18. Citations in this paragraph are taken from David S. Wyman, *The Abandonment of the Jews: America and the Holocaust* (New York: The New Press, 2007), pp. 104-123.
19. Ibid.
20. *New York Times*, 4 May 1943, p. 17.
21. Morgenthau to Roosevelt, January 16, 1944, cited in Bernhard Wasserstein, *Britain and the Jews of Europe, 1939-1945* (Oxford: Oxford Paperbacks, 1988), p. 248.
22. Cited from *www.jewishvirtuallibrary.org/select-quotations-of-david-ben-gurion*.
23. Cited from Jerry A. Grunor, *Let My People Go* (Indiana: iUniverse, 2005), p. 40.
24. Cited from a transcript of the Trial of Adolf Eichmann, Session 59 (Part 5 of 6), reproduced by *http://www.nizkor.org/hweb/people/e/eichmann-adolf/transcripts/Sessions/Session-059-05.html*.
25. Cited from Bruce Hoffman, *Anonymous Soldiers: The Struggle for Israel, 1917-1947* (New York: Knopf, 2015), p. 196.

CHAPTER 8

THE RISE OF JEWISH INSURGENCY

> *We recognize no one-sided laws of war. If the British are determined that their way out of the country should be lined by an avenue of gallows and of weeping fathers, mothers, wives, and sweethearts, we shall see to it that in this there is no racial discrimination. The gallows will not be all of one colour ... Their price will be paid in full"*
>
> —IRGUN PRESS RELEASE, 30 JULY 1947

As victory in Europe was declared on 8 May 1945 with the formal acceptance by the Allies of the unconditional surrender of Nazi Germany's armed forces, jubilant celebrations erupted across the British Empire. In mandatory Palestine, however, the celebrations of the Jewish community were tempered by a crushing sense of horror, shock and mourning as the magnitude of the Holocaust became apparent. The majority now wanted the British to vacate the land of Israel because of a deep sense of betrayal and a conviction that Britain had contributed to the tragedy by her immoral immigration policy and abject failure to provide any meaningful assistance to the Jews during their darkest hour.

Two thirds of the Jewish population of Europe had been slaughtered. Those still clinging to life in territories formerly under Nazi control were in a desperate state. Severely traumatised, homeless, destitute, often the sole survivors of entire families, they had nowhere to go. They were not wanted in the communities from which they had been displaced and were unwelcome elsewhere. Palestine was their only hope, the only life raft promising sanctuary, but the gates were still closed to Jewish refugees. To the boundless shame of Britain, the White Paper of 1939 was apparently more sacred to those in power than life itself.

Faced with British intransigence over immigration, the Jewish Agency was forced to restart the programme of clandestine immigration to rescue the destitute Jews of Europe. This was the beginning of the "golden age" of Aliyah Bet. Typically, these Ha'apala journeys began in mainland European displaced persons camps and continued through one of two collection points in the American occupied sector, Bad Reichenhall and Leipheim. From there, refugees travelled in disguised trucks, on foot, or by train to ports on the Mediterranean Sea, where chartered ships were waiting to transport them to Palestine. Most of the ships were given new names, such as *"You Can't Frighten Us"* and *"To the Victory"*, designed to rally the Jews of Palestine to the cause. Some were named after prominent figures in the Zionist movement or people who had died while supporting Aliyah Bet.

Veteran Aliyah Bet volunteer, American Jew Murray Greenfield, later recalled in an interview with the New York Times how his team took a ship, which was barely seaworthy, and outfitted it with bunks for 1,500 Jews. "We made the shelves and they were gonna slide in Jews like bread in a bakery."[1]

In the dead of night, the ship, renamed *Hatikvah*, landed on a beach where men, women and children were silently taken on board, carrying all their possessions in tiny backpacks. "Most of them ... they were young. Younger than me. A lot of them were alone because they had lost everyone ... they had no mother or father or brothers," Greenfield recalled. "I see these people and they are Jews. They are speaking Yiddish to me. And I started to hear all the stories and I think 'we could have been these people.' Imagine if my parents hadn't come to America." During the voyage, Greenfield was able to spend more time with the survivors, listening with horror as they recounted their experiences: "I almost wish I didn't know Yiddish then ... it was terrible."

Once the shore of Palestine was in sight, excitement mounted for Greenfield and the survivors. Naturally, the British Royal Navy was standing between them and the Promised Land. As was customary, the British proved less than welcoming. They shot the ship with tear gas, boarded and then mercilessly beat those on board. The Holocaust survivors mustered what resistance they could, but it was a forlorn hope. Greenfield recalled, "It was disgusting. It really hurt because the British are nice people ... and we were just fighting along with them. It was ludicrous. And the survivors ... they fought back ... I was thinking 'why are they fighting back ... they have big destroyer ships?' Later, I asked them and they said, 'we've never had a chance to fight back before.'" All those aboard the *Hatikvah* were imprisoned behind barbed wire in Cyprus, Greenfield among them.

The displaced persons camps in the American sector of occupied Germany imposed no restrictions on the movement of Jews out of the camps, and American, French, and Italian officials often turned a blind eye. The United Nations Relief and Rehabilitation Administration (UNRRA), which was founded in 1943 to co-ordinate relief measures for the victims of war, played a major role in helping displaced persons return to their home countries in Europe during 1945-46. Many UNRRA officials openly provided assistance to facilitate the movement of Jews returning to Palestine.

The British government, in stark contrast to the sympathies of other nations, remained determined to prevent Jewish immigration into Palestine. The movement of people in and out of camps under British control was severely restricted, and an extensive network of spies watched over every port in the Mediterranean and Black Seas, reporting on the preparation and movement of Ha'apala ships. Armed naval patrols in the Mediterranean, ordered to intercept Ha'apala ships to prevent immigrants from landing, formed an impressive blockade. Only 12 out of 66 voyages succeeded in running this blockade.

The universal sense of betrayal felt by the Jewish community in Palestine led some to resort to violence against the British. The Irgun, under the leadership of Menachem Begin, became a locus for those inspired to fight as they embarked on a relentless campaign of terror against British instillations and official offices, though operatives were given strict orders to avoid harm to civilian life.

Begin, slight of posture and unimposing in appearance, first came to prominence during World War II as a staunch critic of the dominant Zionist leadership for their cooperation with the British, arguing that the only way to save the Jews of Europe was to compel the British to leave Palestine so that a Jewish state could be established. He joined the Irgun in 1942, and assumed leadership of the group two years later driven by a ferocious determination to force the British government to remove its troops entirely from Palestine.

The official Jewish leadership institutions in Palestine had exercised a policy of restraint during the war and refrained from directly challenging British authority in the belief that the British government would establish a Jewish state after the war. Begin broke away from the official leadership because he was convinced that Britain's history of breaking promises to the Jews and of adopting policies that appeased the Arabs meant that the only hope for the creation of a Jewish state was to launch an armed rebellion against British rule regardless of the war against Nazi Germany.

The strategy devised by Begin involved leveraging international sympathy to create political pressure on Britain. In February 1944, the Irgun began a campaign of guerrilla attacks against government targets, including the offices of the Immigration Department, Income Tax offices and police stations. The aim of the campaign was to humiliate the British in the belief that this would force them to implement repressive measures against the Jewish community. Begin hoped that international media reports of British repression would create global sympathy for the Irgun's cause. Faced with reputational damage if they continued to repress the Jews, Begin believed that ultimately the British would be forced to withdraw.

In the lead up to the British general election of 1945, the Haganah ordered the Irgun to cease their action against the British. Vague rumours were leaking from the opposition Labour party of intentions to open the gates of Palestine should they come to power and to return all the Arabs who had entered the land during the British Mandate to their countries of origin. It is a fact universally overlooked by those who condemn Zionism for being a colonial enterprise responsible for the displacement of native Arabs that throughout the Mandate, Arab immigration into Palestine outstripped Jewish and was largely unregulated. Before the Zionist movement began to encourage Jews to return, Palestine was a land bereft of a population. Hopes ran high among the Jewish community of a change in policy should Labour come to power.

On 26 July 1945, in one of the most seismic political surprises in British history, the Labour party of Clement Attlee won a sensational landslide election victory. Attlee replaced Churchill as Prime

Minister and appointed Earnest Bevin as Foreign Secretary. Bevin, an abrasive character who often caused offence with ill-chosen, insensitive remarks, had grown up in evangelical chapels, but in his early twenties he abandoned his evangelical beliefs and became a dedicated socialist. Before the war, as head of Britain's largest trade-union, the TGWU, he had campaigned to prevent German Jews from migrating to Britain. He favoured the 1939 White Paper's policy of turning Palestine into an Arab state with a Jewish minority, fearing that the creation of a Jewish state would inflame Arab opinion and jeopardize Britain's position as the dominant power in the Middle East. By 1945, contrary to the murmurs of Zionist support leaking from the Labour party, Bevin was determined not to give any form of assistance to the Jews. The war had left Britain close to bankruptcy and dependent on receiving Arab oil supplies at favourable prices. And so Britain's previous policy of Arab appeasement would continue, and once more Jewish hopes were crushed by broken British promises.

The plight of the Holocaust survivors was becoming increasingly desperate, interned in displaced persons camps, robbed of their dignity and freedom, and with the gates to the Promised Land firmly closed.

In August 1945, moved by their continued suffering, US President Henry S. Truman called on Attlee to allow 100,000 survivors to return to Palestine. Bevin, who has been widely condemned as an anti-Semite, responded at a Labour Party meeting, "There has been agitation in the United States, and particularly in New York, for 100,000 Jews to be put in Palestine. I hope I will not be misunderstood in America if I say that this was proposed by the purest of motives. They did not want too many Jews in New York."[2] Defenders of Bevin claim that he was merely restating a comment made by James Byrnes, the United States Secretary of State, but that does not excuse Bevin for making such a crass and insensitive remark.

THE RISE OF JEWISH INSURGENCY

The British government formally responded to Truman's call by simply reiterating the policy of the 1939 White Paper. Britain was roundly condemned in the US for continuing with such an immoral policy in light of the plight of European Jewry. In a poll of interned Jews, when asked where they wanted to go an overwhelming majority chose Palestine. It was the land of their forefathers. When asked where they would choose if they could not return to Palestine, many responded that they would choose the crematorium. Palestine was their only hope.

Under pressure from Truman to allow these Jewish Holocaust survivors to emigrate to Palestine, Bevin made a statement in the House of Commons on 13 November 1945 announcing that an Anglo-American Committee of Inquiry had been appointed to report on the problems of Palestine and European Jewry.

Bevin proposed the joint Committee as a way to outflank the White House. He was sure that a sense of Britain's strategic realities in the Middle East would sway the US to shy away from antagonizing the Arab world. To ensure the desired outcome, however, the British helped to establish an anti-Zionist narrative that crossed over into anti-Semitism, all in the shadow of the Holocaust.

A succession of Arab speakers, who were brought before the Committee, attacked Zionism as an imperialist and racist political doctrine, very much akin to Nazism itself. Princeton Professor Philip Hitti testified that "political Zionism is the rankest kind of imperialism."[3] The director of the Institute for Arab American Affairs, Khalil Totah, added that trouble caused by Zionism "has spread just like the plague, just like the measles, and just like any other disease."[4] Habib Bourguiba of Tunisia, a country where the Nazis had persecuted and murdered Jews just three years earlier, insisted that it was for "Jews to change themselves, to change certain contentions that they hold which make them offensive sometimes to the locality where they live."[5] Jamal al-Husseini, cousin to the exiled grand mufti of Jerusalem Haj Amin, testified that "Anti-Semitism is really our calamity … because had there been no anti-Semitism … the Jews would not have come to Palestine."[6]

Zionist leaders who addressed the Committee, including the likes of Chaim Weizmann, David Ben-Gurion, Moshe Sharett and Golda Meir, pressed for liberalised immigration; all predicted that Jews and Arabs could live together peacefully in a Jewish state while raising political and economic standards throughout the Middle East.

The Committee signed a unanimous report in Lausanne on 20 April 1946 and published it simultaneously in London and Washington 10 days later. British Committee members had pressed for continued immigration restrictions and the dismantling of the Jewish Agency and the Haganah. However, they were overridden by US members who had been greatly impressed by the urgency of Jewish survivors and the progress of Jewish development in Palestine; they also noted with disdain the intransigence of the Arabs.

The Report included ten recommendations; the second was that the 100,000 immigration certificates called for by President Truman should be awarded to Jews who had been victims of Nazi persecution. Recommendation seven stated that the Land Transfer Regulations, which heavily restricted Jewish land acquisition, should be replaced by a policy of free disposal of land, "irrespective of race, community or creed." Recommendation four stated that since "any attempt to establish either an independent Palestine State or independent Jewish State would result in civil strife such as might threaten the peace of the world",[7] until such hostility disappeared, the Government of Palestine should continue to be administered under the Mandate.

On the day that the report was published it received an enthusiastic endorsement by President Truman who issued a statement which read: "I am very happy that the request which I made for the immediate admission of 100,000 Jews into Palestine has been unanimously endorsed by the Anglo-American Committee of Enquiry. The transference of these unfortunate people should now be accomplished with the greatest despatch ... I am also pleased that the Committee recommends in effect the abrogation of the White Paper of 1939 including existing restrictions on immigration and land acquisition to permit the further development of the Jewish national home."[8] Truman's assumption that the Committee's recommendations had brought to an end the tight restrictions on immigration imposed by the 1939 White Paper proved to be premature.

Although Bevin angrily agreed to accept the Committee's recommendations, London postponed implementation under a blizzard of delays, procedural requirements, and imagined political solutions. The British government argued that neither the Jews nor the Arabs would accept the Committee's recommendations. They concluded that the Jews would not accept anything short of partition, and that not only would the guerrilla raids by the Irgun and Lehi paramilitary groups continue, but the more moderate Haganah might also react by launching widespread attacks. In addition, the government believed the Arabs would only accept a unitary state (which would automatically have had an Arab majority). They were concerned that implementing the recommendations would trigger a general Arab uprising in Palestine, with financial and material backing from the surrounding Arab states. Meanwhile, clandestine immigration and Jewish insurgency in Palestine intensified.

By mid 1946, with Ha'apala ships still arriving in Palestine, the detention camps were full to capacity. Britain announced that all future immigrants would continue to be denied access and would be deported to Cyprus, which was at this time still a British colony. Overcrowded ships, bearing refugees suffering in squalid conditions due to inadequate sanitation, were intercepted by the Royal Navy and escorted into Haifa harbour. The distraught people were forced off the ships and manhandled along the dock to transport ships waiting to carry them to Cyprus. The only part of the Promised Land that they set foot on was a short tract of Haifa dock. The scenes were distressing to all who witnessed them, and a veritable shame on the British government.

Most British people today are completely unaware of the cruel treatment received by the returning Holocaust survivors at the hands of the British authorities. On arrival in Cyprus, the survivors were unceremoniously herded into detention camps surrounded by barb-wire fencing and housed in overcrowded dormitories – stark reminders of the horrors they had lived through in the Nazi death camps. It was, of course, not the same horror. Many refugees spoke kindly of the treatment they received from the ordinary British soldiers; their bitterest anger was reserved for the British ruling authorities.

In Palestine, the watching Jewish underground militias became ever more determined to rid the land of the British altogether whatever the cost. Once it became apparent that the new Labour government, contrary to the vague promises leaked before the election, had no intention of establishing a Jewish state and would not allow significant Jewish immigration to Palestine, the Haganah, Irgun and Lehi formed an alliance, known as the Jewish Resistance Movement, to launch a coordinated series of anti-British operations. The alliance operated until August 1946, when it was disbanded by the Jewish Agency in the wake of the King David Hotel bombing.

The King David Hotel Bombing

On Monday 22 July 1946, the Irgun detonated a bomb containing 250 kilos of explosives inside the King David Hotel, Jerusalem, which served as the British administrative headquarters for

Palestine. The death toll from the attack was 91 which included high ranking officials and people of various nationalities. Among the casualties were 15 Jews.

The hotel was the nerve centre of British rule in Palestine, which made it Begin's primary target for an attack. Rooms in the hotel had first been requisitioned in late 1938, on what was supposed to be a temporary basis. The longer term plan was to erect a permanent building for the Secretariat and Army GHQ, but this plan was abandoned at the outbreak of World War II, by which time over two-thirds of the hotel's rooms were being used for government and army purposes.

By 1946, the hotel was the site of the central offices of the British Mandatory authorities of Palestine, principally the Secretariat of the Government of Palestine, and the Headquarters of the British Armed Forces in Palestine and Transjordan. The Secretariat occupied most of the southern wing of the hotel, while the military HQ occupied the top floor of the south wing and the second, third and top floors of the middle section of the hotel. The military telephone exchange was situated in the basement. An annex housed the Military Police HQ and a branch of the Criminal Investigation Department of the Palestine Police force.

Richard Crossman MP stayed in the hotel in March 1946 and described what he witnessed as a scene of intense diplomatic intrigue: "Private detectives, Zionist agents, Arab sheiks, special correspondents, and the rest, all sitting around about discreetly overhearing each other."[9] It was a tempting target for a strike that would devastate the operations of the Mandatory authorities and achieve maximum publicity.

The attack was conceived as a response to the launch of Operation Agatha on 29 June 1946, known in Israel as "Black Saturday", in which some 17,000 British troops carried out a widespread series of raids in a determined attempt by the Mandatory government to uproot sources of terror, violence and anarchy.

Arrests were made in Jerusalem, Tel Aviv, Haifa and several settlements; among those arrested was Moshe Sharrett, a future Minister of Foreign Affairs and Prime Minister of Israel. Targets included Jewish Agency offices from which the British confiscated large quantities of documents, some of which contained details of intelligence activities in Arab countries and others which directly implicated the Haganah in the Jewish insurgency against Britain. The incriminating documentation was taken to the King David Hotel, where it was stored in the offices of the Secretariat in the southern wing.

One week later, news of a massacre of 40 Jews in a pogrom in Poland reached the Jews in Palestine, serving as a bitter reminder of how Britain's restrictive immigration policy was continuing to condemn thousands of European Jews to death.

During the planning phase of the attack, the Haganah leadership expressed reservations, but on 1 July 1946, Moshe Sneh, chief of the Haganah General Headquarters, sent a letter to Menachem Begin instructing him to carry out the attack. Despite this approval for the project, repeated delays in executing the operation were requested by the Haganah in response to changes unfolding in the political situation as the recommendations of the Anglo-American Committee were being dissected, debated and disseminated. Unbeknownst to the Irgun, Haganah approval had been rescinded by the time the operation was carried out.

On the day of the attack, Irgun operatives, disguised as Arab workmen and hotel waiters, entered the hotel through a basement service entrance carrying explosives concealed in milk churns. The churns were placed beside the main columns supporting the southern wing where the majority of the offices used by the British authorities were located. In the final review of the plan, it had been decided that the attack would take place at 11:00 am, a time when there would be no people in the basement coffee shop near to where the bomb was to be planted.

The Irgun later claimed that details of the plan were designed to minimise civilian casualties and that explicit precautions were taken to ensure that the whole area would be evacuated. After placing the bomb, the Irgun operatives slipped out and detonated a small explosive in the street outside the hotel, reportedly to keep passers-by away from the area. However, the police report written in the aftermath of the bombing concluded that this explosion resulted in a higher death toll because it caused spectators from the hotel to gather in its south-west corner, directly over the bomb planted in its basement. Several Arab civilians were injured outside the hotel when the small explosion caused a passing bus to roll onto its side. These Arab casualties were also brought into the hotel.

Three telephone warnings were issued, one to the adjacent French Consulate urging them to open windows to avoid blast damage, another to the Palestinian Post newspaper, and one to the hotel's own switchboard, which staff decided to ignore, possibly because hoax bomb warnings were rife at the time. However, frantic calls from a concerned Palestinian Post staff member to the police caused increasing alarm. The hotel manager was notified, but no evacuation was ordered. In his memoirs, Begin quoted one British official who supposedly refused to evacuate the building, saying, "We don't take orders from the Jews."[10]

For decades the British government denied that any warnings were received. In 1979, however, a Member of the British Parliament produced evidence to the contrary. He offered the testimony of a British officer who heard other officers in the King David hotel bar joking about a Zionist threat to the headquarters. After overhearing their conversation, the officer immediately left the hotel and as a result survived the attack.

The device exploded at 12:37 pm, later than planned and a time when the hotel was relatively busy. The blast caused the collapse of the western half of the southern wing. Ivan Lloyd Phillips, of the Colonial Administrative Service, was sitting in the hotel bar savouring a pink gin when the blast shattered the room. He later recalled, "There was the most appalling roar ... Everything went completely black and there was the noise of smashing glass and wrenching furniture and through the blackness one could feel the atmosphere was full of smoke and dust ... from above came the most terrifying sound I have ever heard: the sound of falling masonry, and we could only assume we were about to be crushed."[11] The final death toll of 91 made it the deadliest attack directed at the British during the entire Mandate era.

The Irgun issued a statement accepting responsibility for the attack and calling into fault the British for their failure to respond to the telephone warnings. The Irgun's radio network announced that it would mourn for the Jewish victims, but not the British because they had not mourned for the millions of Jews who died in the Nazi Holocaust. No mention was made of Arab victims.

The bombing inflamed public opinion in Britain. Newspaper editorials argued that the attack made void statements by the government that it was winning the battle against Jewish paramilitaries. The Manchester Guardian, for example, argued that "British firmness" in Palestine had created the opposite effect that the government had intended by motivating an increase in terrorism and thereby worsening the situation in the country. In Parliament, a succession of speakers rose to express outrage. Winston Churchill also criticised the bombing but, true to his record of staunchly supporting the Zionist cause, he connected the attack with problems created by the Mandatory authorities and advocated for a renewal of Jewish immigration into Palestine.

On a visit to Palestine prior to the attack, Bernard Montgomery had emphasised that British servicemen were "facing a cruel, fanatical and cunning enemy, and there was no way of knowing who was friend and who foe."[12] Because the paramilitary groups included females, he ordered an end to all fraternising with the local population. Within minutes of the King David Hotel bombing, the British commanding officer in Palestine, General Sir Evelyn Barker, gripped by an uncontrollable rage, translated this instruction into an order that "all Jewish places of entertainment, cafes, restaurants, shops and private dwellings" were out of bounds to all ranks. He concluded, "I appreciate that these measures will inflict some hardship on the troops, but I am certain that if my reasons are fully explained to them, they will understand their propriety and they will be punishing the Jews in the way the race dislikes as much as any by striking at their pockets and showing our contempt for them."[13]

Barker's impulsive order, issued with the stench of the worst kind of anti-Semitic trope, instructed his troops to ostracise the entire Jewish community and sparked a wave of outrage. The universal odium directed at Barker almost overshadowed the revulsion caused by the King David atrocity itself. One British newspaper published a caricature of Barker holding *Mein Kampf*. The Zionists earmarked him as their public enemy, second only to Bevin. The British government acted swiftly to relieve Barker of his command, 'promoting' him to a new assignment back in Britain.

In its public declarations following the attack, the British government were at pains to stress that they would not change their stance toward the Anglo-American Committee agreements on Palestine, talks over which were reaching their concluding phase. In a letter dated 25 July 1946, Prime Minister Attlee wrote to President Truman: "I am sure you will agree that the inhumane crime committed in Jerusalem on 22 July calls for the strongest action against terrorism but having regard to the sufferings of the innocent Jewish victims of Nazism this should not deter us from introducing a policy designed to bring peace to Palestine with the least possible delay."[14]

In reality, however, the British administration in Palestine responded to the attack by enacting draconian restrictions on the civil liberties of Jews, which included a renewed use of random personal searches, random house searches, military curfews, road blocks and mass arrests. Such repressive measures, of course, played perfectly into the Irgun's strategy – they were precisely what the Irgun hoped to provoke. They only served to further alienate the Jewish population and to accelerate the shift in British public opinion against the Mandate system.

Mainstream Jewish political organizations universally condemned the attack. Fearing British reprisals of a scale and severity that would eclipse Operation Agatha, the Jewish Agency expressed "feelings of horror at the base and unparalleled act perpetrated today by a gang of criminals."[15] Such protestations were somewhat disingenuous considering that the Haganah had initially sanctioned the bombing, but the loss of life resulted in bitter recriminations. The Haganah claimed that they had specified that the attack should take place later in the day, when fewer people would have been in the offices. David Ben Gurion, in Paris at the time, joined the chorus of condemnation. In an interview with the French newspaper *France Soir*, he declared the Irgun to be "the enemy of the Jewish people." The Haganah, from now on, rarely mounted attacks against British forces and focussed instead on the Aliyah Bet immigration campaign.

The Irgun and Lehi were unrepentant and stepped up their campaign after the bombing, committing a series of further attacks for which they were condemned as terrorist organisations by both the British government and the Jewish Agency. Menachem Begin, however, argued that the Irgun were differentiated from terrorists in that terrorist organisations deliberately target civilians, whereas the Irgun went to great lengths to avoid civilian casualties. On the 60th anniversary of the attack, Benjamin Netanyahu, then the Leader of the Opposition in the Knesset, recapitulated Begin's defence by stating that the attack on the King David Hotel was a legitimate act with a military target, distinguishing it from an act of terror intended to harm civilians. He said, "Imagine that

Hamas or Hezbollah would call the military headquarters in Tel Aviv and say, 'we have placed a bomb and we are asking you to evacuate the area.' They don't do that. That is the difference."[16]

Jewish Armaments

Prime Minister Attlee was opposed to the recommendation of the Anglo-American Committee for mass immigration unless the Jewish community in Palestine were disarmed, but he knew that this was a condition that would never be accepted. Britain had implemented a policy of disarming the Jews from the beginning of the British Mandate, even though on many occasions it had left them defenceless against attacks by the Arabs. Jews caught carrying firearms, even if it were just for self-defence against Arab terrorism, were arrested and liable to imprisonment or the death penalty. The first hanging for possessing a firearm was carried out in 1938, even though there were no allegations that the victim, Shlomo Ben Yusef, had killed anyone.

After the war, the primary concern for the Haganah was to build a viable fighting force. In 1946, Field Marshal Bernard Montgomery was despatched to Palestine to assess the military capability of the underground Jewish organisations to defend the fledgling community from a full-scale assault by the surrounding Arab armies. He concluded that the Jews would be able to hold out for no more than three weeks.

With the prohibition on the Jewish community carrying arms and ammunition, any future Jewish state would be defenceless. The Haganah resorted to creating a network of clandestine weapons manufacturing facilities across the country under the noses of the British authorities. It was a dangerous occupation, for anyone caught was liable to be detained in Acre prison where a number were hanged.

Acre prison was the most tightly-guarded fortress in Palestine, surrounded by walls and encircled to the north and east by a deep moat, and by the sea to the west. It was located in the heart of an Arab town which had no Jewish inhabitants. During the British Mandate, it served as a high security prison for captured insurgents and its gallows as a place of execution for those sentenced to death.

The fortress appeared to be escape proof, but that did not prevent the Jewish underground paramilitaries from planning a breakout. On Sunday, 4 May 1947, the Irgun launched an audacious operation to rescue Irgun and Lehi inmates.

When the idea of a jail break was first mooted, Amichai Paglin, the Irgun's chief operations officer, managed to enter Acre prison in Arab disguise, and carried out a thorough assessment of its internal security. He identified a weak point at the south wall which could be breached by explosives from the outside. The inmates, however, would have to reach the south wall by their own initiative if they were to make good their escape.

Explosives were smuggled into the prison in cans of jam brought by parents of inmates visiting their sons. Incredibly, one can was opened by a British soldier carrying out security checks who spotted the hard lumps of gelignite but he accepted a story that the jam had not gelled correctly and allowed the can to pass. Detonators and a fuse were smuggled into the prison in the false bottom of an oil can. Once more, the oil can was subjected to a security check but the British soldiers failed to discover the false bottom.

The assault team assigned to breaching the outer southern wall entered Acre disguised as British Engineer Corps soldiers and with instructions to conduct themselves in the manner of "His Majesty's troops." One unit entered a Turkish bath house with ladders and explosives, ostensibly to repair telephone lines, and climbed onto a roof adjacent to the prison wall from where they were able to attach the explosives to the prison windows. Other units scattered mines along the roads leading to the southern wall, and a unit of three men disguised as Arabs set up a mortar position north of Acre from where they could fire on the nearby army camp.

At shortly after 4.00 pm, the afternoon stillness of Acre was shattered by a violent explosion that shook the ground and raised a plume of dust, debris and acrid smoke spiralling over the city. On cue, the southern wall had been blasted open.

Inside the prison, the Irgun and Lehi escapees pushed through crowds of confused and panicked Arab inmates, blew open two gates separating them from the breached wall with the smuggled explosive charges, created fires to block the guards from following, and made their way to freedom. In the confusion, 31 Irgun and 11 Lehi fighters escaped through the breach.

A group of 13 escapees boarded a van which headed towards Haifa, but the driver crashed into a wall when fired upon by British soldiers. In the ensuing firefight, 5 escapees were killed and the remaining 8, some of whom were injured, were captured and returned to Acre prison. Of the strike force that breached the southern wall, 5 were taken prisoner in Acre while attempting to withdraw. One other Lehi escapee was wounded during the escape and died later. The remaining 27 escapees and members of the strike force escaped safely and were dispersed throughout Palestine in pre-designated hiding places.

Despite the loss of life, the sensational success of the Acre Prison break drew admiration from around the world. Foreign journalists described the operation as "the greatest jail break in history." The London Ha'aretz correspondent wrote on 5 May: "The attack on Acre Jail has been seen here as a serious blow to British prestige ... Military circles described the attack as a strategic masterpiece."[17] The New York Herald Tribune wrote that the underground had carried out "an ambitious mission, their most challenging so far, in perfect fashion."[18] Back in Britain, Member of Parliament Oliver Stanley asked a stunned House of Commons what action His Majesty's Government was planning to take "in light of the events at Acre prison which had reduced British prestige to a nadir."[19]

Three weeks after the prison break, the five Irgun fighters who had been captured during the operation were put on trial. Three of the defendants were carrying weapons when they were caught close to the prison wall and were convicted on charges of illegal possession of arms, and with intent to kill or cause other harm to a large number of people. All three were sentenced to death. The other two were captured unarmed and the court sentenced them to life imprisonment.

The Irgun responded to the passing of the death sentences on the three Irgun militants by kidnapping two British Army Intelligence Corps NCOs, Sergeant Clifford Martin and Sergeant Mervyn Paice, and threatening to kill them if the death sentences were carried out.

The British resolved to hang the condemned men despite the risk to the two sergeants. Had the Irgun kidnapped British officers, the outcome may have been different. In an incident in June the previous year, death sentences against 2 Irgun fighters were commuted to life imprisonment after 5 British officers were captured in retaliation. In January 1947, another Irgun militant had his death sentence 'indefinitely' delayed after an intelligence officer and a British judge were kidnapped. On both these occasions the British hostages had been released after the death sentences had been commuted. However, the lives of two NCOs were of lower value to the British authorities than those of officers and judges.

On 27 July the High Commissioner, General Sir Alan Cunningham, gave the order for the executions to be carried out. The superintendent of Acre Prison, Major Charlton, refused to preside over the executions because they were to be carried out in secret, rather than in the traditional way, with the execution date announced well in advance and the families of the condemned allowed to visit them prior to the event. He was subsequently relieved of his position.

At the break of dawn on 29 July, the executions were carried out in the same prison from which the Irgun fighters had freed the prisoners. In a letter to Menachem Begin, an Irgun prisoner named Chaim Wasserman described the executions: "Toward evening a party of hangmen arrived. The officers went in and informed the condemned men they were to be executed between four and five in the morning. Their reply was to sing "Hatikvah" and other songs in powerful voices. They then shouted to us that the hangings would begin at four o'clock, in this order: Avshalom Haviv, Meir Nakar, Yaakov Weiss. They added: "Avenge our blood! Avenge our blood!" We shouted back, "Be strong! We are with you, and thousands of Jewish youth are with you in spirit" ... At four in the morning Avshalom began singing "Hatikvah," and we joined in loudly, pressing against the bars. At once armed police came up to the visitors' fence near our cell. At 4:03 Avshalom was hanged. At 4:25 we were shaken by the powerful singing of Meir. Hardly able to breathe, we nevertheless joined in. He was hanged at 4:28. At five o'clock the voice of Yaakov, this time alone, penetrated our cell, singing "Hatikvah." Again we joined in. Two minutes later he was hanged ... At dawn we informed the prison officers through an Arab warder that we would not be responsible for the life of any Englishman who dared enter the jail yard ... Later in the morning we found the following inscription on the wall of the cell of the condemned: 'They will not frighten the Hebrew youth in the Homeland with their hangings. Thousands will follow in our footsteps.'"[20]

That evening, the Irgun carried out their threatened retaliation by hanging the two sergeants. Their booby-trapped bodies were discovered dangling from a tree in a eucalyptus grove outside

Netanya. In a press statement released by the Irgun, they declared, "We recognize no one-sided laws of war. If the British are determined that their way out of the country should be lined by an avenue of gallows and of weeping fathers, mothers, wives, and sweethearts, we shall see to it that in this there is no racial discrimination. The gallows will not be all of one colour ... Their price will be paid in full."[21]

The Irgun were vehemently denounced for committing the hangings by all sections of the Jewish community's official institutions, including the Haganah. The perpetrators were condemned for taking the authority upon themselves to decide matters of life and death by murdering two innocent people.

Enraged British soldiers, seeking vengeance, attacked Jewish civilians in Tel Aviv, killing five. No criminal charges were brought against any of those responsible. Earnest Bevin, never shy of deploying an anti-Semitic trope, declared that it would not surprise him "if the Germans had learned their worst atrocities from the Jews."[22]

The British media described the Irgun's activities as "bestiality." The Times commented that, "It is difficult to estimate the damage that will be done to the Jewish cause not only in this country but throughout the world by the cold-blooded murder of the two British soldiers."[23] The Manchester Guardian, while urging the government that it was "time to go" from Palestine, noted that the hangings were "a greater blow to the Jewish nation than to the British government."[24]

Incensed by the newspaper coverage, anti-Semitic rioters attacked synagogues and Jewish property across Britain. Although nobody was killed, the violence – which was most ferocious in Liverpool and Manchester in northwest England and the Scottish city of Glasgow – shocked a nation that had always valued tolerance. In the Greater Manchester town of Eccles, John Regan, a former sergeant major in the British Army, was fined £15 for inciting an angry crowd: "Hitler was right. Exterminate every Jew – every man, woman and child. What are you afraid of? There's only a handful of police."[25] Although the depths of the horrors uncovered by the liberators of the death camps in 1945 meant that anti-Semitism became taboo, there was a price to pay for the British authorities' tolerance of anti-Semitism during the war. Just two years after British soldiers had liberated Bergen-Belsen, the language of the Third Reich had resurfaced, this time at home. Even the newspapers who had sensationalized the sergeants' murder swiftly called for calm, branding the disturbances "a national disgrace."

The kidnapping and hanging of the two sergeants was a sickening act that was rightly condemned, but it undoubtedly contributed towards pushing the British into a withdrawal from Palestine. With its counter-insurgency strategy failing, and Irgun retaliation mounting, British authority in Palestine was showing signs of unravelling. Their position was becoming untenable. British officials were confined to heavily guarded compounds and forbidden from associating with Jews. In London, the political will to continue the Mandate was bleeding away. Combating the full-scale insurgency being waged by Irgun and Lehi, together with the Haganah's Ha'apala campaign, was forcing the British to commit significant troop levels and finance to Palestine that she could ill afford. British lives were being lost at an alarming rate. With substantial damage being inflicted to her prestige and public opinion at home swaying against remaining in Palestine, Britain was ready to submit the Mandate over to the United Nations.

In mid 1947, UNSCOP, the United Nations committee which was tasked with making recommendations for the future governance of Palestine, arrived to reconnoitre the situation, just in time to witness a heart-rending incident that would overshadow the sergeants' incident and accelerate the creation of the Jewish homeland promised in the Balfour Declaration. The *Exodus 1947*, a Haganah-operated ship laden with 4,554 Jewish refugees, had set sail from France and was steaming towards Palestine, but her cargo of Holocaust survivors was destined to be refused entry, instead being returned first to France, and then onward to Germany, the dreaded country responsible for their suffering. The entire incident would be captured by the world's media and generated a firestorm of protest against Britain.

Endnotes

1. For details see Murray Greenfield, *The Jews Secret Fleet: The Untold Story of North American Volunteers Who Smashed the British Blockade of Palestine* (New York: Gefen House, 1987).
2. Text of speech to the Labour Party conference, 12 June 1946, General Public Statements, FO 371, 52529/E5546.
3. Cited from www.timesofisrael.com/antisemitism-as-anti-zionism-circa-1946.
4. Ibid.
5. Ibid.
6. Ibid.
7. Cited from Michael J, Cohen, *Palestine and the Great Powers, 1945-1948* (Princeton NJ: Princeton University Press, 1982), p. 105.
8. Cited from *www.jewishvirtuallibrary.org/president-truman-statement-on-the-anglo-american-committee-of-inquiry-april-1946*.
9. Cited from Paul H. Jeffers, *The Complete Idiot's Guide to Jerusalem* (Jerusalem: Alpha Books, 2004), p. 149.
10. Ibid., p. 139.
11. Cited from Norman Rose, *"A Senseless, Squalid War": Voices from Palestine; 1890 to 1948* (London: The Bodley Head, 2009), p. 114
12. Tom Segev, *One Palestine Complete: Jews and Arabs under the British Mandate* (London: Picador, 2001).
13. Cited from Michael J, Cohen, *Palestine and the Great Powers, 1945-1948* (Princeton NJ: Princeton University Press, 1982), p. 94.
14. Attlee to President Truman, Truman Presidential Library, *www.trumanlibrary.org*.
15. Cited from Norman Rose, *"A Senseless, Squalid War": Voices from Palestine; 1890 to 1948* (London: The Bodley Head, 2009), p. 116.
16. Cited from *www.jpot.com/features/Reflective-truth*, 27 July 2006.
17. Cited from Jerry A. Grunor, *Let My People Go* (New York: iUniverse, 2005), p. 187.

[18] Ibid., p. 187.
[19] Ibid., p. 187.
[20] "Bygone Days: They Went to the Gallows Singing", *Jerusalem Post*, 25 July 2007.
[21] Cited from the article "The Role of Jewish Defence Organisations in Palestine", *www.jewishvirtuallibrary.org*.
[22] Jerold S. Auerbach, *Brothers at War: Israel and the Tragedy of the Altalena* [ebook] (New Orleans: Quid Pro Books, 2011).
[23] Cited from Paul Bayon, *The Impact of the Jewish Underground upon Anglo Jewry: 1945-1947* (M Phil Thesis, St Anthony's College, University of Oxford), p. 127-128.
[24] Ibid., p. 127-128.
[25] Daniel Trilling, "Britain's last anti-Jewish Riots: Why have the 1947 riots been forgotten", *New Statesman*, 23 May 2012, cited from *https://www.newstatesman.com/2012/05/britains-last-anti-jewish-riots*.

CHAPTER 9

HAGANAH EXODUS 1947

> *The ship looked like a matchbox that had been splintered by a nutcracker. In the torn, square hole, as big as an open, blitzed barn, we could see a muddle of bedding, possessions, plumbing, broken pipes, overflowing toilets, half-naked men, women looking for children. Cabins were bashed in; railings were ripped off; the lifesaving rafts were dangling at crazy angles."*
>
> –RUTH GRUBER

Yet another Conference was convened in London in January 1947 in an attempt to find a peaceful resolution to the future of Mandatory Palestine, but the chasm between the negotiating positions of the Jewish and Arab delegations remained unbridgeable. The Jews were only prepared to accept a partition plan which the Arabs refused to countenance. The only outcome that would satisfy the Arab delegation was the creation of a unitary state of Palestine, but the Jews could not accept this plan as they believed the resulting Arab majority would prevent future Jewish immigration and leave them as a persecuted minority. Neither side were prepared to accept limited autonomy under overall British rule.

With no prospect of an agreement being reached, Earnest Bevin threatened to hand the problem over to the United Nations. The threat failed to move either side, the Jewish representatives because they believed that Bevin was bluffing and the Arabs because they believed that their cause would prevail before the General Assembly of the United Nations. Bevin was not bluffing! British resolve to continue as the Mandatory power in Palestine was cracking under the weight of several converging factors: the strategic rationale for retaining a presence in Palestine was weakened by their intentions to withdraw from the Indian subcontinent; the financial burden imposed on Britain by the fight against Jewish insurgency was unsustainable for an economy ruined by the cost of World War II; there was now a tremendous ground swell of public opinion that opposed keeping troops in Palestine.

In essence, the British government had grown sick and weary of Palestine, although there were no acknowledgements of British culpability for creating the problem through years of bungled administration, imperial thinking, self-interested policy making, procrastination and betrayal. All completed under the veneer of 'fair play' when in reality, barring a few notable exceptions, the higher echelons of government, intelligentsia and the military were riddled with anti-Jewish sentiments.

Earnest Bevin, arguably the most vindictive anti-Semite in government office, accordingly announced that he would ask the United Nations to take the Palestine question into consideration. The decision to allow the United Nations to determine Palestine's future was justified in the House of Commons by Bevin's declaration, delivered in February 1947, that Britain's Mandate in Palestine had "proved to be unworkable in practice … the obligations undertaken by the two communities in Palestine have been shown to be irreconcilable"[1]

The United Nations was born in October 1945 with 51 founding members for the sole purpose, after World War II, of maintaining international peace and preventing wars – something which its predecessor, the League of Nations, had failed to do. The United Nation's inaugural meeting took place in London on 6 January 1946, the birthplace of the Balfour Declaration nearly 30 years earlier.

The British government made a formal request to the United Nations that the General Assembly make recommendations under article 10 of the Charter concerning the future government of Palestine. In response, following the British example of creating special Commissions of Inquiry, the Security Council created the United Nations Special Committee on Palestine (UNSCOP) on 15 May 1947. UNSCOP was charged with investigating the cause of the conflict in Palestine, and, if possible, devising a solution. The Committee was made up of 11 members, none of them permanent members of the Council, and most of them having little knowledge of the Middle East, let alone of Palestine. The Committee members were: Australia, Canada, Czechoslovakia, Guatemala, India, Iran, The Netherlands, Peru, Sweden, Uruguay and Yugoslavia.

The Arab Higher Committee boycotted the Commission, explaining that the Palestinian Arabs' natural rights were self-evident and could not continue to be subjected to investigation, but rather deserved to be recognized on the basis of the principles of the United Nations Charter. They suspected from the outset of its mission that UNSCOP's aim was eventually to recommend the partitioning of Palestine, and accused it of being pro-Zionist. Arab opposition figures were threatened with death if they cooperated with the Committee.

UNSCOP reached the shores of Palestine on 15 June 1947, and three days later embarked on a tour of Palestine courtesy of the Jewish Agency's hospitality. The Agency ensured an enthusiastic welcome reception was organised in each of the Jewish settlements visited, and arranged meetings with settlement members who spoke the same languages as the Committee members. In contrast, the Committee members were ignored and faced with hostility in Arab regions. The regions they visited included Jerusalem, Haifa, the Dead Sea, Hebron, Beersheba, Gaza, Jaffa, the Galilee, Tel Aviv, Acre, Nablus, Beit Dajan, Tulkarm, Rehovot, Arab and Jewish settlements in the Negev, and several Jewish agricultural communities.

The Jewish Agency was playing a masterly diplomatic game. Following their tour of Palestine, UNSCOP held a series of twelve public hearings, from 4 - 17 July, in the course of which 31 representatives from 12 Jewish organizations gave testimony and submitted written depositions. The Jewish Agency representatives included David Ben Gurion, Moshe Shertok and Abba Eban, while Chaim Weizmann also testified as a private citizen. Anti-Zionist Jewish representatives from the Palestine Communist Party and the Ichud party were also involved. Despite the Arab boycott, several Arab officials and intellectuals met privately with Committee members, among them the former Jerusalem mayor, Husseini al-Khalidi.

Ben Gurion opened the Jewish case on 4 July with a survey of Jewish history since biblical times. "With an indomitable obstinacy", he observed, "we always preserved our identity … An unbroken tie between our people and our land has persisted through all these centuries in full force." The core of his argument was that a Jewish state was necessary for their continued survival, "The homelessness and minority position make the Jews always dependent on the mercy of others. The 'others' may be good and may be bad, and the Jews are sometimes treated more or less decently, but they are never masters of their own destiny; they are entirely defenceless when the majority turn against them. What happened to our people in this war is merely a climax to the uninterrupted persecution to which we have been subjected for centuries by almost all the Christian and Moslem peoples in the old world."[2] When his time to testify came, Weizmann described how the Jewish people, in their homeless state, resembled "a disembodied ghost."[3]

With impeccable providential timing, as the UNSCOP public hearings were reaching their conclusion, the pivotal event of the Haganah's Ha'apala operation was unfolding off the shores of Palestine. A dilapidated refugee ship, the *Exodus 1947*, crammed with 4,554 destitute Holocaust survivors, was steaming through the Mediterranean pursued by a flotilla of Royal Navy warships. On the day after the final public hearing, in a perfect illustration of Ben Gurion's argument, the warships attacked and boarded the defenceless *Exodus* with callous disregard for the catastrophic tragedy that could have been precipitated, and steered her to Haifa from where the British authorities planned to deport the despairing refugees to detention camps in Cyprus.

The Committee avidly followed the unravelling of the *Exodus* story. What they witnessed was an epic tragedy founded upon fierce courage, determination and resolution in the face of cold hearted anti-Jewish brutality. Four UNSCOP members were present at the port of Haifa, after being persuaded to go by Abba Eban, to witness the gruesome sight of Jewish immigrants being forcibly removed from the ship and deported back to Europe. The Jewish Agency was making sure they were fully informed of the developing story.

UNSCOP completed its work in Palestine by hearing the eyewitness testimony of the Reverend John Stanley Grauel, a British Church Minister who was on board the *Exodus* during her fateful voyage. The Committee also decided to hear the testimony of the Jewish refugees in British detention camps in Palestine and in European Displaced Persons camps trying to gain admittance to Palestine. Golda Meir, later Prime Minister of Israel, observed that Reverend Grauel's testimony and advocacy for the creation of the Jewish state fundamentally and positively changed the views of UNSCOP members to support the creation of Israel. She commented caustically that they were inclined to give weight to his testimony because he was not a Jew.

Exodus 1947: The Ship that Launched a Nation

With the war at an end, and with the resumption of clandestine immigration by the Haganah, the British committed significant naval resources to the Mediterranean in their determination to prevent Jewish refugees from landing in Palestine. Over half of the Ha'apala voyages attempted were intercepted by British navy patrols, and their human cargos of desolate refugees placed in detention camps. When the Atlit detention camp had reached capacity, the British announced that all subsequent so called 'illegal' immigrants would be deported to Cyprus. The Haganah had no choice but to encourage future Aliyah Bet immigrants to resist capture.

On 9 November 1946, the Haganah purchased *SS President Warfield*, a former packet steamer, for the purposes of Aliyah Bet. The ship, launched in 1928, had carried passengers and freight between Norfolk, Virginia and Baltimore, Maryland in the USA until she was requisitioned in 1942 by the US Navy for service in World War II. She was stationed at Omaha Beach during the Normandy landings but, after being decommissioned by the Navy, she was abandoned to decay, unwanted until she was acquired by agents acting secretly for the Haganah.

The *President Warfield* was selected because she was fast, and taller than the British destroyers which would create problems for any party attempting to board her. The ship was also in a derelict condition. Putting her to sea crammed with passengers would be a risk, but it was felt that this would compel the British to let her pass through the naval blockade because they would fear the reputational damage sustained from international outrage should their interference cause a catastrophe at sea.

President Warfield was renamed as *Exodus 1947*, a reference to the biblical Exodus from Egypt to Canaan. The name was proposed by Moshe Sneh, the head of Aliyah Bet for the Jewish Agency. It was an inspired name, described by Israel's second Prime Minister Moshe Sharett as "a stroke of genius, a name which by itself, says more than anything which has ever been written about it."[4] In America, the name was completely absorbed and even President Truman soon heard rumours about a ship called *Exodus*. The French also made use of the ship's new name, much to the consternation of the British who always made a point of calling her the *President Warfield*.

For months, maintenance teams worked around the clock making adaptations to the *Exodus* designed to make the ship defensible from any British attempt to take her over. Metal pipes were fitted around the ship's perimeter to spray out steam and boiling oil, the lower decks were covered in nets and barbed wire. The machine room, steam room, wheel house and radio room were reinforced to prevent entry by British soldiers.

Once seafaring preparations and embarkations were complete, the *Exodus* set sail for her date with destiny from the port of Sète, near Marseilles on the French Mediterranean coast, on the morning of 11 July 1947. She was carrying 4,554 passengers including 1,600 men, 1,282 women, and 1,672 children. She was captained by Ike Aronowicz, a seasoned Haganah seaman, and was manned by a crew of 35 volunteers, mostly American Jews. Of the 64 vessels that sailed in the Aliyah Bet, she was by far the largest. Her passenger roster constituted the highest number of Jews to sail towards Palestine in a single attempt.

Because of her sheer size and presence, the *Exodus* was not typical of a ship hired for clandestine purposes. She was far too large to go unnoticed. Even as people began boarding her in Sète, an RAF plane was circling overhead and a Royal Navy warship was waiting just beyond the anchorage. It was never going to be possible for her to sneak out of port. From the beginning of her voyage, she was tracked by the Navy until she reached the South Eastern Mediterranean 6 days later. There, she was intercepted off the Egyptian coast, approximately 80 miles south of Tel Aviv, by a flotilla of 5 Destroyers guided by the Royal Navy battle cruiser *Ajax*. The *Ajax* had distinguished herself during the war by her part in sinking the German battleship *Graf Spee*, but now she was stalking the unarmed derelict refugee ship to execute orders for the British battle fleet to stop Jews returning to Palestine.

During the journey, the passengers on board the *Exodus* carried out regular practice drills in preparation for repelling boarders. The general plan was to use the ship's speed and manoeuvrability to burst through the naval blockade, and to beach her on sand banks near Tel Aviv. From there, the refugees could disembark and be dispersed. The British anticipated this, and knowing that the *Exodus* had a much shallower draft than the destroyers who would therefore not be able to follow her in shallow waters, they decided to attack the *Exodus* at sea.

At 2.00 am on 18 July, the *Ajax* approached the *Exodus*, illuminating her with search lights, and challenged her to stop as she was entering territorial waters. The captain of the *Exodus*, Ike Aronowicz, later claimed that this was a lie as the *Exodus* was, at the time, still in international waters. Two of the destroyers then rammed the fragile ship repeatedly, one from either side, in order to steer her away from the coast. The force of the collisions caused a substantial breach in the superstructure of the *Exodus*, which threatened to sink her. She was only able to stay afloat because her excellent pumps were able to expel sufficient water until she made the Port of Haifa. The cruelty of British warships attacking a dilapidated ship carrying destitute refugees in this way is beyond belief. They could have caused an unthinkable catastrophe. It was an action the Haganah believed the British would not risk, but they had underestimated the strength of Britain's ice-cold resolve to stop Jewish immigration at all costs.

In an attempt to gain control of the *Exodus*, Royal Marine commandos jumped aboard the ship from the destroyers on either side. The passengers had no weapons with which to defend the ship, but they put up ferocious resistance arming themselves with a makeshift concoction of missiles, including potatoes and canned kosher bully beef which they hurled at the invading Marines. Some were thrown back into the sea. One British rating reported, "I tried to get on board three times but there was too much opposition in the shape of big Yids. I was forced to draw my revolver and fired eleven warning shots. One of the last shots, I used to stop a lad from collecting my scalp with a meat axe. He got it in the stomach."[5]

Finally, with the Jews refusing to surrender, the Marines opened fire with machine guns and tear gas canisters, and forced their way into the wheel house where crew member Bill Bernstein, an American volunteer, was clubbed to death. Two passengers died from bullet wounds sustained as the Marines raked the decks with machine gun fire, including a 15 year old boy who was the only survivor from the Holocaust of the Yakubowitz family. Over 100 were wounded, many critically. Two British Marines were treated for injuries sustained in the assault, one for a fractured scapula, the other for a head injury and lacerated ear.

The unarmed refugees staged a brave defence against an aggressive attack by an elite force but with the wheel house in British hands the battle-scarred *Exodus*, listing forlornly and riddled with holes, was steered towards Haifa with its weary cargo of Holocaust survivors. As they entered the harbour, where the world's media were waiting, they sang Hatikvah, the Jewish national anthem, and the Star of David was flying proudly above their heads for the whole world to see.

American journalist Ruth Gruber, on assignment in Palestine from the New York Herald Tribune to cover the UNSCOP proceedings, rushed to Haifa and witnessed first-hand the *Exodus* limping into harbour. In a dispatch, she described the horrific state of the ship: "The ship looked like a matchbox that had been splintered by a nutcracker. In the torn, square hole, as big as an open, blitzed barn, we could see a muddle of bedding, possessions, plumbing, broken pipes, overflowing toilets, half-naked men, women looking for children. Cabins were bashed in; railings were ripped off; the lifesaving rafts were dangling at crazy angles."[6]

Once docked, the refugees were forced off the *Exodus* and told they would be deported immediately to Cyprus. Three prison ships, *Runnymede Park*, *Ocean Vigour* and *Empire Rival*, were already waiting to transport them away from the land of Israel. When they saw that they were being expelled, hundreds of the refugees broke down in anguished tears. It was a devastating sight for those who witnessed what happened. British soldiers had to forcefully drag many of the weeping refugees onto the prison ships. Even the wounded were deported, all except those who were critically injured and the dead. Gruber's graphic description of the scene continues: "The people trickled down the gangways in little groups and milled about the dock like frightened animals. They looked weary and shattered … On the pier, the British took off every bandage and examined every wound to make sure that only the serious cases stayed. Some of the wounded screamed in pain as their head dressings were untied … Men looked dazed and ready to collapse as red-bereted soldiers shoved them along the last mile."[7]

Images of the misery of these Holocaust survivors flashed around the world thanks to the presence of the world's press.

Crucially, four members of the UNSCOP Committee were also present on the wharf. What they witnessed would have a profound influence on the Committee's recommendations to the United Nations. The British decision to capture the *Exodus* and the eventual return of the refugees to Germany reinforced the link, in the minds of UNSCOP Committee members, between the survival of European Jews and their eventual settlement in the land of Palestine.

The world stood aghast at the plight of the *Exodus* refugees, but not the British Foreign Secretary Earnest Bevin back in London. His obtuse response was that, due to the high profile of the *Exodus*, it was necessary to make an example of the refugees to both the Jewish community and any European countries which assisted with Jewish immigration. He ordered that they be returned to Europe rather than deported to Cyprus. The three ships left Haifa, laden with the refugees, on 19 July, bound for the French port of Port-de-Bouc.

On arrival in France, the refugees made a defiant stand, refusing to disembark anywhere but Israel. The French government, to the anger of the British, refused to take any refugee who did not disembark willingly. And so, as the world's press looked on, a standoff began which would continue for 4 weeks. The refugees were determined to stand fast even as conditions on board the ships deteriorated. They were tormented by suffocating summer heat and storms, contagion of boils and lesions, privation, with no room below deck to lie down, yet none of these tribulations broke their spirit. Fresh supplies were brought on board by aid agencies as the stalemate continued. The Haganah extolled the refugees for their defiance, "The stand taken in their struggle has written a brilliant page in the history of the Jews' fight for their freedom."[8]

The French authorities adamantly refused to cooperate with repeated British attempts at forced disembarkation, so Bevin, under pressure to find a solution, finally issued an ultimatum which gave the refugees 24 hours to disembark or they would be taken back to Germany, the dreaded country that was the source of their awful suffering, and locked up once again in concentration camps. Only 21 refugees came ashore before the ships departed from France and headed for Hamburg in the British zone of occupation to carry out Bevin's threat.

The British understood that this inhumane decision to return the *Exodus* passengers to camps in Germany would create a public outcry, but concluded that Germany was the only territory under their control that could immediately accommodate so many people. Diplomats in the British Embassy in Paris warned the Foreign Office that the situation was turning into a public relations disaster. John Coulson, one such diplomat, summed by the dilemma in a cable to London in August 1947: "You will realize that an announcement of the decision to send immigrants back to Germany will produce violent hostile outbursts in the press ... Our opponents in France, and I dare say in other countries, have made great play with the fact that these immigrants were being kept behind barbed wire, in concentration camps and guarded by Germans."[9]

When the three ships arrived in Hamburg, the refugees were in a defiant mood and once again refused to disembark. The prospect of being sent to detention camps in Germany was, for these Holocaust survivors, almost impossible to bear. Bevin, with repugnant insensitivity, ordered that they be forcefully removed and placed on trains for transportation to the Displaced Persons camps in Am Stau, near Lübeck, and Pöppendorf. It was a gratuitously repulsive way to handle the pitiful remnants of Auschwitz and the ghettoes. The memories of nightmarish journeys on the Nazi death trains to the concentration camps that must have been stirred are impossible to contemplate. Most of the women and children disembarked voluntarily, but the men were resolved to put up a fight.

Military police and soldiers of the Sherwood Foresters were ordered to board the ships and eject the remaining Jewish immigrants. The officer in charge of the operation, Lt. Col. Gregson, later gave a very frank assessment of the success of the storming of the ships. His report stated, "After a very short pause, with a lot of yelling and female screams, every available weapon up to a biscuit and bulks of timber was hurled at the soldiers. They withstood it admirably and very stoically till the Jews assaulted and in the first rush several soldiers were downed with half a dozen Jews on top kicking and tearing ... No other troops could have done it as well and as humanely as these British ones did." He added, "It should be borne in mind that the guiding factor in most of the actions of the Jews is to gain the sympathy of the world press."[10]

The British soldiers used batons to suppress resistance and turned fire hoses on the Jews. By the completion of the operation, according to official British figures, 33 Jews, including 4 women, had been injured in the melee and 68 were put on trial for disorderly behaviour. The observations of Dr. Noah Barou, present as a representative of the World Jewish Congress, painted a somewhat different picture of the action than that of Lt. Col. Gregson. He described what he called the "terrible mental picture" of young soldiers beating Holocaust survivors: "They went into the operation as a football match ... and it seemed evident that they had not had it explained to them that they were dealing with people who had suffered a lot and who are resisting in accordance with their convictions ... People were usually hit in the stomach and this in my opinion explains that many people who did not show any signs of injury were staggering and moving very slowly along the staircase giving the impression that they were half-starved and beaten up."[11]

As the refugees disembarked, many of them shouted out calling the British troops "gentleman fascists" and "sadists." Dr Barou recalled a particularly impressive young girl who challenged the soldiers, "I am from Dachau", and when they did not react, she roared, "Hitler commandos."[12]

What could have been a more poignant symbol of injustice in the post-war world than Holocaust survivors being barred from Palestine and being redirected so horrifically to Germany? Britain was condemned by the international press. It seemed that the nation that had helped defeat the Nazis were now acting like them. Britain's international reputation was in tatters. Many world leaders, including US President Harry S. Truman, called for an end to Britain's Mandatory control over Palestine.

The refugees were back where they had started, in detention camps in Germany, but their suffering would not be in vain. It has been said that the *Exodus 1947* was 'the ship that launched a nation.' It became a central image in the fight to bring any Jews that wanted back to the land of Israel, helped to unify the Jewish community of Palestine with the Holocaust survivors in Europe, and provoked a powerful reaction in world opinion as they saw the injustice which was done to people who had survived Auschwitz but had no place in the world to call home. Extensive media coverage of the plight of the *Exodus* had opened the world's eyes to the unfair and morally bankrupt policies that guided Britain's control of Palestine. Deepening international sympathy for the plight of the Holocaust survivors inspired an exponential increase in support for the notion of a Jewish state.

The Jewish Agency and pro-Zionist organisations have often been accused of displaying rank opportunism for the manner in which they exploited the misery of the *Exodus* refugees for propaganda purposes. It is certainly true that they made sure UNSCOP and the international media were present to capture the scenes at Haifa. They circulated reports that the refugees were being guarded by Germans, though this was not the case, and encouraged the refugees to stand firm throughout their ordeal. The coverage that the *Exodus* received was a gift to the Zionist cause. The image of Holocaust survivors fighting against one of the West's most august symbols of power, the British Royal Navy, was invaluable on the public relations battlefield. But it must be remembered that they did not provoke the Royal Navy to attack the *Exodus* in such a belligerently ruthless and calculating manner or ask for the refugees to be deported so cruelly to Germany. Responsibility for what transpired is Britain's alone.

In Palestine, on 29 September 1947, the Irgun and Lehi maintained the pressure on the British administration by exploding a bomb at the Central Police HQ in Haifa in retaliation for the British deportation of the Jews from the *Exodus*. Four British policemen, four Arab policemen, an Arab woman and a 16-year-old youth were killed. The building was so badly damaged that it had to be demolished.

The *Exodus* refugees were moved in November 1947 to two new camps at Sengwarden and Emden. From there, many were smuggled into the US zone of occupation from where they made further attempts to reach Palestine. Many were caught and ended up in detention camps in Cyprus, where they were held until Britain formally recognized the State of Israel in January 1949. Eventually, by one means or another, most of these poor, tortured people finally reached the shores of Israel. The battered hull of the *Exodus 1947* remained moored to a breakwater in Haifa harbour, neglected and decaying, until it was sold for scrap to an Italian merchant in 1963.

Endnotes

1. Earnest Bevin, to the House of Commons, February 1947.
2. Cited from Martin Gilbert, *Israel: A History* (London: Black Swan, 2008), p. 146.
3. Ibid., p. 147.
4. Aviva Hamlish, *The Exodus Affair: Holocaust Survivors and the Struggle for Palestine* (New York: Syracuse University Press, 1998), p. 69.
5. Cited from Norman Rose, *"A Senseless, Squalid War": Voices from Palestine; 1890 to 1948* (London: The Bodley Head, 2009), p. 158.
6. Cited from Eric Gartman, *Return to Zion: The History of Modern Israel* [ebook] (University of Nebraska Press, 2015).
7. Ibid.
8. Ibid.
9. Cited from *www.jewishvirtuallibrary.org/quote-exodus-illegal-immigration-ships*.
10. Gerald Ziedenberg, *Blockade: The Story of Jewish Immigration to Palestine* (Indiana: Author House: 2011), p. 155.
11. Ibid., p. 155.
12. Ibid., p. 155.

CHAPTER 10

DYING EMBERS OF BRITISH RULE

> *Hear the word of the* LORD, *you nations; proclaim it in distant coastlands: 'He who scattered Israel will gather them and will watch over his flock like a shepherd.' For the* LORD *will deliver Jacob and redeem them from the hand of those stronger than they"*
>
> —JEREMIAH 31:10-11

For refusing to remove limits on Jewish immigration into Palestine in the aftermath of the war, Earnest Bevin earned the hatred of Zionists. Richard Crossman, a fellow Labour Party Member of Parliament and a pro-Zionist, characterised Bevin's outlook during the dying embers of the Mandate as "corresponding roughly with The Protocols of the Elders of Zion", a notorious forgery which was designed to inflame anti-Semitic prejudice. Crossman intimated that "the main points of Bevin's discourse were ... that the Jews had successfully organised a conspiracy against Britain and against him personally."[1]

UNSCOP left Palestine heading to Germany, Austria and finally Geneva. During the last stretch of this trip, and under Zionist insistence, a subcommittee visited some of the Nazi concentration camps, and toured displaced persons camps in the American and British occupation zones where they interviewed Jewish refugees and local military officials, finding that there was a strong desire among the Jews to emigrate to Palestine. The visits no doubt swayed many UNSCOP members towards the conclusion that Palestine could be the only safe haven for Jews. As the Committee retired in Geneva to write its final report, the images of the concentration camps and the Holocaust could not have been far from their mind. That link was key to UNSCOP's proposed recommendation for the partitioning of Palestine.

It took UNSCOP exactly two and a half months to complete its report. They met in the conference room on the first floor of the Palais des Nations in Geneva where they were subjected to constant Jewish and Arab pressure. Zionist representatives vigorously lobbied the Committee, submitting a stream of memorandums arguing in favour of a Jewish-Transjordan partition. The Arab League liaison demanded a solution satisfactory to the Palestinian Arabs, threatening that catastrophe would result otherwise.

UNSCOP signed their official report on the last hour of the last day of August 1947, just minutes before its term of office expired. The report supported the termination of the British Mandate in Palestine. It contained a majority proposal for a Plan of Partition into two independent states with economic union and a minority proposal for a Plan for one Federal State of Palestine with Jerusalem as its capital.

Bevin commented that, "The majority proposal is so manifestly unjust to the Arabs that it is difficult to see how, in Sir [Alexander] Cardogan's [British Ambassador to the UN] words, we could reconcile it with our conscience."[2] Nevertheless, the British cabinet voted to leave Palestine, and on 26 September 1947, the British

Colonial Secretary, Arthur Creech Jones, conceded defeat by announcing to the UN that, "in the absence of a settlement, the government must plan for an early withdrawal of British forces and of the British administration from Palestine."[3] British officials later cited the financial burden imposed on Britain by fighting against the Jewish insurgency, together with the tremendous public opposition to keeping troops in Palestine that the insurgency generated, as major factors in Britain's decision to evacuate Palestine. Once that decision had been taken, the British could not get out quickly enough. The government wanted to extricate its forces from any obligation to repress disturbances which they expected to arise in response to whichever solution the UN adopted.

An Ad-Hoc Committee was established by the General Assembly to give further consideration to the Palestinian question shortly after the issuance of the UNSCOP report. It released the report of its findings, which essentially supported the Arab position, on 11 November 1947. It observed that with an end to the Mandate and with British withdrawal, "there is no further obstacle to the conversion of Palestine into an independent state" which was the objective of the Mandate in the first place. It found that "the General Assembly is not competent to recommend, still less to enforce, any solution other than the recognition of the independence of Palestine, and that the settlement of the future government of Palestine is a matter solely for the people of Palestine." It concluded that the partition plan was "contrary to the principles of the Charter, and the United Nations has no power to give effect to it."[4]

Had these recommendations been accepted, so that the minority proposal would have been put before the General Assembly, Palestine would have become by default an independent Arab nation with an unwanted Jewish minority, and any hopes for a Jewish homeland would have been crushed. After a series of heated debates, and numerous voting sessions, the recommendations of the Ad-Hoc Committee were eventually rejected by a vote of 25 to 13, with 17 abstentions.

On 29 November 1947, after several days of furious lobbying by the Jewish delegation and delays caused by filibustering designed to buy additional time to persuade nations whose votes were in the balance, the General Assembly approved a final resolution, known as GA Res 181, which was based on the UNSCOP majority plan. Britain abstained in the vote, but despite that, the necessary two-thirds majority carried the resolution. It was a breathtaking outcome that re-contoured the political map of the Middle East.

The outcome of the vote had been very much in doubt – the entire Muslim world was opposed to partition. All of Palestine, Arab and Jew, gathered around radio sets as the votes were called. When the two-thirds majority was reached, spontaneous joyful celebrations erupted in Jewish settlements and quarters. Streets thronged with jubilant crowds, some singing while others, overwhelmed with emotion, openly wept. Moshe Dayan later recalled in his memoirs, "I felt in my bones the victory of Judaism, which for two thousand years of exile from the land of Israel had withstood persecutions, the Spanish Inquisition, pogroms, anti-Jewish decrees, restrictions, and the mass slaughter by the Nazis in our own generation, and had reached the fulfilment of its age-old yearning – the return to a free and independent Zion."[5] For Dayan, however, the moment was tempered by a sense of foreboding, "We were happy that night, and we danced, and our hearts went out to every nation whose UN representative had voted in favour of the resolution. We had heard them utter the magic word 'yes' as we followed their voices over the airwaves from thousands of miles away. We danced – but we knew that ahead of us lay the battlefield."

Under the partition agreement, the original 1922 land mass of Palestine available for Jewish settlement had been reduced by 88 per cent to 5,500 square miles. The Jewish Agency pragmatically acquiesced. Jewish power politics were weak and the lack of Jewish settlement population had to be taken into consideration. There were celebrations across the world as the Jews accepted the partition plan, paving the way for the creation of a Jewish state. The Arabs, however, rejected it outright declaring that they would destroy any Jewish State as soon as it came into being. From a legal perspective, this meant that GA Res 181, which was an advisory resolution, did not attain legal standing under international law and consequently the only standing legal instrument pertaining to the distribution of land in Palestine with international recognition remains the Mandate of 1922. This is overlooked by those today who claim that Israel's 'occupation' of land in disputed territories is illegal.

The rejection of the Partition Plan by the Arabs reflects the crux of the Arab-Israeli conflict today. It was a rejection of the right for a Jewish State to exist at all. On 11 October 1947, Azzam Pasha, Secretary General of the Arab League, was reported by Egyptian media to have warned of "a war of extermination and momentous massacre, which will be spoken of like the Tartar massacre, or the Crusader wars … to win the honour of martyrdom for the sake of Palestine … the shortest road to paradise."[6] This did not seem altogether out of the question. The outrage of the Arabs was palpable, the threat to Jewish bodily integrity real. During the remainder of the British Mandate, fighting between the Jewish and Arab communities intensified.

Civil War in Mandatory Palestine

In the aftermath of the adoption of Resolution 181 by the United Nations, the manifest joy of the Jewish community was counterbalanced by Arab protests throughout Palestine. A 'wind of violence' swept across the country: murders, reprisals, counter-reprisals, dozens of victims killed on both sides. British forces, still obliged to maintain order under the Mandate, did nothing to halt the escalating cycle of violence. They were evidently more concerned with organizing their withdrawal from Palestine.

The Arab Higher Committee declared its intention to thwart by force any attempt to impose partition, announcing confidently on 6 February 1948: "The Palestinian Arabs consider any attempt by Jewish people or by whatever power or group of powers to establish a Jewish state in an Arab territory to be an act of aggression that will be resisted by force … The prestige of the United Nations would be better served by abandoning this plan and by not imposing such an injustice … The Palestinian Arabs make a grave declaration before the UN, before God and before history that they will never submit to any power that comes to Palestine to impose a partition. The only way to establish a partition is to get rid of them all: men, women, and children."[7]

Violence intensified as foreign military units from surrounding Arab nations infiltrated Palestine in support of the Arab cause, an intervention which the British did nothing to impede. On 15 January 1948, Bevin negotiated the Portsmouth Treaty with Iraq which, according to the Iraqi foreign minister Muhammad Fadhel al-Jamali, was accompanied by a British undertaking to withdraw from Palestine in such a fashion as to provide for swift Arab occupation of all its territory.

Jerusalem, which the United Nations had designated an international zone, became a major target. The Arabs attempted to lay siege to the city by cutting off vulnerable access and supply routes. The wider Jewish community had no option other than to organise dangerous relief convoys to carry food and supplies to the beleaguered Jewish inhabitants. Unable to carry arms, the only option for defence was to plate the convoy vehicles with metal sheets to provide protection from sniper fire from the hills overlooking the approach to Jerusalem.

DYING EMBERS OF BRITISH RULE

The British were responsible for providing security, but instead of protecting the convoys, they merely conducted searches of the vehicles for weapons. No action was taken to disarm the Arab militia positioned in the mountains that guarded the approach to Jerusalem from where they were pouring fire down upon the unarmed Jews.

Many of the attacks on the convoys were staged from the otherwise peaceful village of Deir Yassin, close to the Jerusalem neighbourhoods of Givat Shaul, Kyriat Moshe, Beit Hakerrem and Yeffe Nof. Intelligence reports indicated that the village had been infiltrated by foreign Arab soldiers and had become a centre for trafficking weapons. Because of the British refusal to fulfil their legal obligations to defend the convoys, the Irgun decided to take the law into their own hands and proposed an operation against the village as part of the larger operation aimed at clearing the road from Tel Aviv to Jerusalem.

Yosef Nachmias, an Irgun fighter who took part in the operation, described what unfolded, "From there (Deir Yassin), snipers were firing on these neighbourhoods and on the road from Jerusalem to Tel Aviv … The Irgun decided to go and liberate that place."[8]

On the morning of 9 April 1948, on the outskirts of the village, the Irgun addressed the inhabitants through loud speakers to give warning of their attack. Nachmias recalled the message, "You belong to this country, we want to live in peace with you. We are coming to fight the strangers here. You stand aside, we won't harm you."[9]

The Irgun advanced in very painstaking fashion as heavy fire was directed upon them from the village. Nachmias continued, "There were volunteers from Iraq there. They called themselves volunteers but we knew they were Iraqi soldiers dressed in 'civvies'. They used to come and the British turned a blind eye … They didn't let the families leave … Our guys attacked and threw hand grenades into the strongholds there, without knowing there were women and children inside. Unfortunately women and children were killed."[10]

The number of weapons found in Deir Yassin confirmed that the village had indeed been turned into a military post. But that did not prevent the assault becoming a propaganda tool for the Arabs as rumours began to circulate that hundreds of Arabs had been massacred during and after the battle. It is true that the casualty figures were terribly high. Innocent civilians were killed in the fierce house-to-house fighting, including women and children, but exaggerated reports began circulating that spoke of 250 deaths, of pregnant women raped, of captured villagers shot after being paraded through the streets of West Jerusalem, of bodies mutilated by decapitation and disembowelment.

What really happened at Deir Yassin became obscured by lies, exaggerations and contradictions as both sides released inflated casualty figures, but for very different reasons: the Palestinian Arabs embellished the narrative because they wanted to bolster resistance and attract the attention of the Arab nations they hoped would help them; the Israeli left made exaggerated claims of brutality to accuse the Irgun and Lehi of blackening Israel's name by violating the Jewish principle of purity of arms; the Irgun themselves wanted to scare the Palestinian Arabs into flight.

After the dust had settled, studies concluded that 105 Palestinian Arabs and Arab insurgents had died in Deir Yassin, not the 250 reported. But the damage was already done. The reports of a massacre sparked terror amongst the Arabs, leading to a total collapse of morale. Many historians regard the incident as the single biggest catalyst for the Arabs' flight. By United Nations estimates, 750,000 Arabs had fled their homes by the end of the War of Independence, roughly 60 per cent of Palestine's pre-war Arab population.

Hazem Nusseibeh, an editor with the Palestine Broadcasting Service in 1948, admitted in a BBC documentary[11] about the

Arab-Israeli conflict that was aired in 1998 that he had fabricated allegations of a massacre and rapes at Deir Yassin on the direct instructions of Dr. Hussein Khalidi, Secretary of the Palestine Arab Higher Committee. Khalidi told him, "We must make the most of this", and so he embroidered press releases with fictional allegations that the children of Deir Yassin were murdered and pregnant women were raped. Their intention was to encourage the neighbouring Arab countries to join the battle against the Jews. He added that the stories of the atrocity were "our biggest mistake", because of the terror they created amongst the Arab Palestinians who consequently fled the country in large numbers. In the same programme, a former resident of Deir Yassin testified, "'We said, there was no rape.' But Khalidi said, 'We have to say this, so the Arab armies will come to liberate Palestine from the Jews.'" Despite evidence to the contrary, the myths surrounding Deir Yassin persist to this day and are often cited by anti-Israeli activists.

Four days later, a massacre did take place on the other side of Jerusalem. On the morning of 13 April 1948, a convoy carrying patients, medical staff and other hospital workers to the Hadassah hospital on Mount Scopus was stopped and attacked by a group of armed Arabs.

Following the announcement of the United Nations Partition Plan and in anticipation of Israel's declaration of independence, Arab troops had blocked all but one of the access routes to Hadassah Hospital and the Hebrew University campus on Mount Scopus. The only remaining access was via a narrow road, a mile and a half long, which passed through the Arab neighbourhood of Sheikh Jarrah, which the Arabs had seeded with mines that could be detonated from a distance. Arab sniper fire on vehicles moving along the access route had become a regular occurrence.

The hospital, which provided medical care for Jerusalem's 100,000 Jews, was dependent on supplies brought by convoy along this treacherous road. The British Colonial Secretary, Arthur Creech Jones, and the High Commissioner, Sir Alan Cunningham, had given assurances that the relief convoys would be given British protection. On 11 April, the regional British commander gave assurances the road was safe but noted that, in the shadow of the attack on Deir Yassin, tensions were running high. For the previous month, a tacit truce had been in place and the passage of convoys had taken place without serious incident. That truce was about to be obliterated as the Arab militia sought vengeance for Deir Yassin.

At 9.30 am on 13 April, with food and medical supplies dwindling at the hospital, a large convoy comprised of ten vehicles, including two ambulances, set out for the besieged hospital, marked by a "red shield", which should have guaranteed its neutrality. The convoy was accompanied by two lightly armoured Haganah trucks.

At 9.45 am, on a stretch of road in the Sheikh Jarrah quarter, a mine was detonated in front of the leading Haganah truck, forcing it into a ditch. At the same moment, the convoy came under raking fire from Arab forces. Five of the vehicles managed to back out of the ambush, including the second Haganah armoured truck, but the remainder of the convoy, now unarmed and defenceless, were trapped. Just 200 metres from the ambush site, a unit of twelve men from the British Highland Light Infantry were stationed, armed with a heavy machine gun, but they did nothing to intervene.

The attack on the helpless and stricken convoy continued unhindered throughout the day. In the early afternoon, two buses carrying medical staff were enveloped in flames when Molotov cocktails were hurled against them. There were only two survivors from the raging inferno that engulfed the buses, Shalom Nissan and Nathan Sandowsky; the others inside were charred beyond recognition. Sandowsky later testified that passing British convoys refused to help despite their desperate pleas and that he heard Arabs shouting, "for Deir Yassin."

Pleas for the British army to intervene were ignored. The Jewish liaison officer with the British army asked for permission to send in a Haganah relief force, but this was denied on the grounds it might interfere with a cease-fire negotiation. A British army officer, Major Jack Churchill, wanted to launch a rescue mission, but was forbidden by higher authorities. There were reports that ordinary British soldiers under orders not to intervene stood by and wept while the slaughter and carnage continued.

When the British army did eventually receive permission to intervene at 4.00 pm, 78 Jews had been killed by gunfire or burned to death when their vehicles were set on fire. Twenty-three were women. No one in the British army was ever held to account for the appalling loss of life which they could have prevented. Rumours soon began circulating that the Arabs had reached an understanding with the British whereby their operation would not be blocked as long as they refrained from firing on British units, though such stories were never investigated or substantiated. What seems certain is that the attack was motivated by a desire to exact revenge for the Deir Yassin assault four days earlier, and some have postulated that senior British officers allowed the Arabs to take their revenge so as to calm the rage of the Arab world.

The Hadassah convoy was not the only time the British army turned a blind eye to Jews being slaughtered. Even as the full extent of the Holocaust was being uncovered after the liberation of the death camps, Sir John Bagot Glubb, Commander in Chief of the Arab Legion had sent a memorandum to the Foreign Office which glibly stated that the suffering of a few hundred thousand Jews in Palestine, however lamentable that might be, was the price that had to be paid for the future well-being of the British Empire. It appears that the British government, with Earnest Bevin directing foreign affairs, was favourably disposed to follow his advice.

The British hindered Jewish preparations for the expected war with the Arabs by enforcing disarmament, a policy that was not strictly imposed on the Arabs. Bevin knew exactly what would happen to the Jewish community if it did not have the ability to defend itself after the British withdrawal. Based on an audit of military capability conducted by General Montgomery, it was widely assumed that the Jews would not be able to hold out for more than three weeks. No imagination was required to understand what the Arabs would then have done to the Jewish community.

British rule in the dying days of the Mandate was far from neutral. Britain was supplying arms to the Arab armies in the region, and British army officers were advising on training and tactics. Egypt acquired military hardware from Britain, including aircraft and tanks. Glubb was the Commander in Chief of the Jordanian army, supported by 39 British officers of other rank. The British fully expected the Jewish State to be overwhelmed by the neighbouring Arab armies and were placing themselves in a positioning from which they could take advantage of the opportunity that would be afforded to cement their influence in the region.

It is possible to understand, without offering excuse, the favorable position taken by Britain towards the Arabs over the Jews in 1939, but an explanation as to why this position was maintained after the war, in the shadow of the Holocaust, is required. Perception as to what constituted the best interests of the Empire was certainly one pernicious factor, but an altogether more malevolent reason is suggested from the testimony of James MacDonald, the first American Ambassador to Israel. MacDonald said that when he was in the presence of Earnest Bevin, he would hear Bevin ranting against the Jews in a very similar way that Hitler would rant against the Jews and, in some cases, MacDonald thought that Bevin was just as bad in his thinking. Bevin was fully aware that the Arabs were telling their people in Palestine that they were coming to exterminate the Jewish community, and his actions demonstrated that he was implicitly in agreement with that aim.

Taking a wider view of the Civil War, against expectations, the conflict resulted in a remarkably decisive victory for the Jews. They first proved that they could defend themselves, succeeding in consolidating their hold on a continuous strip of territory embracing the Coastal Plain, the Jezreel Valley, and the Jordan Valley. Then, as the Haganah was transformed from a poorly armed militia into a regular army capable of conducting brigade sized offensives, territorial continuity was established by wrestling control of mixed zones. Tiberias, Haifa, Safed, Beisan, Jaffa and Acre fell to the Haganah during an offensive called Plan Dalet.

Ben Gurion made conscription obligatory. Every Jewish man and woman in the country under the age of forty received military training. Thanks to funds raised by Golda Meir from sympathisers in the United States, and Stalin's decision to support the Zionist cause, the Jewish representatives of Palestine were able to purchase vital arms in Eastern Europe. Crucially, the Haganah was gaining the organisational structure, experience and confidence to confront the threatened invasion from neighbouring Arab states.

In comparison, the military capacity of the Palestinian Arabs had never recovered from the mauling they received from the British as they ruthlessly crushed the 1936-39 revolt, and their military capability was now plagued by an inability to organise and coordinate forces. Without cohesive leadership, Arab villages did not come to the help of their neighbouring Arab towns.

The Haganah's move to offensive operations towards the end of the conflict was accompanied by a huge exodus of Arab refugees who fled to neighbouring Arab states. This 'Palestinian exodus', which came to be referred to by the Arabs as the *Nakba*, meaning 'the Catastrophe', generated a considerable amount of press coverage at the time, and its cause remains a controversial topic among Middle East commentators today.

Some attribute responsibility for the *Nakba* to the Arab authorities for issuing instructions to escape with the promise that the refugees could repopulate the land in a matter of weeks after the Arab armies had exterminated the fledgling Israeli state. Iraqi Prime Minister, Nuri as-Said, is quoted as saying, "We will smash the country with our guns and obliterate every place the Jews shelter in. The Arabs should conduct their wives and children to safe areas until the fighting has died down."[12] In his memoirs, Khaled al Azm, Prime Minister of Syria from 1948 to 1949, admitted: "Since 1948 we have been demanding the return of the refugees to their homes. But we ourselves are the ones who encouraged them to leave. Only a few months separated our call to them to leave and our appeal to the United Nations to resolve their return."[13]

Others argue that a policy of expulsion was implemented by Haganah. There is little evidence to support the view that such a policy was generally implemented on a wide scale, though it is entirely plausible that some local commanders may have taken matters into their own hands. Based on belief that Arabs were forcibly displaced, the term '*Nakba*' has become a synonym for Palestinian victimhood; in reality this designation only serves to turn failed aggressors into hapless victims. Significantly, the international press reported extensively on the Arab flight at the time but made no reference to any forcible expulsions by Jewish forces.

Others reject both these assumptions and instead view the *Nakba* as the cumulative effect of many contributing factors – psychological, military and political – which combined to destroy all hope in the hearts of the Arab population and cause a complete collapse in morale. Joseph Schectman, author of *The Arab Refugee Problem*, argued that fear of reprisals played a significant role in the Arab flight, "Arab warfare against the Jews in Palestine had always been marked by indiscriminate killing, mutilating, raping, looting and pillaging ... no quarter whatsoever had ever been given to a Jew who fell into Arab hands ... The Arab population of Palestine expected nothing less than massacres in retaliation if the Jews were victorious."[14] Many Arabs living in Hebron and Safed fled in fear that the Haganah might exact revenge for the massacres of 1929.

My own view is that the *Nakba* was largely a self-inflicted defeat by the Arabs. All wars create refugees, and the suffering of these is a catastrophe, but it is the aggressor who precipitates the conflict that carries the responsibility for their misery. The Arab-Israeli conflicts of 1947–48 were fuelled by Arab governments who rejected the UN plan and encouraged a 'war of extermination and momentous massacre' against the Jews, but who were ultimately defeated.

Jews and their supporters believed that the re-creation of the Jewish State in her ancient homeland was nothing short of a God ordained miracle, the fulfilment of Ezekiel's evocative vision of the valley of dry bones reforming into a vast living army (Ezekiel 37:1-14). After the desolation of the valley death that was the Holocaust the nation of Israel began to breathe again.

On 14 May 1948, as the British Mandate came to an inglorious end, an important milestone in the fulfilment of that miracle took place. The last British High Commissioner, Sir Alan Gordon Cunningham, departed from Government House at 8.00 am and headed for Haifa. That afternoon, as he boarded a Royal Navy warship, the Union Jack flying over Haifa Harbour was lowered, symbolically signalling the end of the British Mandate. At 4.00 pm in Tel Aviv, the leaders of the Jewish Community, led by David Ben Gurion, gathered together to declare the rebirth of the State of Israel.

The Declaration of Independence began by highlighting how the land of Israel was the birthplace of the Jewish people, the never ceasing hope for their return from dispersion among the nations and the restoration of national freedom, and the strivings of those who, in recent decades, had reclaimed a wilderness, revived their language, built cities and villages, and established a vigorous and ever-growing community. The Declaration continued:

"In the year 1897 the first Zionist Congress, inspired by Theodore Herzl's vision of a Jewish state, proclaimed the right of the Jewish people to a national revival in their own country.

This right was acknowledged by the Balfour Declaration of November 2, 1917, and reaffirmed by the mandate of the League of Nations, which gave explicit international recognition to the historic connection of the Jewish people with Palestine and their right to reconstitute their national home.

... The Nazi holocaust which engulfed millions of Jews in Europe proved anew the urgency of the re-establishment of the Jewish state, which would solve the problem of Jewish homelessness by opening the gates to all Jews and lifting the Jewish people to equality in the family of nations.

Survivors of the European catastrophe as well as Jews from other lands, claiming their right to a life of dignity, freedom and labour, and undeterred by hazards, hardships and obstacles, have tried unceasingly to enter Palestine.

... On November 29, 1947, the General Assembly of United Nations adopted a resolution for re-establishment of an independent Jewish state in Palestine and called upon inhabitants of the country to take such steps as may be necessary on their part to put the plan into effect.

... The state of Israel will promote the development of the country for the benefit of all its inhabitants; will be based on precepts of liberty, justice and peace taught by the Hebrew prophets; will uphold the full social and political equality of all its citizens without distinction of race, creed or sex; will guarantee full freedom of conscience, worship, education and culture; will safeguard the sanctity and inviolability of shrines and holy places of all religions."

The Declaration concluded with a plea to the Arab inhabitants of the state of Israel to return to play their part in the development of the state with full and equal citizenship, an offer of peace and amity to all neighbouring states, and finally a call to "the Jewish people all over the world to rally to our side in the task of immigration and development, and to stand by us in the great struggle for the fulfilment of the dream of generations – the redemption of Israel."

The very next day, as predicted, the Arab-Israeli war began as five Arab armies from Egypt, Transjordan, Syria, Lebanon and Iraq invaded the infant State of Israel. Their attempt to annihilate the Jewish State at its birth failed. By the end of the war Israel, in addition to the territory assigned by the United Nations for the creation of a Jewish state, was also in control of much of the Mandatory territory which had been assigned by the United Nations for the creation of an Arab state. The remainder was divided between Jordan and Egypt. Hundreds of thousands of Arab civilians had become displaced.

The prophet Jeremiah proclaimed, *"Hear the word of the LORD, you nations; proclaim it in distant coastlands: 'He who scattered Israel will gather them and will watch over his flock like a shepherd'"* (Jeremiah 31:10). This is a message from God to the nations other than Israel, declaring that He is at work. As He scattered His ancient people Israel among the nations, so He would gather them back. The Word of God is certain to come to pass, and the warning to the nations is to take care not to interfere with the outworking of His purposes.

Britain's ambivalence towards fulfilling its obligations to create a national home for the Jews at the outset of the Mandate over Palestine resulted in the deaths of an inestimable number of Jews who could have escaped from the Holocaust had the gates of Palestine been opened as they should have been. Limitations on Jewish immigration continued to be imposed during and after the Second World War. Displaced death camp survivors, who had no other place to call home, were forcefully prevented from entering Mandatory Palestine and, quite incredibly, interned behind barbed-wire fences. They could not be returned from where they came because they had no citizenship of any other country. By the end of the Mandate, British government officials and senior military commanders, motivated in some cases by deeply rooted anti-Semitic prejudice, were actively supporting the enemies of the Jews who were planning to crush the State of Israel. It was entirely futile, for no power on earth can thwart the purposes of God, but how would God judge Britain for her disgraceful, perfidious and morally bankrupt conduct?

As the British Mandate over Palestine ended, and the Union Jack was symbolically lowered over Haifa harbour, it was flying upside down. The flag is not reflectively symmetrical and when deliberately flown inverted it is a signal that indicates a situation of distress. Was the inversion of the Union Jack at Haifa merely a coincidental act of carelessness or was it a prophetic sign of distress for the British Empire? According to Scripture, God made a promise to Abraham, the father of the Jewish nation, *"I will bless those who bless you, and whoever curses you I will curse"* (Genesis 12:3). Britain had been granted an opportunity to be a nation that were a blessing to the children of Abraham in a similar way to the great Persian king Cyrus and began well by generously supporting the creation of a Jewish national home, but ultimately, they betrayed the Jews in pursuit of their own imperialist agenda. What would this mean for Britain in light of God's promise to Abraham?

Endnotes

1. Cited from Howard Sachar, *A History of Israel from the Rise of Zionism to Our Time*, 2nd Ed (New York: Knopf, 1996), p. 296.
2. *Palestine: memorandum by the Secretary of State for Foreign Affairs*, CAB 129/21, C.P. (47) 259, 18 September 1947.
3. Cited from Michael J Cohen, *Palestine to Israel: From Mandate to Independence* (Abingdon: Frank Cass, 1988), p. 237.
4. *Official Records of the General Assembly, Second Session, Ad-Hoc Committee on the Palestinian Question*, Doc A/AC 14/32 (1947), pp. 276ff.
5. Cited from Martin Gilbert, *Israel: A History* (London: Black Swan, 2008), p. 153.
6. David Bennett & Efraim Karsh, *Azzam's Genocidal Threat*, 18(4) Mid. E. Q. 85, 87 (2011).
7. *United Nations Special Commission, First Special Report to the Security Council: The Problem of Security in Palestine* (16 February 1948), Sec II.6.
8. Transcribed from the DVD "*The Forsaken Promise*" by Hugh Kitson [DVD], 2007, Hatikvah Film Trust.
9. Ibid.
10. Ibid.
11. "Israel and the Arabs: The 50 Year Conflict", BBC, 1998.
12. Cited from Myron Kaufman, *The Coming Destruction of Israel* (New York: The American Library Inc., 1970), p. 26-27.
13. *The Memoirs of Haled al Azm* (Beirut, 1973), Part 1, pp. 386-387.
14. Joseph B. Schectman, *The Arab Refugee Problem* (New York: Philosophical Library, 1952), p. 5-6.

CHAPTER 11

THE RISE OF ISRAEL

> *In Israel, a land lacking in natural resources, we learned to appreciate our greatest national advantage: our minds. Through creativity and innovation, we transformed barren deserts into flourishing fields and pioneered new frontiers in science and technology"*
>
> —SHIMON PERES

Within hours of David Ben Gurion and the leaders of the Jewish Community declaring a new independent State of Israel in the territory assigned by the United Nations partition plan, the leaders of both superpowers, US President Harry S. Truman and Soviet leader Joseph Stalin, formally recognized Israel. Britain, having abstained when the United Nations voted to adopt the partition plan, rather conspicuously did not recognize Israel. Neither, to no one's surprise, did the Arab League of Nations. On 15 May 1948, the day after Israel's declaration of independence, the Arab League member states of Egypt, Transjordan, Syria, Lebanon, Saudi

Arabia, Yemen and Iraq, along with volunteers from Pakistan, Sudan, the Arab Liberation Army and the Muslim Brotherhood marched their forces into what had, until the previous day, been British Mandatory Palestine, proclaiming the right of self-determination for Arabs across the whole of Palestine. And so began the first Arab–Israeli War.

Israel's position was precarious, occupying a narrow strip of land with no strategic depth for defence. British surveys of military capability had estimated that a newly formed Jewish state would not survive for more than three weeks against such a large-scale assault. The American CIA also believed that the Arab states would triumph in case of war. Confident generals in Egypt told their government that the invasion would be "a parade without any risks" and that they would reach Tel Aviv "in two weeks."[1] The Arab Liberation Army field commander Fawzi-al-Qawuqji, who allied to Nazi Germany during World War II, vowed to "drive all Jews into the sea." Three days before the invasion, David Ben Gurion was told by his chief military advisers that Israel's chances of winning a war against the Arab states were only about even. Significantly, however, the Palestinian Arabs, chastened by their experiences during the 1947 civil war, had developed a healthy and demoralising respect for the Jewish community's military capability and, if it came to battle, they expected to lose.

The powerful Egyptian army possessed heavy military equipment, including armoured vehicles, tanks and aircraft supplied by Britain. The army of Transjordan was led and advised by experienced British officers; Sir John Bagot Glubb was Commander in Chief and dozens of British officers resigned their commissions to join with Glubb in Jordan. By contrast, at the outset of war the Jewish forces had no heavy armaments at their disposal. They could not legally purchase any armaments before 15 May because they were not until then a recognized state.

Remarkably, against all international expectation, once battle was joined, Israel stood firm despite some initial loss of territory. Two weeks into the war, on 29 May 1948, the British government initiated United Nations Security Council Resolution 50 declaring an arms embargo in the region. In effect, this ensured that the Arab armies, who Britain supported, would retain their armament superiority by denying Israel the possibility of reaching parity. Furthermore, this regional arms embargo shamefully established a moral equivalence between invader and defender, rewarding the aggressor while punishing the intended victim. Czechoslovakia violated the resolution, supplying the Jewish state with critical military hardware in an airborne arms smuggling mission code-named Operation Balak. Included in these clandestine shipments were Avia S-199 fighter aircraft and heavy machine guns.

British interest, which was formulated by Earnest Bevin, was to control as much territory as possible in the wake of the conflict. Bevin believed that the best means of doing so was through Abdullah, King of Jordan, since a Mufti-led Palestinian state was unacceptable to Whitehall, given the nefarious activities of Haj Amin al-Husseini during the war after he joined the Nazi camp. Bevin and his key advisers also wanted the Negev to be controlled by Jordan and Egypt. They wanted Haifa to be an international zone with special rights for Jordan. The effect would have been to create a very small rump Jewish state as in the 1937 Peel Commission plan whose viability would have been in serious doubt. However, Bevin considered, "It would be too high a price to pay for the friendship of Israel to jeopardize, by estranging the Arabs, either the base in Egypt or the Middle Eastern oil."[2]

In preparation for the declaration of independence, Ben Gurion had united the Haganah with the Palmach, Irgun and Lehi to form the Israeli Defense Forces (IDF). With the gates of Israel finally flung open, large numbers of Jewish immigrants, many of them World War II veterans or Holocaust survivors, flooded into the fledgling state where those able, both men and women, immediately enlisted. They were fighting for the survival of Israel, for their hope, for their own homeland against apparently insurmountable odds, after centuries of oppression and persecution which had culminated in the horror of the Holocaust. There was nowhere to which they could retreat. Rarely had history witnessed such a highly motivated fighting force. By 11 June, the Arab advance had been stalled, and the United Nations negotiated a month-long truce.

By the time hostilities resumed, Israel had established an air force, a navy, and a tank battalion. On 29 June 1948, the day before the last British troops left Haifa, British soldiers sympathetic to the Israeli cause stole two Cromwell tanks from a depot near Haifa harbour, smashing their way through the unguarded gates, and joined the IDF. These two tanks would form the basis of the Israeli Armoured Corps. With remarkable ingenuity, the Israelis supplemented the Cromwell tanks by building three functioning Sherman tanks from spare parts found in abandoned British ordnance depots. In addition to the aircraft supplied by Czechoslovakia, the Israeli air force was supplemented with civilian aircraft converted for military purposes. Many of the pilots were World War II veterans who had enlisted in the RAF as Israeli citizens the fight against the Luftwaffe.

Considering the odds, stopping the initial Arab advance had been a staggering achievement, testimony to the sheer determination of the Jews to defend their land. Then, to the astonishment of observers, when hostilities resumed in July the tide turned in favour of Israel as the IDF switched from a strategy of defence to offense, pushing the Arab armies out of the land assigned to Israel in the partition plan and conquering some territories that had been included in the proposed Arab state.

On 1 December, King Abdullah announced the union of Transjordan with an Arab region of Palestine west of the Jordan River, known today as the 'West Bank'; Britain and Pakistan were the only nations that formally recognized this annexation. The territory occupied by Transjordan included East Jerusalem, which contained the Old City, the Judean hills and Samaria.

Armistice agreements were reached with each of the chastened Arab states between February and July 1949, though no formal peace agreements were signed. By the time that a permanent ceasefire came into effect, Israel had expanded her borders, establishing what came to be known as the Green Line. These borders were never formally recognized as international boundaries at the insistence of the Arab states. The IDF had overrun Galilee, the Jezreel Valley, West Jerusalem, the coastal plain and the Negev. The Syrians remained in control of a strip of territory along the Sea of Galilee originally allocated to the Jewish state, the Lebanese occupied a tiny area at Rosh Hanikra, and the Egyptians retained the Gaza strip. Jordanian forces remained in occupation of the 'West Bank', which they had annexed, and East Jerusalem, which included the Old City and the Western Wall.

On 11 May 1949, Israel was admitted as a member state of the United Nations. With the ceasefire holding, Britain finally released the remaining Jewish detainees held in Cyprus and formally recognized the state of Israel. From a population numbering 650,000, Israel had lost some 6,000 men and women who were killed during the conflict.

The Suez Crisis

There was to be little respite for Israel. They were soon embroiled in another major international crisis which erupted in 1956, when Gamal Abdel Nasser, the pro-Soviet President of Egypt, nationalised the Suez Canal and blockaded the Gulf of Aqaba, preventing Israeli access to the Red Sea. The British and French, who co-owned the Suez Canal, colluded with Israel to create a pretext for regaining control of Suez and overthrowing Nasser. Their plan was for Israel to attack Egypt in response to which Anglo-French forces would invade to restore order and seize the Canal.

On 29 October 1956, Israeli forces, commanded by General Moshe Dayan, attacked Egypt as pre-arranged. Within a matter of days they had overrun the Sinai, and on 5 November the Anglo-French invasion of Suez began.

The United Nations vehemently denounced the actions of Israel, Britain and France, demanding a ceasefire which came into effect on 7 November. At Egypt's request, an Emergency Force (UNEF), consisting of 6,000 peacekeeping troops drawn from 10 nations, was created to supervise the ceasefire. After receiving guarantees of freedom of access to the Suez Canal and the Gulf of Aqaba, the Israelis withdrew to the Negev.

Nasser emerged from the conflict as the clear victor, having strengthened his political grip in the region and seeing his popularity sky-rocket. More significantly, however, the conflict resulted in complete humiliation for the British and French and signalled the end of their imperial dominance in the Middle East.

From an Israeli perspective two important lessons were learnt: militarily, they now knew that with air superiority they could conquer the Sinai Peninsula in a matter of days without British or French support; politically, they learnt that they had only a limited time frame within which to operate militarily before international pressure would restrict Israel's freedom of action. Both lessons would shape Israel's response when faced with another Nasser-inspired crisis a decade later.

The Six Day War

In contravention of the 1949 Armistice agreement, the Jordanian army denied the Jews access to East Jerusalem. Every Jew was expelled from the original Old City and, in order to ensure that Jews would never return to East Jerusalem, Jordanian occupation forces destroyed their homes, synagogues and violated the Jewish cemetery by building army latrines over the ancient grave stones. And so, from the last day of the British Mandate, the Jews had not been able to pray at the Western Wall. On 15 May 1967, the night after Israel's nineteenth Independence Day celebrations, the first public performance of Naomi Shemer's hauntingly beautiful song "Jerusalem of Gold" took place at an Israeli music festival. The song described the Jewish people's 2,000-year longing to return to Jerusalem and over the next few weeks it dominated the Israeli airwaves.

Traditionally, Jerusalem had always been the focus of longing for Diaspora Jews who were forced from their land and the Temple. Psalm 137 is the well-known lament of the Babylonian Jews who wept *"by the rivers of Babylon"* as they remembered Zion and declared, *"If I forget you, O Jerusalem, let my right hand wither."* At the conclusion of every Passover Seder, Jews utter the phrase "next year in Jerusalem" as an expression of future hope. Only three weeks after "Jerusalem of Gold" was released, the Six-Day War broke out, and the song became a morale-boosting battle cry for the Israeli Defense Forces.

Tensions between Israel and Syria had been escalating steadily in the years preceding, marked by frequent border clashes. The rulers of Damascus had transformed the Golan Heights into an extensive military base brimming with bunkers, trenches and artillery positions all pointed south towards northern Israel. Civilians were not permitted to live there, save for a few Druze villages. From these commanding fortifications overlooking the Galilee Syrian artillery routinely terrorized the Jewish Kibbutzim with shelling and took target practice at fishermen on the Kinneret. Syrian engineers had begun from 1964 constructing trenches to divert the headwaters of the Jordan River from flowing into the

Sea of Galilee in an attempt to disrupt Israel's water supply. As the Syrian military bombardment and terrorist attacks intensified, the United Nations did nothing to curb Syrian aggression – even a mild Security Council resolution expressing "regret" for such incidents was vetoed by the Soviet Union. Meanwhile, Israel was condemned by the United Nations whenever she retaliated.

With Syria thus taking the lead in the fight against Israel and Nasser's popularity on the wane, the Egyptian president became determined to resume a belligerent stance towards Israel to wrestle back prestige. His rhetoric became increasingly bellicose, and in 1965 he announced, "We shall not enter Palestine with its soil covered in sand; we shall enter it with its soil saturated in blood."[3]

From mid-May 1967, Egypt and Syria ominously began amassing troops along the Israeli borders, and Egypt closed the Straits of Tiran to Israeli shipping, tantamount to a declaration of war. Nasser demanded that the UNEF, established to secure an end to the Suez crisis, evacuate immediately from Sinai, and threatened an escalation to full scale war. Egyptian radio broadcasts talked about a coming genocide. The Voice of the Arabs radio station proclaimed on 18 May 1967: "As of today, there no longer exists an international emergency force to protect Israel. We shall exercise patience no more. We shall not complain any more to the UN about Israel. The sole method we shall apply against Israel is total war, which will result in the extermination of Zionist existence."[4] An enthusiastic echo was heard on 20 May from Syrian Defence Minister Hafez Assad: "Our forces are now entirely ready not only to repulse the aggression, but to initiate the act of liberation itself, and to explode the Zionist presence in the Arab homeland. The Syrian army, with its finger on the trigger, is united ... I, as a military man, believe that the time has come to enter into a battle of annihilation."[5] On 26 May, Nasser declared, "The battle will be a general one and our basic objective will be to destroy Israel."[6]

Caught between the posturing of Egypt and Syria, the more moderate King Hussein of Jordan, in occupation of the 'West Bank', was forced by geopolitical realities to join their coalition against Israel. Hussein signed a defence pact with Egypt on 30 May. A triumphalist Nasser then announced: "The armies of Egypt, Jordan, Syria and Lebanon are poised on the borders of Israel … to face the challenge, while standing behind us are the armies of Iraq, Algeria, Kuwait, Sudan and the whole Arab nation. This act will astound the world. Today they will know that the Arabs are arranged for battle, the critical hour has arrived. We have reached the stage of serious action and not declarations."[7] President Abdur Rahman Aref of Iraq joined in the war of words: "The existence of Israel is an error which must be rectified. This is our opportunity to wipe out the ignominy which has been with us since 1948. Our goal is clear – to wipe Israel off the map."[8]

Israel responded to the crisis by calling up its civilian reserves and setting up a national unity coalition, including for the first time Menachem Begin's party, Herut, which would later merge into the Likud party. During a national radio broadcast, Prime Minister Levi Eshkol stammered, causing widespread fear in Israel. Talk in the streets from Tel Aviv to Jerusalem was of a return to the terror experienced in Auschwitz and the death camps. To calm public concern Moshe Dayan (Chief of Staff during the Suez crisis) was appointed Defence Minister.

Levi Eshkol spent several tense weeks exhausting all avenues of diplomacy in an effort to avert war. His attempts proved fruitless. Alone, without support from the international community and facing an existential threat that was growing more critical with each passing day, the Israeli government took decisive action, fearing that further delay would have catastrophic consequences for their odds of survival. At dawn on 5 June 1967, the Israeli air force launched a brilliantly executed pre-emptive strike, arriving over Egyptian airbases just minutes after the Egyptian dawn patrol had landed and while its pilots were at breakfast. The Egyptian air force was caught by total surprise and most of its aircraft were destroyed on the ground. Jordanian radar had detected Israeli aircraft taking off and heading out over the Mediterranean, and urgent warnings of an imminent strike were broadcast to her ally, but the communication was accompanied by an outdated codeword which Egyptian commanders did not recognize – the Egyptians had introduced a new codeword for that day but they had not apprised their Jordanian allies of the change – and so the warning went unheeded. Later that day, having decimated the Egyptian air force, Israeli pilots won decisive victories in aerial duels against their Jordanian and Syrian counterparts.

With total air dominance assured, the battle then moved to the ground, and some of history's greatest tank battles were fought between Egyptian and Israeli armour in the blast-furnace conditions of the Sinai desert. The result was the same as the Suez crisis – Egyptian forces in the Sinai, deprived of air support, were destroyed in a matter of days.

Without the resources to fight simultaneously on multiple fronts, Israel made passionate appeals to Jordan to stay out of the war, but to no avail. Jordanian forces fired artillery barrages from Tel Aviv to Jerusalem. Although Israel did not initially respond, not wanting to open a Jordanian front in the war, Jordan continued to attack and occupied the United Nations headquarters in Jerusalem, forcing Israel to fight back. Paratrooper Brigade 55, commanded by Lt. General Mordechai 'Motta' Gur, was sent to Jerusalem and given the impossible task of preparing an assault on the city in just 12 hours. When the paratroopers arrived, raging fires were consuming buildings and the streets were littered with shattered glass. A hazy cloud of smoke from the fires and dust fragments from shell blasts was clinging to the cityscape, creating a surreal atmosphere. Suddenly, out of the destruction, people began to appear from all directions. One of the young paratroopers, Avital Geva, recalled, "They didn't care about the bombings. Women brought food, sweets, coffee, everything. You cannot describe it. It was spontaneous love."[9]

Jordan had committed two battalions of experienced elite soldiers to their assault on the city. The battle fought by the Paratroopers to dislodge them raged for two days, with heavy casualties on both sides. Gradually, after ferocious close-quarter combat, Israeli forces encircled the Old City.

On 7 June 1967, Motta Gur's paratroopers entered the Old City via the Lions' Gate and advanced toward the Temple Mount and the Western Wall, bringing Jerusalem's holiest site under Jewish control for the first time in nearly 2000 years. There are sound recordings of the scene, as Motta Gur announced to his company commanders via loudspeakers, "We're sitting right now on the ridge and we're seeing the Old City. Shortly we're going to go into the Old City of Jerusalem, that all generations have dreamed about. We will be the first to enter the Old City."[10] Motta Gur personally led the charge up to the Temple Mount. A short time later, the crackling radio set at Headquarters burst into life as Motta Gur declared, "The Temple Mount is in our hands! I repeat, the Temple Mount is in our hands and our forces are by the (Western) Wall."[11]

One of the first soldiers to reach the Wall, Zion Karasenti, spoke of the moment 50 years later: "After the 48 hours of battle, we were tired and sweaty, our uniforms were dusty and bloodied, but when we walked down the stairs and saw the stones of the Western Wall, a lot of our guys started crying. It was an extraordinary thing, it's hard to describe."[12] General Rabbi Shlomo Goren, chief chaplain of the IDF, sounded the shofar at the Western Wall to signify its liberation. To Israelis and Jews all over the world, this was a joyous and momentous occasion. Many considered it a gift from God.

For the first time since the end of the British Mandate, Jews could visit the Old City of Jerusalem and pray at the Western Wall. The four-metre wide public alley beside the Wall was later expanded into a massive plaza and worshippers were allowed to sit, or use other furniture, for the first time in centuries.

By 11 June, all Arab forces were routed and a cease-fire was called for by United Nations Security Council Resolutions 235 and 236. The war had resulted in a stunning victory for Israel, victory of a magnitude regarded as miraculous by Jews and Christian supporters of Israel. The international reputation of the IDF as a fighting force to be feared had been secured. In addition to East Jerusalem and the Old City, Israel had gained control of the Sinai Peninsula, the Gaza Strip, the Golan Heights, and the formerly Jordanian-controlled 'West Bank' of the Jordan River. In Hebron, Jews gained access to the Cave of the Patriarchs for the first time since the 14th Century. A third Jewish holy site, Rachel's Tomb in Bethlehem, also became accessible. Once more, taking a line from Shemer's "Jerusalem of Gold", the Jews were able to go down from Jerusalem to the Dead Sea by way of Jericho.

On 22 November 1967, the United Nations Security Council adopted Resolution 242, the "land for peace" formula, which called for the establishment of a just and lasting peace based on Israeli withdrawal from territory – though not all the territories – captured during the war in exchange for the end of all states of belligerency, respect for the sovereignty of all states in the area, and the right to live in peace within secure, recognized boundaries. The resolution implicitly acknowledged that Israel has legitimate territorial claims to at least part of the captured territories. The resolution was accepted by both sides, albeit with different interpretations, and has been the basis of all subsequent peace negotiations.

The Yom Kippur War

In October 1973, the Yom Kippur War, or October War, erupted when Egypt and Syria, smarting from their humiliation in the Six Day War, formed an alliance to launch a surprise attack on Israeli positions in the Sinai and the Golan Heights, on the Day of Atonement, the holiest day in Judaism. Neither specifically planned to destroy Israel, although the Israeli leaders could not be sure of that.

The war began with a large-scale Egyptian crossing of the Suez Canal after which Egyptian forces advanced virtually unopposed into the Sinai Peninsula. It took Israel, who had been caught off guard, three days to mobilize its reserve forces and halt the Egyptian offensive.

Syria coordinated their attack on the Golan Heights to coincide with the Egyptian offensive and initially made threatening inroads into Israeli-held territory. Israel could only muster 180 tanks against an invasion force of 1200 Syrian tanks. After a rapid deployment of reserves, however, Israeli forces succeeded in pushing the Syrians back to the pre-war ceasefire lines within three days. The IDF then launched a counter-offensive deep into Syria. Within a week, Israeli artillery began shelling the outskirts of Damascus.

As Egyptian President Anwar Sadat began to fret about the integrity of his ally, he calculated that capturing two strategic passes located deeper in the Sinai would make his position stronger during post-war negotiations. He therefore ordered two Egyptian army groups to go back on the offensive, but their attack was quickly repulsed. The Israelis counter-attacked at the seam between the two Egyptian armies, crossed the Suez Canal into Egypt, and began advancing southward and westward during a week of bitter fighting that resulted in heavy casualties on both sides.

Egypt was only saved from a crushing defeat when the Soviets invited US Secretary of State Henry Kissinger to Moscow and negotiated terms for ending the war through a UN Security Council Resolution. The United Nations, which had failed to act while the tide was in the Arabs' favour, now acted to save them at the behest of the superpowers. On 22 October 1973, the Security Council adopted Resolution 338 calling for "all parties to the present fighting to cease all firing and terminate all military activity immediately." The vote came on the day that Israeli forces completed an encirclement that isolated the Egyptian Third Army and the city of Suez, placing them in a position to destroy it.

The war had far-reaching implications. Despite impressive operational and tactical achievements on the battlefield, Israel had been caught unprepared and came perilously close to disaster in the early stages of the conflict. Recognition that there was no guarantee that Israel would always dominate the Arab states militarily paved the way for negotiations that led to the first peaceful recognition of Israel by an Arab country.

On 17 September 1978, Israel and Egypt signed a peace treaty on the lawn of the White House in Washington, DC. Israeli Prime Minister Menachem Begin, despite intense opposition from within his own Likud Party, agreed to return to Egypt the strategically important Sinai Peninsula, 91 percent of the territory won by Israel during the Six-Day war, in exchange for Anwar Sadat's promise to make peace. In recognition of his willingness to join Sadat in making compromises for peace, Begin shared the 1978 Nobel Peace Prize with the Egyptian leader.

The Israeli-Palestinian Conflict

A final settlement to the Israeli-Palestinian conflict has proven to be more elusive. A popular uprising, known as 'intifada' (Arabic for 'shaking off'), began in 1987 as Palestinian Arabs protested violently against Israeli settlements in the 'West Bank'. However, alongside the violence, a political pragmatism began to crystallise. The Palestinian National Council finally accepted the two-state solution in 1988, as envisaged by the United Nations resolution 181 in 1947. It renounced terrorism and started to seek a negotiated settlement based on Resolution 242, which called for Israel to withdraw from territory captured in the Six-Day War.

Following secret talks facilitated by the Norwegian government, Israeli Prime Minister Yitzhak Rabin and Palestine Liberation Organization (PLO) negotiator Mahmoud Abbas signed a 'Declaration of Principles' on Interim Self-Government Arrangements, commonly referred to as the "Oslo Accord", at the White House in September 1993. Israel accepted the PLO as the representative of the Palestinians, and the PLO renounced terrorism and recognized Israel's right to exist in peace. Both sides agreed to a five-year transitional period in which Israeli forces would withdraw from disputed territories and in which a Palestinian Authority (PA) would be established and assume governmental responsibilities in the 'West Bank' and Gaza Strip. After this, permanent status talks on the issues of borders, refugees and Jerusalem would be held. The Oslo agreement was followed by an Israeli–Jordan peace treaty which was concluded on 26 October 1994 without Palestinian involvement.

The "Oslo II Accord", signed in September 1995, divided the 'West Bank' into separate areas under Israeli control, Palestinian control, and Israeli military responsibility with Palestinian civil administration, respectively. Oslo II also spelled out provisions for elections, civil and legal affairs, and other bilateral Israeli–Palestinian cooperation on various issues, the most important of which were the borders of Israel and Palestine, the Israeli settlements, the status of Jerusalem, the question of Israel's military presence in and control over the remaining territories, and the Palestinian right of return. The Oslo Accords, however, fell short of creating a Palestinian state, leaving open the question of whether Palestinian self-determination could be achieved by alternative means.

The agreement was denounced by hard-liners among both the Israelis and Palestinians as a sell-out and talks on the process of implementation quickly stalled. US President Bill Clinton brought together Yasser Arafat, a relative of Haj Amin al-Husseini,[13] and Israeli Prime Minister Ehud Barak for talks at Camp David in 2000 in an effort to revive the agreement, but these talks broke down over the final-status issues of Jerusalem and the future of Palestinian refugees.

Most accounts of the Camp David summit, and the months of Israeli-Palestinian negotiations that followed, talk of Barak making a series of unprecedented offers, each of which were met with an uncompromising "no" by Arafat. The failure to reach a final agreement is therefore attributed, without notable dissent, to Arafat. Barak portrayed Arafat's behaviour as a "performance geared to exact as many Israeli concessions as possible without ever seriously intending to reach a peace settlement or sign an end to the conflict."[14] President Clinton also blamed Arafat after the failure of the talks, stating, "I regret that in 2000 Arafat missed the opportunity to bring that nation into being and pray for the day when the dreams of the Palestinian people for a state and a better life will be realized in a just and lasting peace."[15] Clinton was said to have been enraged with the Palestinians over their refusal to make compromises or counter offers.

Opposition to the Oslo agreement was led on the Palestinian side by the Islamist militant group Hamas who incited a deadly campaign of suicide bombing, the 'Second Intifada', during which dozens of Israeli civilians were killed. Having passed on the opportunity for peace at Camp David, Arafat pursued this path of terror in hopes of creating pressure on the Israelis and repositioning the

Palestinians as victims in the eyes of the world. His strategy has proven to be largely effective, particularly amongst left-wing progressives who are pre-conditioned by their worldview to regard Israel, with its strong sense of national identity and capitalist culture, as the oppressor irrespective of the objective reality. Israeli counter-strikes against the terrorists killed many Palestinians and the parts of the 'West Bank' from which Israel had withdrawn were swiftly re-occupied. Although Israel was acting to protect her own citizens and the majority of Palestinian casualties were combatants, these responses fuelled narratives of Israeli aggression. Israeli academic Efraim Karsh described the Oslo Accords as "the starkest strategic blunder in [Israel's] history," creating the conditions for "the bloodiest and most destructive confrontation between Israelis and Palestinians since 1948" and radicalizing "a new generation of Palestinians" living under the rule of the PA and Hamas with "vile anti-Jewish (and anti-Israel) incitement unparalleled in scope and intensity since Nazi Germany."[16]

The battles for the state of Israel's existence stretch beyond those contested with rockets, bullets and terrorist bombs. Israel has also been forced to withstand a blizzard of propaganda and information warfare designed to bring about its economic, cultural and political isolation. The origins of these assaults can be traced to September 2001 when a forum of NGOs was convened in Durban, South Africa, under the auspices of the United Nations World Conference against racism. More than 1500 organizations were represented. The conference attained infamy for the appalling racism that marred an event that was supposed to combat such conduct. Posters displaying Jewish caricatures were placed alongside Nazi icons, and participants circulated copies of the notorious anti-Semitic fabrication, *Protocols of the Elders of Zion*. Tom Lantos, a US Congressman and Holocaust survivor who was present at the conference, commented, "the occasion was hijacked by hate-filled and venomous leaders who perverted the noble idea of ending racism, and turned the conference into a lynch mob against Israel ... Having experienced the horrors of the Holocaust firsthand, this was the most sickening and unabashed display of hate for Jews I had seen since the Nazi period."[17]

Against this backdrop, the conference adopted a resolution that defined Israel as a "racist, apartheid state" and called for the launch of a "global solidarity campaign" targeting governments, the United Nations and civil society to achieve the "complete and total isolation of Israel." This co-ordinated attack on Israel's very existence and legitimacy has become the vehicle through which new generations of thought leaders, often naively ignorant of the campaign's insidious roots, are exposed to the characterization of the Jewish state as a uniquely wicked, unjust project that must be unwound for the good of humanity.

During the Second Intifada, the 'Road Map for Peace' was introduced, which explicitly called for a two-state solution and the establishment of an independent Palestinian state living side by side with Israel in peace. The 'Road Map' plan was proposed by the United States, the European Union, Russia and the United Nations. A draft version of the plan was published by the administration of George W. Bush on 14 November 2002, and a final text was released on 30 April 2003. However, as happened with the Oslo Accords, talks on the process rapidly reached a state of deadlock and the plan was never implemented, though the United Nations remain committed to it as a solution.

The Road Map plan was devised while Israel was engaged in decisive action to crush Arab terrorism during the Second Intifada, and from a cynical viewpoint it represents an attempt to appease Arabs at a time when the Bush administration was launching its own war on terror in Iraq.

In 2003, the PA established the office of prime minister in an attempt to circumvent Arafat and restart the peace process with Israel and Mahmoud Abbas, considered to be a moderate, was installed in the post. Following Arafat's death in 2004, Abbas was elected chairman of the PLO and president of the PA. In 2005, Israel withdrew soldiers and settlers from parts of the 'West Bank' and from all the Gaza Strip, which then came under Palestinian control, raising genuine hopes for new peace talks.

However, when the hard-line militant group Hamas won a surprise election victory over Fatah in 2006, violence between their forces escalated in the Gaza Strip and, after a week of fighting, Ḥamas defeated Fatah and took control of Gaza. The Ḥamas takeover of Gaza added a new element of uncertainty to Israeli-Palestinian relations. Instead of building a state, Hamas immediately declared its intention to seek the destruction of Israel and set to work constructing terror tunnels into Israeli territory as a means of infiltration and launching rockets towards Israel. The Israeli government responded by declaring Gaza under Ḥamas rule a hostile entity and imposed a blockade, sealing border crossings and placing heavy restrictions on imports. Indiscriminate rocket attacks by Hamas became commonplace, terrorizing residents in southern Israel, in response to which Israeli forces launched retaliatory strikes against rocket sites and Hamas infrastructure.

In September 2008, Israeli Prime Minister Ehud Olmert offered proposals to Mahmoud Abbas that would have given the Palestinian Authority 93.7 percent of the West Bank, and a corridor connecting the West Bank to Gaza. He even offered to relinquish Israeli control of the Old City – home to Jerusalem's most sensitive holy sites – and place it under international control. His offer was made at a turbulent time, for Olmert was enveloped in a corruption scandal that would eventually lead to his conviction on bribery and corruption charges. Abbas not only rejected the proposal but, like Arafat in 2000, refused to even make a counter proposal. Many commentators have subsequently lamented that thus was spurned the last chance for a two-state solution.

On 27 December 2008, a ferocious conflict erupted in the Gaza Strip as Israeli forces launched Operation Cast Lead, which included an incursion by ground forces, with the aims of putting a stop to indiscriminate Palestinian rocket fire against Israel and weapons smuggling into the Gaza Strip. The conflict resulted in over 1,000 Palestinian deaths and 13 Israeli deaths. A significant contributing factor towards these appalling casualty figures was an Israeli decision to target military instillations and weapon caches in the densely populated cities of Gaza, Khan Yunis and Rafah. Amid concern at the casualty rate and rising international criticism, Israeli politicians declared a unilateral ceasefire on 18 January and completed a withdrawal of all forces from Gaza on 21 January.

In September 2009, a UN special mission, headed by Justice Richard Goldstone of South Africa, published a report on the Gaza conflict which accused both Palestinian militants and the IDF of war crimes and crimes against humanity. The Israeli government issued a vigorous response which criticised the Goldstone Report and disputed its findings, after which Goldstone retracted the report's conclusion that Israel had intentionally targeted civilians.

Relations between Israel and the Palestinians soured further in May 2010 when Israeli commandos raided a civilian ship carrying pro-Palestinian activists to the Gaza Strip in defiance of Israel's blockade. Nine people aboard the ship were killed when the commandos opened fire after being attacked by activists armed with clubs and knives.

A terrorist attack in the 'West Bank' on 12 June 2014, in which three teenage yeshiva students were kidnapped and murdered by Ḥamas operatives, brought a new escalation of tension in and around the Gaza Strip. In response to an Israeli crackdown against Hamas after the murders, rockets and mortars were fired from Gaza into Israel. On 8 July 2014, Israel launched a large-scale assault against Ḥamas and other militants in Gaza, known as 'Operation Protective Edge', which began with a week of aerial bombardment and progressed to another incursion by ground troops with the stated aims of destroying Gaza's terror tunnels and preventing further rocket attacks. After several weeks of fighting, Israel withdrew all forces from Gaza, declaring that their mission had been fulfilled. The conflict cost the lives of 72 Israeli soldiers and civilians, and over 2,000 Palestinians, including civilians, though the number of civilian casualties is disputed.

Against this backdrop, the Obama administration presented plans for restarting negotiations between Israel and the Palestinians in a final effort to reach a two-state solution, taking Olmert's 2008 proposal as a starting point. Yet again, the Palestinian Authority refused to engage in bilateral negotiations with the Israeli government despite stipulations in the Oslo Accords that they must do so. And so the Palestinian leadership have continued to follow precedents of refusing opportunities for statehood that have stretched as far back as the Peel Commission Report of 1937.

At the time of writing, Israel is being pushed to the brink of another Gaza war as rockets continue to be fired from Gaza into southern Israel without censure from the UN. Incendiary balloons released from Gaza are destroying thousands of acres of farm land in a new form of terrorism and regular riots at the border are being instigated by Hamas and seeded with terrorist operatives seeking incursion into Israel. Border violence began at the end of March 2018 with a six week campaign of protests called by organizers the 'Great March of Return' that was intended to end on Nakba Day, 15 May 2018, but which has continued intermittently thereafter. The protests culminated in the deadliest day since the Gaza war of 2014 when, on 14 May, 62 Palestinians were killed by Israeli forces. Hamas claimed 50 of the dead as its militants; Islamic Jihad claimed 3 as belonging to its military wing. These admissions did not stop propaganda claims that Israel was killing innocent civilian protestors.

A new peace proposal is being prepared by Jared Kushner for the Trump administration, the so called 'deal of the century', but has been widely rejected by the Palestinian Authority before its official release. The prospect of a broader Middle Eastern conflict directed against Iran by the United States, into which Israel would inevitably be drawn, is looming ominously large. Thus, the struggles of Israel for a peaceful existence continue.

The Modern State of Israel – Fulfilling Herzl's Vision

After the first Zionist Congress, held in 1897, Herzl noted in his diary, "At Basel I founded the Jewish State. If I said this out loud today, I would be answered by universal laughter. If not in five years, certainly in 50, everyone will know it."[18] His prediction proved to be accurate. Fifty years on from that conference, the United Nations voted to create a Jewish State which paved the way for the birth of the modern state of Israel. If the birth-pangs were traumatic, they have been followed by an arduous childhood.

The name Israel, which was first given to Jacob, means to wrestle for the blessing of God (Genesis 32:28). The history of the Jewish people has demonstrated the prophetic import of this name, and the preceding summary of the struggle to establish the modern state of Israel, from the Arab wars, to the intifada and conflict with Palestinians, has proven once more the truth of this name. Israel was forced into a bitter fight for survival in its infancy. Military strategists arrogantly talk of losing a battle but winning the war. Israel was in a position, encamped on the precipice of extinction, where she could not afford to lose a single battle. Yet Israel prevailed, securing her borders by taking possession of strategically important territory, and since the Six Day War, with US support and the development of a nuclear capability, she has become the foremost military power in the region.

Despite the constant threats to security, both internally and on her borders, Herzl's vision of the state of Israel, which was for a neutral, peace-seeking, advanced society that would utilize science and technology to develop the land, has largely come to pass. Israel has established the national home for the Jewish people promised in the Balfour Declaration. It is an advanced democratic society with a high standard of living comparable to that in Western Europe, a vigorous free press and exceptional educational and health facilities.

If any nation has ever had cause to adorn a victim mentality, it is Israel in the aftermath of the Holocaust. And yet, despite all the challenges from without and the opportunities for division within between religious and secular Jews, reformed and ultra-orthodox, Sephardic and Ashkenazi, the Jewish people have striven to settle, develop and build a successful state that contributes positively to the world. This is reflected in the disproportionate number of Nobel Prize Laureates Israel has produced comparative to its small size. Despite comprising less than 0.2 per cent of the world's population, 22 per cent of the total prize winners are Jewish, including Elie Wiesel, an Auschwitz survivor who became an eloquent witness for the six million Jews slaughtered in World War II and who, more than anyone else, seared the memory of the Holocaust on the world's conscience. In the aftermath of the systematic massacre of Jews, no voice had emerged to drive home the enormity of what had happened. For almost two decades, the traumatized survivors seemed frozen in silence. But by the sheer force of his personality and his gift for the haunting phrase, Wiesel exhumed the Holocaust from the burial ground of the history books. "Wiesel is a messenger to mankind," the 1986 Nobel Peace Prize citation stated. "His message is one of peace, atonement and human dignity. His belief that the forces fighting evil in the world can be victorious is a hard-won belief."[19]

Shimon Peres, the late former Prime Minister of Israel, declared, "In Israel, a land lacking in natural resources, we learned to appreciate our greatest national advantage: our minds. Through creativity and innovation, we transformed barren deserts into flourishing fields and pioneered new frontiers in science and technology."[20] As the prophet Isaiah said, *"look to Abraham, your father, and to Sarah, who gave you birth. When I called him he was only one man, and I blessed him and made him many. The Lord will surely comfort Zion and will look with compassion on all her ruins; he will make her deserts like Eden, her wastelands like the garden of the Lord"* (Isaiah 52:2-3). Again, speaking of the return of the Ransomed to Zion, Isaiah prophesied, *"The desert and the parched land will be glad; the wilderness will rejoice and blossom like the rose"* (Isaiah 35:1).

During the later years of the Ottoman Empire, large tracts of the land had been owned by absentee landlords who, through neglect, allowed desert and swamp to overwhelm cultivatable soil. Numerous travellers who passed through Palestine during this forlorn period described its utter desolation. The 18th Century French historian, Count Constantine Frangois Volney, called Palestine a "ruined" and "desolate" land, reporting that, "In consequence of such wretched government, the greater part of the Provinces are impoverished and laid waste."[21] According to Volney, "We with difficulty recognize Jerusalem ... remote from every road, it seems neither to have been calculated for a considerable mart of commerce, nor the centre of a great consumption ... [the population] is supposed to amount to twelve to fourteen thousand."[22]

The abandonment and dismal state of the terrain continued to be lamented throughout the 19th Century. J. S. Buckingham described his visit of 1816 to Jaffa, which "has all the appearances of a poor village, and every part of it that we saw was of corresponding meanness."[23] In a German encyclopaedia published in 1827, Palestine was depicted as "desolate and roamed through by Arab bands of robbers."[24] In 1840, a writer, who was travelling through Syria, observed that the once populous area between Hebron and Bethlehem was "now abandoned and desolate" with "dilapidated towns."[25] Jerusalem consisted of "a large number of houses ... in a dilapidated and ruinous state," and "the masses really seem to be without any regular employment."[26] The "masses" of Jerusalem were estimated at less than 15,000 inhabitants, of whom more than half were Jews.

The British Consul in Palestine reported in 1857, "The country is in a considerable degree empty of inhabitants and therefore its greatest need is that of a body of population."[27] In the 1860s, H. B. Tristram noted in his journal, "The north and south [of the Sharon plain] land is going out of cultivation and whole villages are rapidly disappearing from the face of the earth. Since the year 1838, no less than 20 villages there have been thus erased from the map [by the Bedouin] and the stationary population extirpated."[28]

Mark Twain, in his inimitable fashion, expressed scorn for what he called the "romantic" and "prejudiced" accounts of Palestine after he visited the Holy Land in 1867. He described the land as "a desolate country whose soil is rich enough, but it is given over wholly to weeds ... a silent mournful expanse ... a desolation ... hardly a tree or shrub anywhere. Even the olive tree and the cactus, those fast friends of a worthless soil, had almost deserted the country." In one location after another, Twain registered gloom at his findings: "Stirring scenes ... occur in the valley [Jezreel] no more. There is not a solitary village throughout its whole extent – not for thirty miles in either direction. There are two or three small clusters of Bedouin tents, but not a single permanent habitation. One may ride ten miles hereabouts and not see ten human beings." To find "the sort of solitude to make one dreary," one must, "Come to Galilee for that ... these unpeopled deserts, these rusty mounds of barrenness, that never, never do shake the glare from their harsh outlines, and fade and faint into vague perspective; that melancholy ruin of Capernaum: this stupid village of Tiberias, slumbering under its six funereal palms … We never saw a human being on the whole route … Nazareth is forlorn … Jericho the accursed lies a mouldering ruin today, even as Joshua's miracle left it more than three thousand years ago: Bethlehem and Bethany, in their poverty and their humiliation, have nothing about them now to remind one that they once knew the high honour of the Saviour's presence … Bethsaida and Chorzin have vanished from the earth, and the "desert places" round about them, where thousands of men once listened to the Saviour's voice and ate the miraculous bread, sleep in the hush of a solitude that is inhabited only by birds of prey and skulking foxes … Palestine sits in sackcloth and ashes … desolate and unlovely."[29]

Many writers, such as the Reverend Samuel Manning, mourned the atrophy of the coastal plain of Sharon, "The exquisite fertility and beauty of which made it to the Hebrew mind a symbol of prosperity." He continued, "But where were the inhabitants? This fertile plain, which might support an immense population, is almost a solitude … Day by day we were to learn afresh the lesson now forced upon us, that the denunciations of ancient prophecy have been fulfilled to the very letter – 'the land is left void and desolate and without inhabitants.'"[30] W. M. Thomson reiterated the Reverend Manning's observations: "How melancholy is this utter desolation! Not a house, not a trace of inhabitants, not even shepherds, seen everywhere else, appear to relieve the dull monotony … Isaiah says that Sharon shall be wilderness (Isaiah 33:9), and the prediction has become a sad and impressive reality."[31]

Yet the prophet Ezekiel spoke of the revival of this desolate wasteland, *"This is what the Sovereign* Lord *says: "On the day I cleanse you from all your sins, I will resettle your towns, and the ruins will be rebuilt. The desolate land will be cultivated instead of lying desolate in the sight of all who pass through it." They will say, "This land that was laid waste has become like the garden of Eden; the cities that were lying in ruins, desolate and destroyed, are now fortified and inhabited""* (Ezekiel 36:33-36). God has made possible the impossible, and Israel stands as a testimony to His power to fulfil his promises. As His people have been reunited with the land promised as their inheritance, so the land has responded and become fruitful once more.

Many challenges remain. Over time, the United Nations has developed an extremely one-sided pro-Palestinian position that is grossly unfair to Israel, focussing exclusively on the controversial issue of Israeli settlements in the 'West Bank' and East Jerusalem while ignoring the security threat posed to Israel by Palestinian terrorism. Addressing a UN conference on anti-Semitism in 2003, Anne Bayefsky, the human rights scholar and activist, said: "There has never been a single resolution about the decades-long repression of the civil and political rights of 1.3 billion people in China, or the more than a million female migrant workers in Saudi Arabia being kept as virtual slaves, or the virulent racism which has brought 600,000 people to the brink of starvation in Zimbabwe. Every year, UN bodies are required to produce at least 25 reports on alleged human rights violations by Israel, but not one on an Iranian criminal justice system which mandates punishments like crucifixion, stoning, and cross-amputation. This is not legitimate critique of states with equal or worse human rights records. It is demonization of the Jewish state."[32] A report in 2005 by the United States Institute of Peace on UN reform said that, contrary to the UN Charter's principle of equality of rights for all nations, Israel is denied rights enjoyed by all other member-states, and that a level of systematic hostility against it is routinely expressed, organized, and funded within the United Nations system.[33] In an interview on 16 December 2016, the former UN General Secretary, Ban Ki Moon, acknowledged that

"Decades of political manoeuvrings have created a disproportionate volume of resolutions, reports and conferences criticizing Israel ... rather than helping the Palestinian cause, this reality has hampered the ability of the UN to fulfil its role effectively."[34]

In parallel with the hostility towards Israel exhibited by sections of the UN, in many parts of the world the anti-Semitic Boycott, Divestment and Sanctions (BDS) movement, chillingly reminiscent of the Nazi call to boycott Jewish business in 1933, is gaining traction, indicating that the lessons of the Holocaust have not been heeded by all. The BDS movement, which is a distortion of the anti-Apartheid campaign that was waged against South Africa, seeks to pressurize Israel economically and isolate it politically. Many people who support it do so sincerely believing that they are fighting for 'social justice', but in reality, it is a shield for a type of reputational warfare against Israel. Marc Greendorfer, founder of the legal think tank the Zachar Institute, has highlighted the connections between the BDS movement and Palestinian terror organizations. He writes, "BDS is a proxy for foreign terror groups ... (It) promotes discrimination and normalizes the message of terror groups by cloaking it in the vernacular of civil rights ... (It) is the non-violent arm of terror groups whose ultimate goal is to disenfranchise Jews from their right to their own country."[35] A report by Israel's Ministry of Strategic Affairs has provided conclusive evidence that terrorist organisations have infiltrated, and are even driving, BDS activities. The report details over 100 links between the prescribed terror groups Hamas and the Peoples Front for the Liberation of Palestine (PFLP) and Western backed groups promoting BDS, stating, "Hamas and PFLP operatives have infiltrated and adopted seemingly benign NGOs in the Palestinian Authority, Europe, North America and South Africa, for the purpose of advancing their ideological goal: the elimination of the state of Israel ... Convicted terrorist operatives who have served prison sentences currently hold senior positions in NGOs which delegitimize and promote the BDS campaign against Israel."[36]

It is not only from 'social justice' groups that pressure is being applied to Israel and the Jewish community in Britain. In politics, on both the resurgent radical left and extreme right, the spectre of anti-Semitism is re-emerging at an alarming rate, reaching levels not seen in Britain for decades. Issues with left wing groups in particular have injected anti-Semitism into mainstream politics. Michael Gove MP, a pro-Israeli Conservative cabinet minister, delivered a withering Chanukah message in December 2017 in which he opined, "There is no abatement in the threat to Israel." He wrote of a movement against Israel "fuelled by a dark and furious energy" that "hopes to take advantage not only of fading memories and youthful ignorance, but of residual and nascent bigotries of the worst kind."[37]

On the extreme right, anti-Semitism manifests in tropes about Jewish conspiracies to control the world. Myths are perpetuated of Jews acting with malice as they wield power, of 'Zionist bankers' manipulating financial markets and of Mossad nefariously interfering in the affairs of other nations. On the radical left, where being anti-Israel has become quite the fashion, it is expressed in ways that resonate with the local narrative. For example, in Britain, with its colonial past, left wing political groups talk about Israeli imperialism. In the US, Israel is accused of being a white supremacist country (which is ironic considering that right wing anti-Semitism is based on Jews not being white). In Canada, Israel is charged with ethnically cleansing the indigenous population (such charges originate from anti-Semitic attempts to equate Zionism with Nazism). In South Africa, Israel is called an apartheid state. All these narratives are palpably false, but when projected onto Israel they gain traction among those who either have little knowledge of, or interest in, the historical reality or who wilfully choose to ignore it.

Yossi Klein Halevi wrote the following in response to a student who asked him whether 'humanizing' Zionists was comparable to asking African Americans to 'humanize members of the KKK':

"Anti-Semitism is not simply hating the other – the Jew as the other. Anti-Semitism works a little bit differently. What anti-Semitism does is turn the Jews – 'the Jew' – into the symbol of whatever it is that a given civilization defines as its most loathsome qualities. And so, under Christianity – before the Holocaust and Vatican II – the Jew was the Christ-killer. Under Communism, the Jew was the capitalist. Under Nazism, the ultimate race polluter.

Now we live in a different civilization, where the most loathsome qualities are racism, colonialism, apartheid. And lo and behold, the greatest offender in the world today, with all the beautiful countries of the world, is the Jewish state. The Jewish state is the symbol of the genocidal, racist, apartheid state ... An Israeli political philosopher named Yakov Talmon once put it this way: "The state of the Jews has become the Jew of the states." Criticism of Israel is not anti-Semitism. Criticism of Israel's existence – denying Israel the right to exist, calling Israel the Zionist entity – that is anti-Semitism. That is a classical continuity of thousands of years of symbolizing the Jew. So, using that kind of language places you in very uncomfortable company. That kind of language can come today from the far left. It can come from white supremacists. It can come from Islamist extremists. It can come from many sources, but all of those groups converge on one idea: The Jew remains humanity's great problem."[38]

It lies beyond the scope of this work to present detailed arguments to address all these charges levelled against Israel, but a few brief comments will suffice to demonstrate their absurdity. If Israel is a colonial venture, who exactly is it a colony of? The Oxford Dictionary defines 'colonization' as "the action or process of settling among and establishing control over the indigenous people of an area." But the Jews *are* the indigenous people of

Israel. In essence, Israel is a colony of – Israel. Contrary to claims of ethnic cleansing, the Arab population within Israel has actually *increased* since 1948 at a rate that has matched the growth of the Jewish population. And those who accuse Israel of being an Apartheid state should consider the following foundational precepts from Israel's declaration of independence: "The state of Israel will promote the development of the country for the benefit of all its inhabitants; will be based on precepts of liberty, justice and peace taught by the Hebrew prophets; will uphold the full social and political equality of all its citizens without distinction of race, creed or sex; will guarantee full freedom of conscience, worship, education and culture."

Arabs residing in Israel have the right to vote, to hold political office, travel without restriction, serve in the armed forces and have the same access to education and healthcare as Jews. Arabs constitute 20% of Israel's university population, a precise echo of their percentage of the general population. Many Arabs have risen to the most senior levels in the judiciary, military and civic realms. Polling indicates that a majority of Israeli Arabs are proud to be citizens of Israel. By contrast, Palestinians residing in the surrounding Arab states are denied citizenship and trapped in a perpetual refugee status, denied the right to vote, forced to endure severe travel restrictions, and are blocked from accessing education and healthcare. Under the Palestinian Authority, it is illegal to sell land to Jews, a crime punishable by life imprisonment. It is blindingly obvious against whom the accusations of Apartheid should be levelled.

Geo-politically, Israel faces direct hostility on its borders from Hamas and Hezbollah, and fears that Iran is preparing one day to develop nuclear weapons with the intent to destroy Israel. With the menacing spread of Islamist terrorism across the Middle East, Israel cannot afford to relinquish security control west of the Jordan River or to countenance the creation of a Palestinian state in the 'West Bank' if there is a risk that it may fail and degenerate into a terrorist state as has happened in Gaza. From a political perspective, the prospects for lasting peace seem as remote now as they did in 1948.

Of course, the political nuances of Israel's modern history are much more complicated than can be represented in this brief overview. It has been said that if anyone believes that they understand the Israeli-Palestinian conflict, then they clearly don't understand the problem. Also, it must be recognized that admiration for Israel and belief that her re-emergence is a miraculous fulfilment of biblical prophecy do not absolve its leaders from responsibility for acting justly. At least by embracing true democracy, the kind in which Israeli Arabs serve in the Knesset, those elected as leaders are rigorously held to account.

Such has Israel fared since the end of the British Mandate. To anyone not blinkered by hatred or visceral prejudice, it is a miraculous, inspirational story of a downtrodden and dispossessed people who, after enduring centuries of persecution, hardships and terror, have returned to their ancient home and built a thriving and free democratic state, retaining dignity in the face of a challenging political climate and discriminatory opposition. But what about Britain? How has she fared since the end of the Mandate?

Endnotes

1. Cited from Benny Morris, *1948, A History of the First Arab-Israeli War* (New Haven: Yale University Press, 2008), p. 185.
2. Cabinet Middle East Policy Note by Secretary of State for Foreign Affairs Ernest Bevin, on Israel: Bevin's report reviewing meetings with England's representatives in the Middle East, to Cabinet, August 25, 1949, PRO CAB 129/2 (CP/49 183).
3. Cited from Howard Sachar, *A History of Israel: From the Rise of Zionism to Our Time* (New York: Knopf, 1979), p. 616.
4. Cited from Isi Leibler, *The Case for Israel* (Australia: The Globe Press, 1972), p. 60.
5. Ibid., p. 60.
6. Nasser speech to the General Council of the International Confederation of Arab Trade Unionists, Cited from Samir A. Matawi, *Jordan in the 1967 War* (Cambridge: CUP, 2002), p. 95.
7. Isi Leibler, *The Case for Israel*, p. 6.
8. Cited from Mark A Tessler, *A History of Israel in Palestinian Conflict* (Indianapolis: Indiana University Press, 1994), p. 393.
9. Cited from *www.jewishvirtuallibrary.org/background-and-overview-six-day-war*.
10. Voice of Israel Radio, 7 June 1967, live broadcast.
11. Ibid.
12. Cited from Israeli Defense Forces Facebook page, *https://www.facebook.com/idfonline/posts/what-does-it-mean-to-be-an-idf-soldier-let-instagram-tell-the-story-with-our-10-/607875715901969/*
13. "Arafat's actual name was Abd al-Rahman abd al-Bauf Arafat al-Qud al-Husseini. He shortened it to obscure his kinship with the notorious Nazi and ex-Mufti of Jerusalem, Haj Amin al-Husseini." Howard M. Sachar, *A History of Israel* (New York: Knopf, 1976). The Bet Agron International Centre in Jerusalem interviewed Arafat's brother and sister, who described the Mufti as a cousin with tremendous influence on young Yassir after the Mufti returned from Berlin to Cairo. Yasser Arafat himself kept his exact lineage and birthplace secret.

[14] Cited from Benny Morris, "Camp David and After: An Exchange 1. An Interview with Ehud Barak", 49 (10) The New York Review of Books, 13 June 2002.

[15] Cited from Gabriel G. Tabarani, *Israel-Palestinian Conflict: The Balfour Promise to Bush Declaration* (Indiana: Author House, 2008), p. 214.

[16] Efraim Karsh, "Why the Oslo Process Doomed Peace", *Middle East Quarterly* 23(4), Autumn 2016, pp. 1-17.

[17] Cited from *https://www.lantosfoundation.org/news/2015/9/17/tom-lantos-un-speech-for-holocaust-rememberance-day-delivered-by-daughter-dr-katrina-lantos-swett*.

[18] Theodor Herzl Diaries, entry for 3 September 1897.

[19] Cited from *https://www.nobelprize.org/prizes/peace/1986/press-release*.

[20] From an Op-Ed in the Los Angeles Times, 18 June 2012.

[21] Count Constantine F. Volney, *Travels Through Syria and Egypt in the Years 1783, 1784, 1785* (London, 1788), Vol. 2, p. 147.

[22] Ibid., pp. 303-325.

[23] J.S. Buckingham, *Travels in Palestine* (London, 1821), p. 146.

[24] Brockhaus, Alig. *Deutsch Real-Encyklopaedie, 7th ed.* (Leipzig, 1827), Vol. VIII, p. 206.

[25] S. Olin, *Travels in Egypt, Arabia Petraea and the Holy Land* (New York, 1843), Vol. 2, pp. 438-439.

[26] Ibid., pp. 77-78.

[27] James Finn to the Earl of Clarendon, Jerusalem, September 15, 1857, F.O. 78/1294 (Pol. No. 36).

[28] H.B. Tristram, *The Land of Israel: A Journal of Travels in Palestine* (London, 1865), p. 490.

[29] Mark Twain, *The Innocents Abroad* (American Publishing Company, 1869), pp. 336, 349, 375, 441-442.

[30] The Reverend Samuel Manning, *Those Holy Fields* (London, 1874), pp. 14-17.

[31] W. M. Thomson, *The Land and the Book* (London: T. Nelsons & Sons, 1866), p. 506ff.

[32] Anna Bayefsky, "Perspectives on Anti-Semitism Today". Lecture at conference "Confronting Anti-Semitism: Education for Tolerance and Understanding", United Nations Department of Information, New York, 21 June 2004.

[33] *American interest and UN reform. Report of the Task Force on the United Nations*, United States Institute of Peace, 2005.

[34] Cited from *https://www.un.org/sg/en/content/sg/statement/2016-12-16/secretary-generals-briefing-security-council-situation-middle-east.*, 16 December 2016.

[35] Cited from Sean Savage, "Evidence Mounting that US BDS Groups are Fronts for Terror Organisations", *Jewish News Syndicate*, 18 January 2019, *https://www.jns.org*.

[36] Cited from Aaron Bandler, "New Report Details pro-BDS NGOs ties to Terrorism", *Jewish Journal*, 6 February 2019, *https://jewishjournal.com/news/world/293482/*.

[37] Cited from Conservative Friends of Israel, "Michael Gove Celebrates Israel's 'Light to the World' at CFI's Annual Business Lunch Attended by 170 Conservative Parliamentarians", *https://cfoi.co.uk/michael-gove-celebrates-israels-light-to-the-world-at-cfis-annual-business-lunch-attended-by-170-conservative-parliamentarians.*, 12 December 2017.

[38] Yossi Klein Halevi, "Defining the Root of Anti-Semitism", *Jewish Journal [online]*, 16 April 2019, *https://jewishjournal.com/culture/lifestyle/first_person/242334/the-root-of-anti-semitism/*.

CHAPTER 12

THE DECLINE OF BRITAIN

> "*If my people, who are called by my name, will humble themselves and pray and seek my face and turn from their wicked ways, then I will hear from heaven, and I will forgive their sin and will heal their land*"
>
> –2 CHRONICLES 7:8

Herzl's dream of an independent State of Israel came to pass just over 50 years after the publication of *Der Judenstaat*. In a fraction under 50 years after the end of British Mandatory rule over Palestine, the transfer of Hong Kong from British rule to China, completed on 1 July 1997, marked the end of the British Empire.

Though Britain and her Empire had emerged victorious from World War II, a victory which would not have been possible had Britain not stood alone in the summer of 1940 against a known anti-Semitic tyranny, in reality the defeat of Germany had been mainly the work of Soviet and American power, whilst that of Japan had been almost entirely an American triumph. The effects of the conflict were profound, both at home and abroad. Much of Europe, a continent that had dominated the world for centuries, lay in ruins, and was host to the armies of the United States and the Soviet Union who now held the balance of global power.

Britain had survived and recovered the territory lost during the war. But its prestige and authority, not to mention its wealth, had been severely reduced. Britain was left essentially bankrupt, with insolvency only averted in 1946 after the negotiation of a $US 4.33 billion loan from the United States, the last installment of which was repaid in 2006.

The British now found themselves locked into an imperial endgame from which every exit was blocked except the trapdoor to oblivion. Anti-colonial movements were rising in every corner of the Empire. The US, themselves locked in an increasingly bitter rivalry with the Soviets, continued to support the existence of the British Empire as a buttress against Communist expansion. Ultimately, however, so ferocious were the "winds of change" sweeping across the world that the British Empire was swept into a deadly funnel that tore it apart. Britain attempted to keep a dignified appearance by adopting a policy of peaceful disengagement from its colonies once stable, non-Communist, governments were available to assume power. In reality, she rarely had any choice. Across the planet, the Union Jack came down, from Malaya to Malawi, from Singapore to Suez. Between 1945 and 1965, the number of people living under British rule outside the UK fell from 700 million to 5 million, most of whom were in Hong Kong.

Many explanations for the collapse of Britain's power have been postulated and debated. Several convergent factors contributed which are summarised below. In truth, it must be acknowledged that the process was far more complex than can be represented in this short appraisal, but the validity of each factor discussed is generally accepted.

THE DECLINE OF BRITAIN

An early symptom of the weakness of Britain was her withdrawal in 1947 from India, the jewel in the crown of the British Empire. During World War II, Britain had mobilised India's resources for their imperial war effort. They ruthlessly crushed an attempt by Mahatma Gandhi and the Indian National Congress to force them to 'quit India' in 1942. Nonetheless, in an earlier bid to win Congress support, Britain had promised to give India full independence once the war was over.

Within months of the end of the war, it became glaringly obvious that Britain lacked the means to defeat a renewed campaign for independence by the Indian National Congress. Its officials were exhausted and troops were lacking. Britain still harboured hopes that a self-governing India would remain part of their system of 'imperial defence'. For this reason, Britain was desperate to keep India united but their efforts came to nothing. By the time that the last Viceroy, Lord Louis Mountbatten, arrived in India, Congress and its leader, Jawaharlal Nehru, had accepted that unless they agreed to partition, they risked a descent into chaos and communal war before power could be transferred from Britain into Indian hands. It was left to Mountbatten to stage a rapid handover to two successor governments, India and Pakistan, before the ink was dry on their post-imperial frontiers.

Despite the rhetoric from politicians, mutual back-slapping and pretence of dignity, nothing could disguise the fact that the end of the Raj was a staggering blow for British world power. Britain had lost the colony that had provided much of its military muscle east of Suez. The burden of defending the Empire shifted back to a Britain that was both weaker and poorer than it had been before 1939. Britain was now overshadowed by the emerging super states of America and the Soviet Union, her domestic economy had been seriously weakened and the Labour government had embarked on a huge and expensive programme of social reform.

Prime Minister Clement Attlee and his cabinet colleague, Ernest Bevin, who dominated Labour's foreign policy at the time, concluded that Britain's economic recovery and the survival of sterling as a great trading currency required closer integration with the old 'white' dominions, especially Australia, New Zealand and South Africa. The 'sterling area', which included the Empire and Commonwealth, accounted for half of the world's trade in the early post-war years. The British were also determined to exploit the tropical colonies more effectively because their cocoa, rubber and tin could be sold for much-needed dollars.

The desire to maintain what remained of the Empire was not motivated solely by the economic imperative. Britain's strategic defence against the new Soviet threat required forward air bases from which to bomb Southern Russia – the industrial arsenal of the Soviet Union. That meant staying in the Middle East even after the breakdown of British control in Palestine and its hasty evacuation in 1948. In Egypt, Iraq, Jordan and the Gulf, the British were determined to hang on to their treaties and bases, including the vast Suez Canal zone.

Across the whole spectrum of political party opinion, British leaders had no doubt that Britain must uphold its status as the third great power, and that it could only do so by maintaining its Empire and Commonwealth links. Europe, by contrast, they saw as a zone of economic and political weakness.

In the 1950s, Britain struggled to achieve this post-war imperial vision. Successive governments invested heavily in up-to-date weaponry and fretted over the slowness of the British economy to resume its old role as the great lender of capital. By the end of the decade, things were not going well.

Staying in the Middle East inevitably led to confrontation with President Nasser of Egypt and the disastrous decision to seek his overthrow by force in collusion with France and Israel. The 1956 Suez Crisis was a savage revelation of Britain's financial and military weakness and destroyed much of what remained of Britain's influence in the Middle East.

As the 1950s drew to a close, and with her old Empire tottering, Britain's position as the third great power and 'deputy leader' of the Western Alliance was under serious threat from the resurgence of France and West Germany, who jointly presided over the new European Economic Community (EEC). Britain's claim on American support, the indispensable prop of imperial survival, could no longer be taken for granted. And Britain's own economy, far from accelerating, was stuck in a depressing rut.

Throughout the 1960s, it become increasingly difficult to maintain even a semblance of British world power as successive governments attempted forlornly to make bricks without straw. Britain tried and failed twice to enter the EEC, hoping to galvanise its stagnant economy and to smash the Franco-German 'alliance'.

To avoid being trapped in a costly struggle with local nationalist movements, Britain backed out of most of the remaining colonies with unseemly haste. As late as 1959, it had publicly scheduled a degree of self-government for Kenya, Uganda and Tanganyika. All became independent between 1961 and 1963.

British leaders gamely insisted that Britain would remain at the 'top table' of world power, a status guaranteed by its nuclear deterrent and its continuing influence in the ex-colonial world, but things did not go as planned. Britain's failure to stop the white settler revolt in Southern Rhodesia in 1965 was a huge embarrassment and drew fierce condemnation from many new Commonwealth states. In South East Asia, protecting the new federation of Malaysia against Indonesian aggression required ever spiralling resources that drained the treasury.

Meanwhile the British economy staggered from crisis to crisis and the burden became unsustainable. Devaluation of the pound in November 1967 was followed within weeks by the decision to withdraw Britain's military presence east of Suez. When Britain finally entered the European Community in 1973, the line had been drawn under Britain's imperial age. But the ending of an Empire is rarely a tidy affair. The Rhodesian rebellion was to last until the late 1970s and Hong Kong continued, with tacit Chinese agreement, as a British dependency until it was transferred to China in 1997, formally marking the end of the British Empire. It had suffered a spectacular and rapid fall from grace.

Such are the political and economic factors that contributed to Britain's decline. But what about the spiritual dimension?

The factors explored above, though relevant, are not sufficient to explain the savagery and speed of Britain's demise as a global power. Scripture teaches that it is God who causes nations and kingdoms rise and fall, *"He makes nations great, and destroys them; he enlarges nations, and disperses them"* (Job 12:23).[1]

The Lord made a promise to Abraham, the father of the nation of Israel, *"I will make you into a great nation, and I will bless you; I will make your name great, and you will be a blessing. I will bless those who bless you, and whoever curses you I will curse; and all peoples on earth will be blessed through you"* (Genesis 12:2-3).

On 2 November 1917, the pro Zionist government of David Lloyd George made a contract with world Jewry, publishing the Balfour Declaration which promised that Britain would endeavour to facilitate the creation of a Jewish homeland in Palestine in return for Jewish support for Britain during her desperate struggle against the Central Powers in the Great War. The Bible makes it abundantly clear that God takes very seriously the making of solemn declarations of intent and any subsequent breaking of them. There are many biblical references that speak of this, but to give just a couple of examples, *"If you make a vow to the Lord your God, you shall not delay fulfilling it, for the Lord your God will surely require it of you, and you will be guilty of sin ... You shall be careful to do what has passed your lips, for you have voluntarily vowed to the Lord your God what you have promised with your mouth"* (Deuteronomy 32:21-23); *"But above all, my brothers, do not swear, either by heaven or by earth or by any other oath, but let your "yes" be yes and your "no" be no, so that you may not fall under condemnation"* (James 5:12).

World Jewry kept its word and delivered everything that was promised. However, as previously set out, successive British governments broke faith with the Jews, culminating in the publication of the 1939 MacDonald White Paper which abrogated the promise of the Balfour Declaration. It was a bitter betrayal delivered at the worst possible time as Europe's Jews were falling into the abyss of the Holocaust. The gates of Palestine were closed, cutting off the Jews' only escape route and condemning them to the gas chambers. Even after the war, the Labour government of Clement Attlee, soaked in anti-Semitism, continued to enforce the prohibitions of the White Paper with ruthless determination.

Britain has on its hands the blood of countless thousands of Jews. There is always a price to pay for breaking vows, and Archbishop William Temple had warned Britain in March 1943, "We stand at the bar of history, of humanity and of God." Britain was found wanting. Following a hasty and undignified withdrawal from Palestine, Britain was systematically stripped of her Empire.

There are two particularly pertinent passages in Scripture that explain why the blessing of God has been removed from Britain because of the conduct of her commitments towards Mandatory Palestine. God's Word will always come to pass. He watches over it diligently to perform it, and His Word stands as our Judge.

Through the prophet Joel, speaking of the last days in which we are now living, God declares, *"In those days and at that time, when I restore the fortunes of Judah and Jerusalem, I will gather all nations and bring them down to the Valley of Jehoshaphat. There I will put them on trial for what they did to my inheritance, my people Israel, because they scattered my people among the nations and divided up my land"* (Joel 3:1-2).

Take note of the second part of the charge against the nations in this passage, that they *"divided up my land."* Within two years of assuming Mandatory control of Palestine, Britain divided the land along the Jordan River, severing nearly four-fifths of Palestine – some 35,000 square miles – to create a new Arab emirate, Transjordan, which was closed to Jewish immigration. A further division of Mandatory Palestine occurred in 1923 when the Golan Heights were ceded to the French Mandate of Syria. Further erosion of land available for Jewish settlement was proposed by the Peel Commission of 1937 which recommended the partitioning of what remained of Palestine into Jewish and Arab states, with a retained British Mandate under international supervision over Nazareth, Bethlehem, Jerusalem and a corridor from Jerusalem to Jaffa.

Under the Peel partition plan, the Jewish state that would have been created was astonishingly small, including only the coastal strip stretching from Mount Carmel to south of Be'er Tuvia, the Jezreel Valley and the region of Galilee. The Peel partition was not enacted for pragmatic reasons, but the conceptual groundwork had been laid for the future United Nations partition plan which would be recommend ten years later in 1947.

Britain, followed by the United Nations, is very clearly at the forefront of the nations who are charged by the Word of God with "dividing up" the land. Britain is also heavily implicated in the "Road Map for Peace" agreement which requires a further division of the land. This plan, aimed at resolving the Israeli–Palestinian conflict, was proposed by the United States, the European Union, Russia and the United Nations, and calls for an independent Palestinian state living side by side with Israel in peace.

As set out in the previous chapter, the Road Map plan was devised following decisive action taken by Israel to crush Palestinian Arab terrorism during the 'Second Intifada' and represents an attempt to appease Arabs at a time when the Bush administration was launching its own war on terror in Iraq. The concern motivating many of the nations implicated in the plan was to placate Muslim voters in their own countries by supporting an Arab cause against Israel.

Speaking of the days in which the fortunes of Israel would be fully restored during the reign of the Messiah, the prophet Isaiah declared, "*Foreigners will rebuild your walls, and their kings will serve you. Though in anger I struck you, in favour I will show you compassion. Your gates will always stand open, they will never be shut, day or night, so that people may bring you the wealth of the nations – their kings led in triumphal procession. For the nation or kingdom that will not serve you will perish; it will be utterly ruined*" (Isaiah 60:10-12).

There is a striking promise contained in this passage, "*Your gates will always stand open, they will never be shut, day or night.*" Throughout the period of Mandatory rule, Britain constantly imposed restrictions on Jewish immigration to Palestine, despite this being the very purpose for which the Mandate was given. Finally, the 1939 White Paper imposed a policy that effectively closed the gates of Palestine to Jewish immigration both during and after the Second World War, a policy that was rigorously enforced by the Royal Navy blockade that prevented ships laden with Holocaust survivors from landing on the shores of Palestine and a dispassionate Labour government, riddled with anti-Semitism, who ordered that survivors from the death camps be interned in overcrowded detention camps.

By closing the gates of Palestine to Jewish immigration in this way, Britain placed herself in direct opposition to the declared purposes of God. No man can close a door that God has opened;

the defeat of Britain in Palestine was inevitable. The passage from Isaiah closes with a warning to the nation that will not serve Israel, *"it will be utterly ruined."* Though the largely secularised governmental institutions and intelligentsia of modern Britain, including leading representatives from many mainstream Christian denominations, would be dismissive of such warnings, the Christian community who base their values upon the Bible must consider that the evident demise of Britain following the Second World War is a consequence of God fulfilling His Word. Britain may not have been *"utterly ruined"* in the way Isaiah described, for that is a fate awaiting those nations who will not serve Israel during Messiah's reign, but the principle of ruin being associated with a nation's attitude towards Israel is undoubtedly valid and pertinent. Britain, because of her conduct of the Mandate for Palestine, has brought upon herself the curse contained in the promise to Abraham, *"I will make you into a great nation, and I will bless you; I will make your name great, and you will be a blessing. I will bless those who bless you, and whoever curses you I will curse"* (Genesis 12:2-3).

Britain's Future?

What does the future hold for Britain? There is hope.

From the reformation onwards, and particularly during the 19th Century, the British Evangelical churches were at the forefront of a movement that took seriously prophetic scriptures that told of the restoration of Israel and were praying ardently for their fulfilment. The influences of this movement were deeply rooted in British political circles at the moment that British forces were sweeping through Palestine during World War I.

In the early years of the Mandate, the British government did much that was good to support the restoration of Israel. Had it not been for the Balfour Declaration and the protection afforded to the Jewish community in Palestine from the Arab population, despite objections from some British military commanders and civil servants, there would not have been an Israel for the Jews. In the crucial early period of the Mandate, His Majesty's Government facilitated Jewish immigration, encouraged Jewish settlement, subsidised Jewish defence and protected the vulnerable Jewish community. Since the time of Cyrus the Great, no major world power had supported a Jewish return to their ancient homeland in such a concrete way.

There were a number of prominent British politicians, military commanders and clergy who contributed to the Zionist cause during the Mandatory period. Men of calibre, who waded against the tide to support the Jews: David Lloyd George, Arthur James Balfour, Herbert Samuel, Winston Churchill, Richard Meinertzhagen, Charles Orde Wingate, William Temple. Beyond these influential figures, many Jewish veterans of Aliyah Bet and the detention camps testify that the treatment they received from the ordinary British soldiers was, on the whole, kind. Young British soldiers who wept as their commanding officers forbade them from intervening while Jews were being massacred on the road to Hadassah, or who rushed to the rescue of Jews on the stricken *Patria*. The fault lay not with the ordinary British people, but with a cold and impersonal administration in London, with those haughty politicians who strutted imperiously through Whitehall and those bellicose military commanders who strode through the Empire imbued with a sense of superiority, all engaged in an imperial game of thrones.

The ordinary people of Britain today have little idea of the story of Israel's restoration, and the part that Britain played. Stories are not told in Britain of the Acre prison break or the *Haganah Exodus 1947*. They do not know of how their governments broke promises to both Arabs and Jews, or of the 1939 White Paper by which the Chamberlain government abandoned the Jews to their terrible fate in the Holocaust.

Britain's decline reached its nadir with the humiliating transfer of Hong Kong, against the wishes of its population, to China. Since then, over the last two decades, the British economy has finally begun to recover something of its former swagger. Old imperial links still survive, particularly those based on language and law, which may assume growing importance in a globalised world. Even the Commonwealth, bruised and battered in the 1960s and 1970s, has retained a surprising utility as a dense global network of informal connections, valued by its numerous small states.

On 23 June 2016, the ordinary people of Britain stunned the world by voting in a referendum to sever political ties with the European Union against the advice of virtually the entire spectrum of the political, economic and educational establishment. It was a people's revolution against the forces of globalisation which will deliver in time a return of independent sovereignty and control over our own destiny. Economic analysts have forecast ruin for the British economy, politicians are so grieved that many are attempting to subvert the result, though a minority see a brighter vision of renewed hope for Britain. It is my contention that the future for post-Brexit Britain will be determined less by economics and politics, and more by the spiritual dimension that underscored those 50 years of decline.

God speaks through the prophet Jeremiah, *"If at any time I announce that a nation or kingdom is to be uprooted, torn down and destroyed, and if that nation I warned repents of its evil, then I will relent and not inflict on it the disaster I had planned"* (Jeremiah 18:7-8). This is the hope for Britain, if it will hear the Word of God, take its warnings seriously and repent of our former attitudes in the light of it. If we will begin once again, as we did in the days of the Balfour Declaration, to bless the people whom God blesses, the descendants of Abraham, Isaac and Israel, and adopt the same view that God holds towards His inheritance, which is His land and His people, then the ruin that we have brought upon ourselves may be reversed. If we repent for all our broken promises, we may confidently expect to see a return of God's blessing on our nation. If we will not do this, we may expect to see continuing decline.

The Word of God is clear that judgment begins with the household of God. He has promised, *"If my people, who are called by my name, will humble themselves and pray and seek my face and turn from their wicked ways, then I will hear from heaven, and I will forgive their sin and will heal their land"* (2 Chronicles 7:8). The fate of Britain lies in the hands of the church. According to our choice, the post-Brexit Britain will either prosper or decline into further ruin. We must rise to support Israel, and pray that our government will deal honourably and justly towards Israel, particularly in the United Nations which continues to scapegoat Israel by passing unjust resolutions against her. That does not mean that we should approve of every decision taken by the Israeli government, but that we must earn the right to be a friend that takes responsibility for challenging Israel openly and with the best of intentions, not motivated by self interest. We can do nothing to change the past, but as Eleanor Rathbone MP implored the House of Commons at the height of the Holocaust, "What is past is past but the future is still within our control."

On 21 December 2016, in a recent edition of what has become a surreal annual assault on Israel marked by a torrent of one-sided resolutions, the United Nations General Assembly wrapped up its annual legislative session in New York by adopting a disproportionate 20 resolutions against Israel and only 4 resolutions on the rest of the world combined, one each on Syria, Iran, North Korea and Crimea. Not a single United Nations General Assembly resolution was even introduced to address the victims of gross human rights abusers such as Saudi Arabia, Turkey, Venezuela, China, or Cuba.

Hillel Neuer, executive director of 'UN Watch', a Geneva-based non-governmental watchdog, commented, "Even as Syrian president Bashar Assad is preparing for the final massacre of his own people in Aleppo, the UN adopted a resolution—drafted and co-sponsored by Syria—which falsely condemns Israel for 'repressive measures' against Syrian citizens on the Golan Heights. It's obscene … At a time when Palestinian President Mahmoud Abbas and his state-controlled media incite to the continued stabbing and shooting of Israeli Jews, the United Nation's response is to reflexively condemn Israel in 20 separate resolutions, each of them one-sided, each of them utterly silent on Palestinian abuses."[2]

The clear aim of this annual session is to delegitimize the state of Israel. Each resolution was passed with overwhelming support. This despite the fact that Israel accepted the 1947 United Nations partition plan, whereas it was rejected by the Palestinian independence movement and the Arab League of nations. On each occasion that the Arab-Israeli conflict has flared, in 1948, 1967 and 1973, the Arab nations were the aggressors. When Israel did withdraw its citizens from the Gaza strip to facilitate Palestinian governance in 2005, the region was taken over by Hamas who are devoted to the destruction of Israel, yet the United Nations call on Israel to complete a similar transfer of power in the 'West Bank' close to the heart of Israel. Psalm 83, which speaks of the nations conspiring against Israel, could have been written to describe the United Nations in our generation: *"With cunning they conspire against your people; they plot against those you cherish. 'Come,' they say, 'let us destroy them as a nation, so that Israel's name is remembered no more.' With one mind they plot together; they form an alliance against you"* (Psalm 83:4-5).

In truth, during our involvement in Palestine, Britain broke promises made to both the Jews and the Arabs. The intractable nature of the violence in the region is largely of our making. Former Foreign Secretary, Jack Straw, in an interview in 2002 with The New Statesman, observed: "A lot of the problems we are having to deal with now ... are a consequence of our colonial past ... The Balfour Declaration and the contradictory assurances which were being given to Palestinians in private at the same time as they were being given to the Israelis ... present an interesting history for us but not an entirely honourable one."[3]

What is it that drives our governments to support the Palestinian cause so fastidiously? In this case part of the answer to the present lies with the past. The Chamberlain government supported the Arabs over the Jews out of fear that the Arabs would otherwise align with Nazi Germany, while the Attlee government was terrified of compromising Britain's regional military bases and access to Middle Eastern oil. Similar strategic interests still determine British policy. Saudi Arabia, for example, exports oil to Britain on very favourable terms that were agreed as part of a lucrative arms deal. Britain routinely votes in favour of the unjust, one-sided, United Nations resolutions against Israel, not because of conscience or the validity of resolutions, but by reason of realpolitik. Upsetting the wider Arab world is considered bad for British interests.

Post-colonial guilt is also a factor. While the British Empire achieved much that was beneficial, there can be no denying that often its subjects were exploited mercilessly and the Arab people are perceived to be among the greatest victims.

Sympathy for the plight of the Arab refugees displaced during the Arab-Israeli war of independence, estimated at 750,000, and the subsequent suffering of Palestinian Arabs in Gaza, the 'West Bank' and neighbouring Arab states is a legitimate concern. As the Israeli author Amos Oz puts it, "The Israeli-Palestinian conflict has been a tragedy, a clash between one very powerful, very convincing, very painful claim over this land and another no less powerful, no less convincing claim."[4] The situation of those trapped in Gaza is a particularly terrible tragedy that demands a response from the civilized world. Placing the blame exclusively upon Israel as many have done is, however, nothing short of a new form of political anti-Semitism that does nothing to solve the real cause. There is no prospect for achieving freedom for Gazans without the oppressive and murderous Hamas regime, who routinely target Israeli civilians with rocket fire and use women and children as human shields to protect against retaliation, first being overthrown. As long as Hamas brutality continues, the border fence will continue to be tightly controlled for the paramount concern of Israel is, quite rightly, the security of her people.

The refugee problem has been exploited as a symbol of Palestinian victimhood and used as a propaganda tool to undermine the legitimacy of the state of Israel, when in reality it was largely a self-inflicted disaster. Although Arab leaders talk passionately about their support for an Arab state west of the Jordan River, Egypt, Syria and Jordan, who occupied Gaza, Golan, Judea and Samaria after 1949 never considered transferring these lands to the Palestinians. Instead, they held Palestinian Arabs who had fled across their borders in perpetual refugee status for use as political pawns in their fight against the legitimacy of an Israeli State. It is also often overlooked that a greater number of Jewish refugees, estimated at 850,000, were forced to flee from Arab nations in what was an unequivocal act of ethnic cleansing, with no reparations ever made for land and property lost.

So far, I have mainly highlighted the political and economic decline of Britain. But what of the Church, substantial elements of which had provided the rocket fuel that propelled Zionism during the 19th Century, and which at the same time contributed so vigorously to World Mission? Things have not gone well for the denominational churches in Britain since World War II, a period marked by declining influence, alarming collapses in attendance and aging congregations. Social changes in the aftermath of two bitter world wars are usually cited as the causes for an aggressive rise of secularism that has pushed the Church to the margins of society.

It is commonly accepted that Britain is becoming an increasingly godless society. Data from a survey in 2016 by the National Centre of Social Research found that more than half the population described themselves as having 'no religion.' In an article published by the Huffington Post in 2011, Rabbi Shmuley Boteach commented, "(Britain's) principle religious exports today are thinkers who despise religion. From Richard Dawkins, who has compared religion to child abuse, to my friend Christopher Hitchens, who titled his 2007 book *"God Is Not Great: How Religion Poisons Everything"*, the British have cornered the market on being anti-God, at least the Christian and Jewish varieties."[5] Historically, Britain has been the seat of many significant gospel revivalist movements that have impacted the world – now we are exporting liberal secularism and anti-God philosophy. The rate of decline in religious affiliation has been as startling as the collapse of Britain's global power. Could this be another symptom of the withholding of God's blessing from the nation? Interestingly, when current Church attitudes towards Israel and the Jews are considered, it soon becomes apparent that they often parallel, or have been influenced by, those in British politics and media, and are contrary to the Zionist traditions that prevailed in both government and Church during the 19th and early 20th Centuries.

Despite the relentless trend towards 'godlessness' in British society, there are pockets of Christian communities that are thriving and standing resolutely in defiance against this trend, propped up in some locations by immigrants who have imported a vibrant faith. The churches that are growing tend to be those that take seriously the authority of scripture, and from that perspective support for Israel is not a question of political choice, it is a biblical imperative!

There are many Christians who would not accept that statement. Several denominations, including the Church of England's General Synod, have issued vehemently anti-Israeli and anti-Judaic statements, though it must be acknowledged that more balanced statements have also been issued by the Church of England. The picture is mixed; there are many great people who are connected to each of the Christian denominations and organizations referred to in the remainder of this chapter, but there are also 'worst case' examples where each of them have used emotive language to accuse Israel of ethnically cleansing Palestine and even of Judaising Jerusalem – the city whose ancient Jewish origins predate the arrival of Christian, Muslim and other invaders by a millennium. They have encouraged their people to support the BDS movement by refusing to purchase Israeli products, especially those produced in Judea and Samaria. This despite the fact that not all Israelis are actually Jews, and it is often the Palestinians employed by Israeli businesses that suffer most from boycotting.

Highly influential Christian organizations have whipped up the hysteria against Israel. Chief among these is Christian Aid, who propagate hard-left views that seek to delegitimize the state of Israel and that have heavily influenced the Middle East policy of many British churches. On numerous occasions it has distributed material that depicts Israelis as rapacious settlers whose only aim is to seize Palestinian land. Its website has displayed images of Palestinian homes destroyed by Israel but says nothing about the devastation wrought by the suicide bombers who lived in them or of the generous financial payments made to the bombers' families by the Palestinian Authority, Hamas and Hezbollah in compensation for having a 'martyr' in the family. Israeli measures to protect its people against terrorist attacks are presented as an entirely oppressive attempt to ruin the Palestinian economy, yet Palestinian incitement to murder Israelis is overlooked and no acknowledgement is given of the vast amount of humanitarian aid that Israel allows into Gaza. The blame for Palestinian suffering is laid at Israel's 'occupation' and supposed failure to comply with international law, but there is no recognition that hardships inflicted on Palestinians, such as the security barrier, have been caused entirely by the need to protect Israeli citizens from Palestinian suicide bombings, sniper fire and other violence – and the barrier has proven to be very successful in fulfilling its purpose.

Christian Aid is not alone in propagating such misinformed and one-sided opinions. The official magazine of the United Reformed Church, titled *Reform*, published a slanted Christmas article in its December 2010 issue which stated, "The broken town of Bethlehem is not what the popular Christmas carol proclaims: the 'security' wall, the checkpoints, the refugee camps, the towering Jewish settlement of Har Homa ... are the realities of daily life in 'the little town' ... and the 'water shortages' that Palestinians are forced to suffer while their Israeli neighbours enjoy a plentiful supply."[6] The picture being painted is a complete misrepresentation of reality. The checkpoints, which Palestinians cross on their way to work in Israel or for medical services provided by Israel, serve the same purpose as the security fence, protecting Israeli citizens from terrorist attacks. The refugee camps were constructed by the Jordanians because they refused to integrate the Palestinians when they illegally annexed the 'West Bank' – Israel attempted to disband the camps and develop higher quality housing, but these plans were vehemently opposed by the Palestinian Authority. The suburb of Har Homa does have high-rise buildings, but is actually situated below the entrance to Bethlehem. Water shortages are a complex issue not simply of Israeli making; they are a consequence of failure by the Palestinian Authority to adequately maintain infrastructure despite the billions of dollars they receive each year in international aid.

Other major denominations have, from time to time, joined in the rhetoric against Israel. The Methodist Church, for example, issued an annual conference report in June 2010, which contained a wide-ranging section titled "Justice for Palestine and Israel." The report condemned the 'occupation' and 'settlements', and urged a theological redefinition of the biblical covenant relationship between God and the Jewish people. It also contained a lengthy 'historical' section that presented the Arab-Israeli conflict from a skewed pro-Palestinian standpoint, with many significant omissions. Of its numerous errors and misrepresentations, one example will suffice to illustrate the point. The report states: "In December 2008, tensions between Israel and Hamas resulted in war." What it omits to say is that hundreds of Hamas rockets and mortars had rained down on southern Israel, indiscriminately targeting civilians, including women and children, and turning life into a nightmare of constant alarms and explosions. Israel was forced to respond to protect her people, as any other state would have done. To refer to this as "tensions" is somewhat euphemistic and creates a false moral equivalence between Hamas and Israel.

The propagandizing of history was only one part of the report; more significantly the Methodists became the first British church group to advocate for the far-left BDS position by accepting a resolution to boycott Israeli settlement goods. As is usual, boycotting was directed solely against Israel. Why, for example, did the report contain no recommendations for such sanctions against Iran for human rights violations committed while suppressing protests after elections in the previous year? The conference report was greeted with dismay by the British Jewish community (and many members of the Methodist community). The former Chief Rabbi, Jonathan Sacks, criticized it for being "unbalanced, factually and historically flawed," and offering "no genuine understanding of one of the most complex conflicts in the world today."[7]

The Church of Scotland, known informally as 'the Kirk', offered on its website a list of suggested activities in an article titled "Invest in Peace-Action for a just peace in Israel and Palestine" which included, among other things, donating to Christian Aid and studying the Kairos Palestine document, a controversially one-sided text that calls upon Christians everywhere to fight against Israeli occupation. The Simon Wiesenthal Institute criticised this document for casting "a political agenda in theological garb, re-writing history, ignoring Jewish roots and presence in the Holy Land for thousands of years," and placing "all blame for the tragic circumstances of Palestinians on Israel, and none on the actions of Palestinians who blew up innocent Israelis in restaurants and launched rockets at school buses."[8]

Another Kirk document that denigrated Israel was published in November 2010 under the title: "IF ONE SUFFERS: World Mission Council's Report concerning Christians living in a minority situation." The document, produced while Christian minorities were suffering savage persecution in Egypt, Iran, Iraq, Pakistan, and many other areas beyond the Middle East, disingenuously began its description of communities in danger with Israel, citing the plight of Palestinians under occupation. Yet, while it is true that the Christian populations living under the remits of the Palestinian Authority in the 'West Bank' and Hamas in Gaza are declining at an alarming rate, the causes have been persecution and pressure applied by Islamic fundamentalists. The Christian community accounted for 80 per cent of Bethlehem's population when it was handed over by Israel to the Palestinian Authority in 1995. By 2018, at the time of writing, it accounted for only 20 per cent. Meanwhile, the Christian community in Israel itself is thriving, the only one in the entire Middle East that is growing, with full freedom of worship and expression protected under Israeli law.

I have written this book for two reasons. Firstly, to examine Britain's betrayal of the Jews in light of a conviction that the restoration of Israel is aligned to the purposes of God, and in so doing to set straight historical narratives that are often twisted and distorted according to political agendas that reflect visceral anti-Semitic bias. That does not mean that I do not also deplore the way Britain broke faith with promises made to the Palestinian Arabs that were just as ambiguous and contradictory as those made to the Jews, and were I to tell more of that story, the narrative would be just as bleak for the British. Nor does it mean that I give carte blanche approval to all actions taken by Israel. Indeed, many Israelis are themselves critical of the actions of their government as they are free to be in an advanced democracy. Israel's political system, like those of every other nation, is beset with corruption and dysfunctionality. But excessive, non contextualised, one-sided criticism that uses a higher standard against which to judge Israel compared to the rest of the world, serves only to demonize Israel and to reveal disturbing anti-Semitic trends; and all this is emanating from mainstream elements of British politics, media and society, including broad sections of the Christian Church.

Naturally, in a nation where most citizens no longer believe in the Bible as a source of truth, we cannot expect foreign policy to be determined on the basis of the Bible alone. However, any evenhanded assessment of the historical narrative presented in this work would have to conclude that there is a strong case for a foreign policy that is supportive of Israel, based on the internationally accepted legality of the State (international consensus, expressed through UN resolutions that challenge the legality of Israel, is not the same thing as international law), historical connection and basic moral obligation.

My second purpose in writing is to challenge Britain, and particularly the Church, to repent of ingrained anti-Semitism, and to stop creating false distinctions between being anti-Jewish and anti-Israel considering that half of the world's Jews reside in Israel and the majority of the Diaspora support Zionism. Anti-Zionists generally claim not to be anti-Semitic but equate Zionism with colonialism and profess to be anti-colonialist. However, anti-Zionism is intrinsically anti-Semitic because it singles out the Jews uniquely as having no right of self-determination in their own country. It does this on the basis of falsehoods that write Jews out of their own history as the only people for whom the land of Israel was ever their national kingdom. It is, in fact, the Arabs who are the colonialists, intent on driving Jews out of a land to which Jews have lawful, historic and moral claims.

A report by the Institute for Jewish Policy Research, published on 29 January 2019, using data collected in 2017, established a statistical correlation between anti-Israel and anti-Jewish attitudes, with those who focus activism against Israel more likely than not to hold anti-Semitic views, such as those relating to money, divided loyalties and the nefarious use of power.[9] Loathing of Israel has all the same unique characteristics of Jew hatred throughout the ages. It obsessively singles out Israel as a uniquely wicked nation through false historical narratives akin the 'blood libels' and other ancient anti-Jewish tropes; it reverses victim and oppressor in the conflict with the Palestinians; it holds Israel responsible for a global conspiracy of evil; and it seeks to deprive the Jewish people of their right to self-determination and to remove them from the land in which they alone are the indigenous people.

The Church must disengage from hard left politically motivated organizations, often disguised as 'humanitarian' or 'Christian', that propagate these false narratives about Israel (the 'ravenous wolves in sheep's clothing' from the expression coined by Jesus (Matthew 7:15)), and take seriously the Word of God at a time when the future spiritual and material prosperity of the nation hangs precariously in the balance.

Theologically, if the church is to return to a biblical foundation, then it must also disengage from unbiblical replacement teaching, in all its various guises, that assumes the church is now the 'true' or 'spiritual' Israel, and thereby inheritors of the biblical promises made to Israel, whereas there is no longer any place for disinherited Jews or the nation of Israel in the purposes of God. Historically, such thinking has birthed many terrible acts against the Jews, and since 1948 has been used as a tool for delegitimizing the State of Israel. R. C. Sproul Jr., in an article penned for Table Talk magazine, summed up his replacement ideology: "We believe that the Church is essentially Israel. We believe that the answer to, 'What about the Jews?' is 'Here we are.'"[10] Arnold Fruchtenbaum, director of Ariel Ministries and a leading expert in Messianic Theology, responded to this outlandish statement quite brilliantly with this piercing riposte: "To bad you were not declaring this on the streets of Berlin around 1941."[11]

Replacement theology is constructed from complex systems of allegorical interpretation of the bible, yet from a plain reading of scripture it is evident that many of the promises to Israel have been fulfilled historically in a very literal way. Promises that the Jews would continue as a distinct people during their long dispersion among the nations,[12] that they would be re-gathered to the Promised Land, that this land would become a desolate wasteland after which it would be restored, that the desert would blossom like a rose and the mountains shoot forth branches.[13]

A corollary to rejecting replacement theology is a return to, or rediscovery of, the Church's Jewish roots. Jesus was not, as some claim, a Palestinian. He was an orthodox Jewish Rabbi whose teaching was firmly entrenched in the Law and the Prophets, notwithstanding that he had deep disagreements with some of his rabbinical contemporaries, though that is not untypical amongst Rabbis. He worshiped at the Temple, participated in the Jewish festivals and attended his local synagogue. The early church was very much located as a sect within Judaism until the two separated during the early part of the 2nd Century AD, after which the encroachment of replacement theology set in. A deeper awareness of the Jewishness of Jesus is essential for understanding who he is. Those who claim to have faith in Jesus ought, at the very least, to have respect for the faith of Jesus.

From a political perspective, what would restoration for Britain look like? Nobody would seriously countenance a return to Imperialism and Empire. The world has changed, and the exploitation that marked Britain's colonial past is now a source of shame. The pursuit of Imperial aims caused so much suffering and humiliation. But at our best, Britain was a great trading nation, a centre of learning, innovative, soaked in Christian values and internationally recognized for providing leadership to the world. Britain has an opportunity to rise to greatness once again, not in the sense of Empire, but with a global vision to promote free trade and business innovation. Indeed, the British economy is being shaped to become a world leading centre for technological innovation. That being so, who better to partner with than Israel, the archetypal start up nation? After Brexit, it will be imperative for Britain to forge new alliances.

In a recent blog for *The Spectator*, Stephen Daisley wrote, "the beginnings of a new partnership can be glimpsed."[14] Israel is one of Britain's leading trading partners – Brexit presents an opportunity to develop economic ties and the two countries have already signed a contingency deal to trade on preferential terms after Britain leaves the EU. From the time of Earnest Bevin onwards, who created an institutionally hostile foreign policy apparatus, the relationship with Israel has at best been cordial, sometimes ambivalent, but there is an opportunity to build a new special relationship. To do so, we must acknowledge culpability for bungling the administration of the Mandate for Palestine, seek forgiveness for the broken promises that marred our relationship with the land of Israel, the Jews, and the Arabs, and begin once more to be a blessing to the children of Abraham. We cannot expect God to restore spiritual, economic or political health to the nation until we acknowledge culpability for breaking faith with Israel and the consequences we have reaped.

It is imperative that Britain finds the courage to face our past; indeed, to try and redeem it. We need to acknowledge, with honesty and humility, the reprehensible attitudes and unethical behaviour in our nation that contributed to the enduring impasse in the ongoing quest for the peace of Jerusalem.

Endnotes

1. See also Daniel 2:21; 5:21, 26-27.
2. *www.unwatch.org/unga-adopts-20-resolutions-israel-4-rest-world-combined.*
3. *https://www.newstatesman.com/node/156641.*
4. Cited from a transcript of an interview with PBS, "Coping with Conflict: Israeli Author Amos Oz", *https://www.pbs.org/newshour/show/coping-with-conflict-israeli-author-amos-oz.*
5. Cited from *Huffington Post*, "Is Godlessness Dooming Britain?" 7 March 2011.
6. Cited from *www.reform-magazine.co.uk/index.php/2010/11/peace-on-earth/#comment-516.*
7. Cited from Jerusalem Center for Public Affairs, "Major UK Churches Adopt Christian Aid's Anti-Israel BDS Agenda" *http://jcpa.org/article/major-uk-churches-adopt-christian-aid-anti-israel-bds-agenda.*
8. Cited from "SWC Extremely Concerned By Flawed Presbyterian Palestinian 'Kairos' Study Guide", *www.wiesenthal.com*, 24 June 2011.
9. David Graham & Jonathan Boyd, "The Apartheid Contention and calls for a Boycott", Institute for Jewish Policy Research, 29 January 2019.
10. Cited from an Editorial by R. C. Sproul Jr., in *Table Talk*, Ligonier Ministries, December 1998, p. 2.
11. Cited from *https://www.ariel.org/pdfs/magazine/summer-2018.pdf*, p. 11.
12. Isaiah 49:14-16; Jeremiah 30:11, 31:35-37.
13. Isaiah 35:1; Ezekiel 36:8.
14. Stephen Daisley, "When will Britain recognize Jerusalem as the capital of Israel?" *The Spectator*, *www.blogs.spectator.co.uk*, 3rd July 2019.

APPENDIX 1

BRITISH PALESTINE MANDATE: TEXT OF THE MANDATE (24 JULY 1922)[1]

The Council of the League of Nations

Whereas the Principal Allied Powers have agreed, for the purpose of giving effect to the provisions of Article 22 of the Covenant of the League of Nations, to entrust to a Mandatory selected by the said Powers the administration of the territory of Palestine, which formerly belonged to the Turkish Empire, within such boundaries as may be fixed by them; and

Whereas the Principal Allied Powers have also agreed that the Mandatory should be responsible for putting into effect the declaration originally made on November 2nd, 1917, by the Government of His Britannic Majesty, and adopted by the said Powers, in favour of the establishment in Palestine of a national home for the Jewish people, it being clearly understood that nothing should be done which might prejudice the civil and religious rights of existing non-Jewish communities in Palestine, or the rights and political status enjoyed by Jews in any other country; and

Whereas recognition has thereby been given to the historical connection of the Jewish people with Palestine and to the grounds for reconstituting their national home in that country; and

Whereas the Principal Allied Powers have selected His Britannic Majesty as the Mandatory for Palestine; and

Whereas the mandate in respect of Palestine has been formulated in the following terms and submitted to the Council of the League for approval; and

Whereas His Britannic Majesty has accepted the mandate in respect of Palestine and undertaken to exercise it on behalf of the League of Nations in conformity with the following provisions; and

Whereas by the afore-mentioned Article 22 (paragraph 8), it is provided that the degree of authority, control or administration to be exercised by the Mandatory, not having been previously agreed upon by the Members of the League, shall be explicitly defined by the Council of the League Of Nations;

Confirming the said Mandate, defines its terms as follows:

ART. 1.

The Mandatory shall have full powers of legislation and of administration, save as they may be limited by the terms of this mandate.

ART. 2.

The Mandatory shall be responsible for placing the country under such political, administrative and economic conditions as will secure the establishment of the Jewish national home, as laid down in the preamble, and the development of self-governing institutions, and also for safeguarding the civil and religious rights of all the inhabitants of Palestine, irrespective of race and religion.

ART. 3.

The Mandatory shall, so far as circumstances permit, encourage local autonomy.

ART. 4.

An appropriate Jewish agency shall be recognized as a public body for the purpose of advising and co-operating with the Administration of Palestine in such economic, social and other matters as may affect the establishment of the Jewish national home and the interests of the Jewish population in Palestine, and, subject always to the control of the Administration to assist and take part in the development of the country.

The Zionist organization, so long as its organization and constitution are in the opinion of the Mandatory appropriate, shall be recognized as such agency. It shall take steps in consultation with His Britannic Majesty's Government to secure the co-operation of all Jews who are willing to assist in the establishment of the Jewish national home.

ART. 5.

The Mandatory shall be responsible for seeing that no Palestine territory shall be ceded or leased to, or in any way placed under the control of the Government of any foreign Power.

ART. 6.

The Administration of Palestine, while ensuring that the rights and position of other sections of the population are not prejudiced, shall facilitate Jewish immigration under suitable conditions and shall encourage, in co-operation with the Jewish agency referred to in Article 4, close settlement by Jews on the land, including State lands and waste lands not required for public purposes.

ART. 7.

The Administration of Palestine shall be responsible for enacting a nationality law. There shall be included in this law provisions framed so as to facilitate the acquisition of Palestinian citizenship by Jews who take up their permanent residence in Palestine.

ART. 8.

The privileges and immunities of foreigners, including the benefits of consular jurisdiction and protection as formerly enjoyed by Capitulation or usage in the Ottoman Empire, shall not be applicable in Palestine.

Unless the Powers whose nationals enjoyed the afore-mentioned privileges and immunities on August 1st, 1914, shall have previously renounced the right to their re-establishment, or shall have agreed to their non-application for a specified period, these privileges and immunities shall, at the expiration of the mandate, be immediately re-established in their entirety or with such modifications as may have been agreed upon between the Powers concerned.

ART. 9.

The Mandatory shall be responsible for seeing that the judicial system established in Palestine shall assure to foreigners, as well as to natives, a complete guarantee of their rights.

Respect for the personal status of the various peoples and communities and for their religious interests shall be fully guaranteed. In particular, the control and administration of Wakfs shall be exercised in accordance with religious law and the dispositions of the founders.

ART. 10.

Pending the making of special extradition agreements relating to Palestine, the extradition treaties in force between the Mandatory and other foreign Powers shall apply to Palestine.

ART. 11.

The Administration of Palestine shall take all necessary measures to safeguard the interests of the community in connection with the development of the country, and, subject to any international obligations accepted by the Mandatory, shall have full power to provide for public ownership or control of any of the natural resources of the country or of the public works, services and utilities established or to be established therein. It shall introduce a land system appropriate to the needs of the country, having regard, among other things, to the desirability of promoting the close settlement and intensive cultivation of the land.

The Administration may arrange with the Jewish agency mentioned in Article 4 to construct or operate, upon fair and equitable terms, any public works, services and utilities, and to develop any of the natural resources of the country, in so far as these matters are not directly undertaken by the Administration. Any such arrangements shall provide that no profits distributed by such agency, directly or indirectly, shall exceed a reasonable rate of interest on the capital, and any further profits shall be utilised by it for the benefit of the country in a manner approved by the Administration.

ART. 12.

The Mandatory shall be entrusted with the control of the foreign relations of Palestine and the right to issue exequaturs to consuls appointed by foreign Powers. He shall also be entitled to afford diplomatic and consular protection to citizens of Palestine when outside its territorial limits.

ART. 13.

All responsibility in connection with the Holy Places and religious buildings or sites in Palestine, including that of preserving existing rights and of securing free access to the Holy Places, religious buildings and sites and the free exercise of worship, while ensuring the requirements of public order and decorum, is assumed by the Mandatory, who shall be responsible solely to the League of Nations in all matters connected herewith, provided that nothing in this article shall prevent the Mandatory from entering into such arrangements as he may deem reasonable with the Administration for the purpose of carrying the provisions of this article into effect; and provided also that nothing in this mandate shall be construed as conferring upon the Mandatory authority to interfere with the fabric or the management of purely Moslem sacred shrines, the immunities of which are guaranteed.

ART. 14.

A special commission shall be appointed by the Mandatory to study, define and determine the rights and claims in connection with the Holy Places and the rights and claims relating to the different religious communities in Palestine. The method of nomination, the composition and the functions of this Commission shall be submitted to the Council of the League for its approval, and the Commission shall not be appointed or enter upon its functions without the approval of the Council.

ART. 15.

The Mandatory shall see that complete freedom of conscience and the free exercise of all forms of worship, subject only to the maintenance of public order and morals, are ensured to all. No discrimination of any kind shall be made between the inhabitants of Palestine on the ground of race, religion or language. No person shall be excluded from Palestine on the sole ground of his religious belief.

The right of each community to maintain its own schools for the education of its own members in its own language, while conforming to such educational requirements of a general nature as the Administration may impose, shall not be denied or impaired.

ART. 16.

The Mandatory shall be responsible for exercising such supervision over religious or eleemosynary bodies of all faiths in Palestine as may be required for the maintenance of public order and good government. Subject to such supervision, no measures shall be taken in Palestine to obstruct or interfere with the enterprise of such bodies or to discriminate against any representative or member of them on the ground of his religion or nationality.

ART. 17.

The Administration of Palestine may organist on a voluntary basis the forces necessary for the preservation of peace and order, and also for the defence of the country, subject, however, to the supervision of the Mandatory, but shall not use them for purposes other than those above specified save with the consent of the Mandatory. Except for such purposes, no military, naval or air forces shall be raised or maintained by the Administration of Palestine.

Nothing in this article shall preclude the Administration of Palestine from contributing to the cost of the maintenance of the forces of the Mandatory in Palestine.

The Mandatory shall be entitled at all times to use the roads, railways and ports of Palestine for the movement of armed forces and the carriage of fuel and supplies.

ART. 18.

The Mandatory shall see that there is no discrimination in Palestine against the nationals of any State Member of the League of Nations (including companies incorporated under its laws) as compared with those of the Mandatory or of any foreign State in matters concerning taxation, commerce or navigation, the exercise of industries or professions, or in the treatment of merchant vessels or civil aircraft. Similarly, there shall be no discrimination in Palestine against goods originating in or destined for any of the said States, and there shall be freedom of transit under equitable conditions across the mandated area.

Subject as aforesaid and to the other provisions of this mandate, the Administration of Palestine may, on the advice of the Mandatory, impose such taxes and customs duties as it may consider necessary, and take such steps as it may think best to promote the development of the natural resources of the country and to safeguard the interests of the population. It may also, on the advice of the Mandatory, conclude a special customs agreement with any State the territory of which in 1914 was wholly included in Asiatic Turkey or Arabia.

ART. 19.

The Mandatory shall adhere on behalf of the Administration of Palestine to any general international conventions already existing, or which may be concluded hereafter with the approval of the League of Nations, respecting the slave traffic, the traffic in arms and ammunition, or the traffic in drugs, or relating to commercial equality, freedom of transit and navigation, aerial navigation and postal, telegraphic and wireless communication or literary, artistic or industrial property.

ART. 20.

The Mandatory shall co-operate on behalf of the Administration of Palestine, so far as religious, social and other conditions may permit, in the execution of any common policy adopted by the League of Nations for preventing and combating disease, including diseases of plants and animals.

ART. 21.

The Mandatory shall secure the enactment within twelve months from this date, and shall ensure the execution of a Law of Antiquities based on the following rules. This law shall ensure equality of treatment in the matter of excavations and archaeological research to the nationals of all States Members of the League of Nations.

6. "Antiquity" means any construction or any product of human activity earlier than the year 1700 A. D.

7. The law for the protection of antiquities shall proceed by encouragement rather than by threat.

    Any person who, having discovered an antiquity without being furnished with the authorization referred to in paragraph 5, reports the same to an official of the competent Department, shall be rewarded according to the value of the discovery.

8 No antiquity may be disposed of except to the competent Department, unless this Department renounces the acquisition of any such antiquity.

No antiquity may leave the country without an export licence from the said Department.

9 Any person who maliciously or negligently destroys or damages an antiquity shall be liable to a penalty to be fixed.

10 No clearing of ground or digging with the object of finding antiquities shall be permitted, under penalty of fine, except to persons authorised by the competent Department.

11 Equitable terms shall be fixed for expropriation, temporary or permanent, of lands which might be of historical or archaeological interest.

12 Authorization to excavate shall only be granted to persons who show sufficient guarantees of archaeological experience. The Administration of Palestine shall not, in granting these authorizations, act in such a way as to exclude scholars of any nation without good grounds.

13 The proceeds of excavations may be divided between the excavator and the competent Department in a proportion fixed by that Department. If division seems impossible for scientific reasons, the excavator shall receive a fair indemnity in lieu of a part of the find.

ART. 22.

English, Arabic and Hebrew shall be the official languages of Palestine. Any statement or inscription in Arabic on stamps or money in Palestine shall be repeated in Hebrew and any statement or inscription in Hebrew shall be repeated in Arabic.

ART. 23.

The Administration of Palestine shall recognize the holy days of the respective communities in Palestine as legal days of rest for the members of such communities.

ART. 24.

The Mandatory shall make to the Council of the League of Nations an annual report to the satisfaction of the Council as to the measures taken during the year to carry out the provisions of the mandate. Copies of all laws and regulations promulgated or issued during the year shall be communicated with the report.

ART. 25.

In the territories lying between the Jordan and the eastern boundary of Palestine as ultimately determined, the Mandatory shall be entitled, with the consent of the Council of the League of Nations, to postpone or withhold application of such provisions of this mandate as he may consider inapplicable to the existing local conditions, and to make such provision for the administration of the territories as he may consider suitable to those conditions, provided that no action shall be taken which is inconsistent with the provisions of Articles 15, 16 and 18.

ART. 26.

The Mandatory agrees that, if any dispute whatever should arise between the Mandatory and another member of the League of

Nations relating to the interpretation or the application of the provisions of the mandate, such dispute, if it cannot be settled by negotiation, shall be submitted to the Permanent Court of International Justice provided for by Article 14 of the Covenant of the League of Nations.

ART. 27.

The consent of the Council of the League of Nations is required for any modification of the terms of this mandate.

ART. 28.

In the event of the termination of the mandate hereby conferred upon the Mandatory, the Council of the League of Nations shall make such arrangements as may be deemed necessary for safeguarding in perpetuity, under guarantee of the League, the rights secured by Articles 13 and 14, and shall use its influence for securing, under the guarantee of the League, that the Government of Palestine will fully honour the financial obligations legitimately incurred by the Administration of Palestine during the period of the mandate, including the rights of public servants to pensions or gratuities.

The present instrument shall be deposited in original in the archives of the League of Nations and certified copies shall be forwarded by the Secretary-General of the League of Nations to all members of the League.

Done at London the twenty-fourth day of July, one thousand nine hundred and twenty-two.

Endnotes

[1] Cited from The Avalon Project, Lillian Goldman Law Library, Yale Law School, <*avalon.law.yale.edu/20th_century/palmanda.asp*>.

APPENDIX 2

LEGAL CONSIDERATIONS REGARDING THE 'WEST BANK'

The majority of mainstream political and media commentators routinely repeat a canard that originates from anti-Israeli activists that refers to the 'West Bank' and Gaza as 'occupied' territories, and references Israeli settlements in the 'West Bank' as 'illegal' under international law. However, the British Mandate for Palestine remains the only internationally agreed and legally binding document relating to settlement of the land, and under the terms of the Mandate, Israeli presence in the 'West Bank' is neither an 'occupation' nor 'illegal.' A correct designation would be to label the 'West Bank' as a disputed territory. It seems befitting for a book in which the British Mandate has been central to the narrative to give a brief overview of how the Mandate relates to the present conflict between Israel and the Palestinian Arabs over this most bitterly contested strip of land.

Critics of Israel's policy of encouraging its citizens to settle in the regions of Judea and Samaria point to a UN Security Council resolution, allowed to pass by the United States during the final days of Barak Obama's presidency, that declared Israeli homes, built in the region of Judea and Samaria, a "flagrant violation of international law." Bold words, but in reality, this resolution was merely a political statement that is non-binding under international law, and is it actually true?

In order for Israeli settlements to be in violation of international law Israel must be considered an occupier of foreign territory. Yet, Israel's legal claim to the territory in question has been recognised by the international community on several occasions. First, the land on both sides of the river Jordan was recognized as part of the Jewish National Home by the 1920 San Remo Conference. This was endorsed by the 1922 League of Nations Mandate to Britain and affirmed by Article 80 of the United Nations charter in 1945. After Israel's leaders declared sovereignty in 'all' territory relinquished by Britain on 15 May 1948 it was recognized as the State of Israel by the General Assembly and Security Council in May 1949.

Jordan invaded and conquered the regions of Judea and Samaria in 1948, annexed it in 1950, and gave it a new name: 'West Bank' (of the river Jordan). Britain and Pakistan were the only nations in the entire world that recognized Jordan's annexation; not a single Arab country joined them. Furthermore, the so called 'Green Line' that separated the 'West Bank' from Israel was never recognized as an international border. Article 2 of the United Nations charter forbids the acquisition of territory through war. Thus, Jordan's acquisition and annexation of the territory was indisputably illegal under international law. Jordan expelled all Jews who were legitimately living in the newly termed 'West Bank' territory from homes built on Jewish owned land, without reparations, dispossessing Jewish communities that had existed for centuries. Jewish homes and synagogues were destroyed to ensure they would never return and Jewish cemeteries desecrated. It was an unequivocal act of ethnic cleansing.

LEGAL CONSIDERATIONS REGARDING THE 'WEST BANK'

In 1967, Jordan again initiated a war against Israel with the intention of annihilating the Jewish State in conjunction with Egypt and Syria. By the conclusion of hostilities Jordan had been pushed out of Judea and Samaria by Israel. This re-acquisition of the territory by Israel must be considered legal because Article 51 of the United Nations charter permits a nation to defend itself from attack. It is also understood that national self-defence often necessitates control of any territory from which the initial aggression was launched.

Had the 'West Bank' been recognized as within the borders of the State of Jordan either by Israel or the international community between 1949 and 1967, then Israel's return to the territory would have been an occupation, regardless of previous title. However, Jordan's annexation was not recognized by the international community, nor did the Israeli-Jordanian ceasefire agreement in 1949 represent acquiescence to new borders by either side: "No provision of this Agreement shall in any way prejudice the rights, claims and positions of either Party hereto in the ultimate peaceful settlement of the Palestine question, the provisions of this Agreement being dictated exclusively by military considerations."[1]

Given the fact that Israel had legal title to the territory that was recognized by the international community and Israel's final control of the territory was a result of self-defence rather than aggression, as opposed to Jordan's control of the territory which was the result of aggression and which was not recognized as legitimate by the international community, common sense shows that Israel merely won back territory that legitimately belonged to it in the first place.

Alan Dershowitz, formerly professor of Law at Harvard University, highlights how many of the fathers of modern Israel were experts in legal affairs and went to great lengths to ensure that the nation state was founded on solid legal ground. As he expresses it, "Lawyers, not generals, were the midwives of Israel's birth – or more accurately re-birth, since it had existed as an independent country twice before in history."[2] One of the false narratives used to perpetuate Palestinian claims to the 'West Bank' argues that UN Resolution 181 gave that part of Mandatory Palestine to the Arabs, and Israel is therefore violating international law by settling Judea and Samaria. However, Res 181 did not give the Arabs an unqualified right to a state. The resolution proposed two states joined by economic union, with a joint currency system, joint telephone and postal service, common ports and airports, shared water and power facilities, and more. The condition under which the Jews accepted Res 181 was that the other side would cooperate.

There are many facts that are generally accepted under international law that are ignored by critics of Israeli settlement policy. Firstly, General Assembly resolutions are not legally binding, but are only intended as policy recommendations. Secondly, such resolutions are only binding in any sense if both parties agree. The Arabs rejected Res 181 in both word and deed, waging war in 1948 with the goal of annihilating Israel. As such, the resolution never took effect and is not binding. Thirdly, the party that rejects an agreement does not retain any rights based on that agreement.

The insistence that Res 181 remains valid with the option of a Palestinian state being open to the Arabs is simply not true from a legal perspective. The British Mandate is therefore the only legally binding document regarding the formerly named territory of Palestine, and Article 6 of this document explicitly states that the Mandate should encourage the close settlement of Jews in the whole of Palestine, which included Judea and Samaria (and at the time of the agreement, the Golan Heights).

That is not to say that the Israeli policy on settlements is justified. There are many in Israel who oppose this policy on the grounds that it is both provocative and an obstacle to progressing a peaceful resolution to conflict with the Palestinians. The settlements may not be illegal, but an action being legal is not necessarily the same as it being the right thing to do. The ultimate solution to the problems created by Jewish settlements in Judea and Samaria is a matter for political agreement.

Endnotes

[1] General Armistice Agreement between Israel and Jordan, 3 April 1949
[2] Alan Dershowitz, "Israel's Legal Founding", cited from assets.ctfassets.net/dershowitz, accessed 28 February 2020.

APPENDIX 3

BRITISH GOVERNMENT DOCUMENTS OF THE MANDATORY PERIOD

Table of British Government Documents referenced in this work, including Commission Reports and White Papers:

DATE ISSUED	NAME OF DOCUMENT
July 1920	Palin Commission Report
October 1921	Haycraft Commission Report
June 1922	Churchill White Paper
March 1930	Shaw Commission Report
October 1930	Hope Simpson Report
October 1930	Passfield White Paper
July 1937	Peel Commission Report (Royal Commission)
November 1938	Woodhead Commission Report
March 1939	Macdonald White Paper
April 1946	Anglo-American Committee of Inquiry Report

Bibliographic References

Churchill White Paper: Correspondence with the Palestine Arab Delegation and the Zionist Organisation, June 1922, Cmd 1700. His Majesty's Stationery Office, London, 1922

Haycraft Report, Palestine: Disturbances in May, 1921. Report of the Commission of Inquiry with Correspondence Relating Thereto, Cmd 1540, His Majesty's Stationery Office, London, 1921

Hope Simpson Report: Palestine: Report on Immigration, Land Settlement, and Development. His Majesty's Stationery Office, London, 1930

Palin Commission, Report of the Court of Inquiry Convened by Order of His Excellency the High Commissioner and Commander in Chief. His Majesty's Stationery Office, London, 1920

Peel Report: Palestine Royal Commission Report Presented by the Secretary of State for the Colonies to Parliament by Command of His Majesty, July 1937. His Majesty's Stationery Office, London, 1937

Shaw Report: Report of the Commission on the Palestine Disturbances of August 1929, Cmd. 3530. His Majesty's Stationery Office, London, 1930

White Paper of 1939: Palestine: Statement of Policy Presented by the Secretary of State for the Colonies to Parliament by Command of His Majesty, May 1939, Cmd 6019. His Majesty's Stationery Office, London, 1939

Bibliography

Auerbach, Jerold S., Brothers at War: Israel and the Tragedy of the Altalena (New Orleans: Quid Pro Books, 2011)

Auerbach, Jerold S., Hebron Jews: Memory and Conflict in the Land of Israel (Plymouth: Rowman & Littlefield, 2009)

Barr, James, A Line in the Sand: The Anglo-French Struggle for the Middle East, 1914-1948 (London: W. W. Norton & Co, 2013)

Bauer, Yehuda, Rethinking the Holocaust (New Haven, CT: Yale University Press, 2001)

Bayliss, Thomas, How Israel Was Won: A Concise History of the Arab–Israeli Conflict (Maryland: Lexington Books, 1999)

Biger, Gideon, The Boundaries of Modern Palestine, 1840–1947 (London: Routledge, 2004)

Churchill, Winston S., Winston Churchill Speeches: Never Give In (London: Pimlico, 2007)

Cohen, Hillel, Army of Shadows: Palestinian Collaboration with Zionism, 1917–1948 (Berkeley Ca: University of California Press, 2009)

Cohen, Michael J., Palestine to Israel: From Mandate to Independence (Abingdon Oxon: Frank Cass, 1988)

Cohen, Michael J., Palestine and the Great Powers, 1945-1948 (Princeton NJ: Princeton University Press, 1982)

Douglas, J. D., et al, New Bible Dictionary 2nd Ed (Leicester: IVP, 1982)

El-Eini, Roza I. M., Mandated Landscape: British Imperial Rule in Palestine, 1929–1948 (London: Routledge, 2006)

Elpeleg, Zvi, The Grand Mufti Haj Amin Al-Hussaini (London: Frank Cass, 1993)

Fromkin, David, A Peace to End all Peace: The Fall of the Ottoman Empire and the Creation of the Modern Middle East (New York: Holt Paperbacks, 2009)

Gartman, Eric, Return to Zion: The History of Modern Israel (University of Nebraska Press, 2015)

Gilbert, Martin, Israel: A History (London: Black Swan, 2008)

Goldschmidt Jr., Arthur, A Concise History of the Middle East, 11th Ed (Boulder Col: Westview Press, 2015)

Greenfield, Murray, The Jews Secret Fleet: The Untold Story of North American Volunteers Who Smashed the British Blockade of Palestine (New York: Gefen House, 1987)

Gruber, Ruth, Exodus 1947: The Ship That Launched a Nation (New York: Times Books, 1999)

Grunor, Jerry A., Let My People Go: The Trials and Tribulations of the People of Israel, and the Heroes who Helped in their Independence from British Colonization (New York: iUniverse, 2005)

Halamish, Aviva, The Exodus Affair: Holocaust Survivors and the Struggle for Palestine (London: Valentine Mitchell, 1998)

Hilberg, Raul, The Destruction of the European Jews, 3rd Ed (New Haven, CT: Yale University Press, 2003)

Hoffman, Bruce, Anonymous Soldiers: The Struggle for Israel, 1917-1947 (New York: Knopf, 2015)

Ingrams, Doreen, Palestine Papers 1917-1922, Seeds of Conflict (London: John Murray, 1972)

Jeffers, Paul H., The Complete Idiot's Guide to Jerusalem (Jerusalem: Alpha Books, 2004)

Kamel, Lorenzo, Imperial Perceptions of Palestine: British Influence and Power in Late Ottoman Times (London: British Academic Press, 2015)

Katz, Shmuel, Battleground: Fact and Fantasy in Palestine (New York: Bantam Books, 1973)

Khalidi, Rashid, The Iron Cage: The Story of the Palestinian Struggle for Statehood (Boston Mass: Beacon Press, 2006)

Korda, Michael, Hero: The Life and Legend of Lawrence of Arabia (New York: Harper Perennial, 2011)

Laqueur, Walter, The History of Zionism 3rd Ed. (London: Taurisparke Paperbacks, 2003)

Laqueur, Walter, The Israel-Arab Reader: A Documentary History of the Middle East Conflict (London: Penguin, 1979)

Leibler, Isi, The Case for Israel (Australia: The Globe Press, 1972)

Lewis, Geoffrey, Balfour and Weizmann (London: Continuum, 2009)

Makovsky, Michael, Churchill's Promised Land: Zionism and Statecraft (New Haven: Yale University Press, 2007)

Mansfield, Peter, A History of the Middle East: 3rd Ed. (London: Penguin Books, 2010)

Meinertzhagen, Richard, Middle East Diary: 1917-1956 (London: Cresset Press, 1959)

Miller, Rory, ed., Britain, Palestine and Empire: The Mandate Years (Abingdon: Routledge, 2010)

Morris, Benny, 1948: A History of the First Arab–Israeli War (New Haven: Yale University Press, 2008)

Morris, Benny, Righteous Victims: A History of the Zionist–Arab Conflict, 1881–1999 (New York: Knopf, 2001)

Quigley, John, The International Diplomacy of Israel's Founders (Cambridge: CUP, 2016)

Reynold, Nick, Britain's Unfulfilled Mandate for Palestine (London: Lexington Books, 2014)

Rose, Norman, "A Senseless, Squalid War": Voices from Palestine; 1890 to 1948 (London: The Bodley Head, 2009)

Sachar, Howard, A History of Israel from the Rise of Zionism to Our Time, 2nd Ed (New York: Knopf, 1996)

Schechtman, Joseph B., The Life and Times of Vladimir Jabotinsky: Rebel and Statesman (Silver Springs, MD: Eshel Books, 1986)

Schmidt, David W., Partners together in this Great Enterprise (Jerusalem: Xulon Press, 2011)

Schneer, Jonathan, The Balfour Declaration: The Origins of the Arab-Israeli Conflict (London: Bloomsbury, 2010)

Segev, Tom, One Palestine, Complete: Jews and Arabs under the British Mandate (London: Picador, 2001)

Shapira, Anita, Land and Power: The Zionist Resort to Force, 1881–1948 (Palo Alto Ca.: Stanford University Press, 1999)

Shepherd, Naomi, Ploughing Sand: British Rule in Palestine 1917-48 (London: John Murray, 2000)

Sherman, A. J., Mandate Days: British Lives in Palestine, 1918–1948 (London: Thames & Hudson, 1998)

Sicker, Martin, Pangs of the Messiah: The Troubled Birth of the Jewish State (Westport CT: Greenwood Publishing Group, 2000)

Stewart, Ninian, The Royal Navy and the Palestine Patrol (London: Frank Cass Publishing, 2002)

Tabarani, Gabriel G., Israel-Palestinian Conflict: The Balfour Promise to Bush Declaration (Indiana: Author House, 2008)

Tessler, Mark A., A History of Israel in Palestinian Conflict (Indianapolis: Indiana University Press, 1994)

Teveth, Shabtai, Ben-Gurion: The Burning Ground, 1886–1948 (Boston: Houghton Mifflin Harcourt, 1987)

Thurley, Roy, Ed., Partners in this Great Enterprise (Nottingham: New Life Publishing, 2017)

Wasserstein, Bernhard, Britain and the Jews of Europe, 1939-1945 (Oxford: Oxford Paperbacks, 1988)

Wasserstein, Bernard, Israel and Palestine (London: Profile Books, 2004)

Wyman, David S., The Abandonment of the Jews: America and the Holocaust (New York: The New Press, 2007)

Zertal, Idith, From Catastrophe to Power: The Holocaust Survivors and the Emergence of Israel (Los Angeles, Ca: University of California Press, 1998)

Ziedenberg, Gerald, Blockade: The Story of Jewish Immigration to Palestine (Indiana: Author House: 2011)

Video/DVD Media

"*Against all Odds: Israel Survives*" by William McKay, 2006, American Trademark Pictures

"*Partners in this Great Enterprise*" by Balfour100 Ltd [DVD], 2017, Hatikvah Films Trust

"*The Forsaken Promise*" by Hugh Kitson [DVD], 2007, Hatikvah Films Trust

Websites Consulted

American-Israeli Cooperative Enterprise, Jewish Virtual Library, <*http://www.jewishvirtuallibrary.org*>

Avalon Project, Lillian Goldman Law Library, Yale Law School, <*avalon.law.yale.edu*>

Bickerton, Ian J., et al, "Palestine", Encyclopaedia Britannica, <*https://www.britannica.com/place/Palestine*>

Khalidi, Rashid, "Palestinian Arab Revolt (1936-1939)", Encyclopaedia of the Modern Middle East and North Africa, *http://www.encyclopaedia.com*.